SCAPA FLOW

SCAPA FLOW

THE REMINISCENCES OF MEN AND WOMEN WHO SERVED IN SCAPA FLOW IN THE TWO WORLD WARS

MALCOLM BROWN AND PATRICIA MEEHAN

First published in the UK in 1968 by Allen Lane The Penguin Press
This paperback edition published 2019

The History Press
97 St George's Place
Cheltenham, GL50 3QB
www.thehistorypress.co.uk

British Library Cataloguing in Publication Data.
A catalogue record for this book is available from the British Library.

ISBN 978 0 7509 9208 4

Typesetting and origination by The History Press
Printed and bound in Great Britain by TJ Books Limited

Contents

List of Illustrations

1. Winter dawn, Stromness.
2. Evening view of Scapa Bay.
3. The cliffs at Yesnaby.
4. The Old Man of Hoy.
5. The old town, Stromness.
6. A street in Kirkwall.
7. St Magnus' Cathedral, Kirkwall.
8. The Churchill Barrier in Water Sound.
9. Water Sound, 2001.
10. The Ness Battery during the Second World War.
11. The Ness Battery in the 1960s.
12. Exterior of the Italian Chapel.
13. Interior of the Italian Chapel.
14. The *St Ninian*.
15. Marines drilling on a quarter-deck during the First World War.
16 The 'Green Room' of a battleship.
17. Concert-party programme from H.M.S. *Benbow*.
18. Coaling ship.
19. 'Holystoning' the decks.
20. Lord Kitchener leaving the *Oak*.
21. Marwick Head, with Kitchener Memorial.
22. Surrender of the German Fleet, 21 November 1918.

23. SMS *Friederich der Grosse, König Albert and Kaiserin*.
24. SMS *Grosser Kurfurst, Kronpriz Wilhelm* and *Markgraf*.
25. König class battleship in Scapa Flow.
26, 27. SMS *Seydlitz* taking up her moorings.
28. German High Seas Fleet in Scapa Flow.
29. Deck-scene on an interned German destroyer.
30. German sailors abandoning ship.
31. SMS *Bayern*, 21 June 1919.
32. The scuttling of the German destroyer *G.102*.
33. The scuttling of SMS *Hindenberg*.
34. Scapa Flow after the Great Scuttle of 1919.
35. British soldiers guarding a beached German ship.
36, 37. Salvage operations between the wars.
38. Libertymen leaving the *Royal Oak*.
39. 'Libertymen at Lyness', by Charles Cundall.
40. The triumphant return to Germany of *U-47*.
41. Commander of *U-47* being congratulated on his return to Germany.
42. The commander and engineer of *U-47*.
43. The *Royal Oak* memorial bell, St Magnus' Cathedral.
44. Concrete block casting yard at St Mary's Holm.
45. 'Boom Defence Vessels', by Charles Cundall.
46. A typical front page from *The Orkney Blast*.
47. A cartoon by Strube envisioning the worst exile for Hitler.
48. Dame Vera Laughton Mathews inspecting Wrens at Lyness.
49. Convoy PQ18 under attack.
50. The effects of ice in northern waters.
51. Capital ships steaming ahead in heavy weather.
52. A film show below decks, in a drawing by Gordon Rowland.
53. Scapa Flow at the end of the Second World War.
54. Peaceful Scapa Flow. The view from Houton, 2001.

Acknowledgements

The authors and publishers are indebted to the following for their help in the provision of illustrations: Mr A. F. B. Bridges (17); the Ministry of Defence (48); Mr and Mrs Robertson Easton (32, 41), from the collection of G. Gordon Nicol; William Hourston of Stromness (36, 37); the Trustees of the Imperial War Museum (5, 16, 18, 19, 23, 24, 25, 26, 27, 31, 32, 33, 41, 49, 50, 51); Herbert Johnston (38); Evan MacGillivray, Librarian of Orkney County Library (34, 35), from the Thomas Kent Collection; the former Mansell Collection (20); Ernest W. Marwick of Kirkwall (3, 5, 7); Gerald G. A. Meyer, Editor of the *Orcadian*, for the page from the *Orkney Blast* and the Strube cartoon (46, 47); the National Maritime Museum for the paintings by Charles Cundall (39, 45); the North of Scotland, Orkney and Shetland Shipping Company (14); the Hulton-Getty Collection (22); Gordon Rowland, who served in the convoys to north Russia in 1942 (52), his picture was drawn specially for this book; Vice-Admiral Friedrich Ruge (29); the Scottish Tourist Board (2, 4, 6, 8, 10), from the collection of William S. Thomson; Douglas Shearer of Kirkwall (13), Jenny Suddaby (9, 43, 54) and the estate of Hans Wessels (40, 42).

We would also like to thank George Mackay Brown and B.B.C. Scotland for permission to print an extract from 'The Winter Islands', and Allie Windwick for permission to print 'Lonely Scapa Flow'.

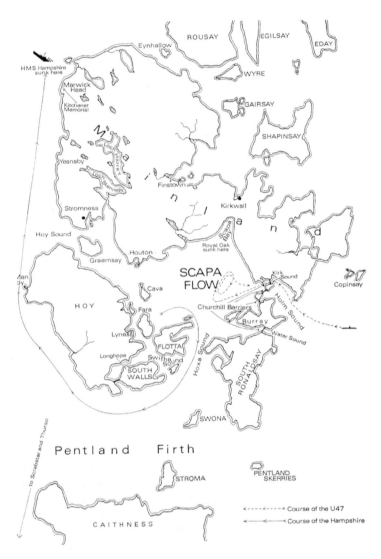

A Map of Scapa Flow showing the course of the *Hampshire* and *U-47*.

Extracts from A Memorial to the Lords Commissioners of Admiralty

Proposal for Establishing a Temporary Rendezvous for Line of Battle-Ships in a National Roadstead called Scapa Flow Formed by the South Isles of Orkney – most humbly submitted to the consideration of the Rt Hon. the Lords Commissioners of the Admiralty and Presented to their Lordships by their most obedient and most humble Servant Graeme Spence late Maritime Surveyor to their Lordships.

If the peculiar situation of the Orkney Isles and the numerous Harbours they contain be duly considered with reference at the same time to Britain and Ireland and the West Coast of Europe as laid down in the annexed charts, it will not be at all surprising that the Northern maritime Nations of Europe such as the Danes, Swedes and Norwegians, should, from the earliest accounts we have of them have looked upon the Conquest of Orkney as an object of the first importance towards their obtaining that footing and possession which they ultimately got in Britain and Ireland . . .

Even the Romans so famed for their choice of eligible military stations, thought the Orkneys of so much importance that on the Division of the Empire among the sons of Constantine the Great, the Kingdom of the Orcades fell to the share of Constantine . . .

Our Neglect of them hitherto appears to me to Consist in our not availing ourselves of the Use that Nature seems to have intended them for, namely, a Northern Roadstead in which a Fleet of Men of War might Rendezvous and be ready to Act either on the offensive or defensive, from this Advanced post as circumstances might require. . . .

Scapa Flow is, in my opinion, admirably well adapted for a Northern Roadstead for a Fleet of Line-of-Battle-Ships; and it is doubtless the finest natural Roadstead in Britain or Ireland except Spit-Head, if all the Qualities which constitute a good Roadstead be properly considered . . .

Nature seems to have given every degree of Shelter to Scapa Flow that could possibly be expected in a Roadstead of such extent; and therefore it wants no artificial Shelter, a circumstance greatly in its favour.

The depth of Water is great, there being from 10 to 20 fathoms all over the Flow; the which in a more confined Anchorage would be rather a disadvantage; but as there is plenty of room here to stow the Anchor, I shall call it, in the Sailors' phrase, a Good fault . . .

If we had a strong Fleet there in War time, it would prevent the Enemy from going North-about Britain to Ireland or elsewhere should he ever attempt it. Our Fleet there would also intercept and prevent all the Enemy's Trade North-about Britain to Russia, Sweden, Norway, Denmark, Holland and Flanders, a Route which those Nations often take especially in War time.

When our Fleet, which is Blockading the Baltic and the Northern Ports of the Enemy, has occasion to quit these Stations, it might Rendezvous in Scapa Flow, in the greatest shelter and safety and secure from danger . . .

I have thus presumed to Present this Work to the Rt Honorable the Lords Commissioners of the Admiralty (whose Servant I have been in this line alone for the last 8 years of my life) from an idea that I could not discharge my Duty better than by submitting to their consideration a Scheme and Plan which has for its Object the Extension of the Maritime Power and Greatness of Britain; which, I beg, they will graciously condescend to Accept from the hands of their Lordships' most obedient and most humble Servant Graeme Spence.

London, 4 June 1812

Introduction

This is a book of voices. They are the voices of men and women who served in two world wars in one of the bleakest and most remote places in Britain – Scapa Flow, in the islands of Orkney. They are the voices of the lower deck, the barrack room, the lonely gunsite and they are as fresh and alive as when we first heard them forty years ago.

It all began with a BBC TV documentary. The idea had come from the well-known writer and broadcaster Ludovic (now Sir Ludovic) Kennedy. He had been based in Scapa Flow as a lieutenant in destroyers from 1940 to 1943 and had never forgotten the enduring and particular fascination of the place. While planning the programme we, the producers, published an appeal in the *Radio Times* asking people who had served in Scapa Flow to send in their accounts of life there during the two world wars. What we were hoping for was a modest crop of nicely written reminiscences from which a handful of pungent and evocative quotations might be extracted for use in the programme. What we got was something quite extraordinary.

After a few days two or three letters arrived. The following day there were a dozen more. And then they came in a prolonged avalanche – everything from anecdotes pencilled on the backs of postcards to semi-autobiographies many pages long. It was an amazing and moving response. Altogether well over seven hundred replies were received. Roughly half the letters were about the First War, half about the Second. The Navy, as was inevitable, predominated, but the Army was extremely well represented, as were, to a slightly lesser degree, the Women's Services and the RAF.

But it was not only the quantity which was impressive. Our appeal had somehow touched a nerve in the people who had responded to it. It had given the rank and file their chance and they had taken it.

What impressed us above all was the vividness of the material, and the vigour and energy with which so much of it was written. In many cases it was as though people had carried around their experiences with them for years waiting for someone to express an interest and at last somebody wanted to listen. But we were soon aware of something else: the freshness of the angle from which so much of it was written. This was war glimpsed from the lower deck or the ordinary barrack-room. Here was a view of war with the rawness and the sentiment, and the humour, left in. It showed that life in uniform was as likely to lead to boredom as to bravery. In short, this was war as it really was.

The programme was also enriched by the on-screen accounts by a number of witnesses of crucial moments in the history of Scapa Flow. One was a German naval officer present at the scuttlng of the German fleet in 1919. Another had served in *U-47*, the U-boat which penetrated the Flow in 1939 and sank the battleship *Royal Oak*, with the loss of over 800 lives. Yet another was a British sailor who was one of the *Royal Oak*'s survivors.

A key feature throughout was the reading, by a range of sympathetic actors, one of whom had himself served in the Flow as a naval officer, of memorable and often moving extracts from the letters we had received. Add to these elements historic film and stills from the archives, and some fine photography by an accomplished BBC cameraman of Orkney's striking landscapes and seascapes, and it is scarcely surprising that the film received considerable acclaim when it was shown in Christmas week of 1966, being credited with the exceptionally high audience figure for a programme of eleven and a half million viewers.

However, even at sixty minutes a TV documentary could include only a limited number of extracts from the mass of material we had acquired. Yet it was unthinkable to shelve what was basically a treasure trove of historical evidence, much of it vividly, movingly and often beautifully recorded. Hence our desire to put some of the best of the evidence we had acquired into a book to which we would supply the frame while the quotations would supply the flesh. It was our great good fortune that our proposal should have found its way to the desk of a publisher so sympathetic to its concept and style as Sir Allen Lane, creator of that remarkable phenomenon the Penguin paperback, at a time when he was moving into the publication of high-quality hardbacks.

Scapa Flow was first published by Allen Lane The Penguin Press, in 1968. We were especially gratified that when the book appeared it was well received in Orkney, a proud society not always happy with the literary intrusions of strangers who fail to show proof of adequate knowledge or research. The editor of its principal newspaper, the *Orcadian*, wrote of it that it presented 'a picture that every former sailor, soldier and civilian will instantly recognize – mirroring accurately, vividly and movingly the 60-year period when Orkney was in the mainstream of world events.'

It is especially pleasing to us, the authors, that this book should now be reprinted, in a fine hardback, forty years after its first publication. Whether this allows us to claim 'classic' status for it is not for us to judge, nor is it a matter of importance. It is good enough for us to see the book back on the shelves. The republication of *Scapa Flow* is not simply a matter of plucking an ancient book from a dusty shelf because it has a decent yarn to tell. It gives new life and recognition to a work which, we believe, can genuinely be seen as a book of quality which is also an early example of a distinguished and vibrant tradition of popular history.

Malcolm Brown and Patricia Meehan

APPROACH TO SCAPA FLOW

A winter people, far in the north,
Severed from brilliant cities
By the slash and jab of the Pentland Firth –
Island severed from island
By crested Sounds . . .

The Atlantic, restless, nudges the western crags,
Till Yesnaby, Hoy, Marwick
Are loaded with thunder, laced with spindrift.
Twice a day, ebb and flow
Its slow pulse beats through the Sounds
Till the islands brim like swans,
Till the islands lie in their seaweed like stranded hulks.
You would not think this grey empty stretch
Where fishermen haul their creels
Sheltered the British Navy in two great wars,
And after the first holocaust
Imprisoned the Kaiser's warships
Until the prisoners opened their veins and drowned.
Here Gunther Prien in his U-boat
Pierced the defences and sank the Royal Oak.
Then Irish labour sealed the Sounds
And exiled Italian prisoners
Returned their thanks to God with a tin chapel
Ablaze inside with saints and martyrs.
Old winters saw that agony, that glory . . .

From *The Winter Islands,* by George Mackay Brown

1

Scapa

Scapa left its mark on all who served there. To go to Scapa was to join a club whose membership you could never quite disown. Like Poona, Alexandria or Singapore, Scapa was a place to which it was impossible to have a neutral reaction. You either hated it, or you loved it. The evidence is that people usually did both. There were times when men spat the name out like a four-letter word. There were other times when they wondered how homely, familiar Great Britain ever came to have within its boundaries a place so serene, so different and of so special a flavour. Writing about it years afterwards some could still not surmount their loathing, but many remembered it with an almost surprised pleasure and discovered in themselves a deep longing to return. Yet side-by-side with the longing there was often a certain anxiety – that the place might be unrecognizable, that it would be so changed that they would feel they had ceased to belong.

To call it a place is a mistake, of course. Scapa – which should be pronounced to rhyme with 'sapper', in spite of the long 'a' given to the word by Cockney rhyming slang – is really just a sheet of water. It is a vast, almost landlocked anchorage, fifteen miles in length from north to south and eight miles broad from east to west, which on the map looks like a jagged hole punched in the southern half of the Orkney Islands. It is so big that it could have housed all the navies of the world in the great days of sea-power. It has three main entrances. Hoxa Sound, between the islands of

South Ronaldsay and Flotta, was the front gate through which the battleships came and went. Switha Sound, between Flotta and South Walls, the fat little peninsula that juts eastwards from the southern end of the island of Hoy, was the narrower gate for the destroyers. Hoy Sound, between the northern end of Hoy and the large island which is known as the Mainland, was rarely used by naval vessels in time of war, though now it is the regular route through which the daily mail steamer approaches Orkney on its often boisterous journey from Caithness.

Until a generation ago, there were several other entrances to the Flow – tiny ones on the eastern side which were only wide enough to admit fishing boats or naval ships of the size of a submarine. Within six weeks of the outbreak of war in 1939 a German U-boat slipped unperceived through the northernmost of these entrances, Kirk Sound, and sank a battleship at anchor with the loss of over eight hundred lives. Subsequently a road was constructed, carried on huge concrete blocks from island to island, effectively ensuring that nothing so audacious could happen again. Called after the man who ordered that they should be built, these causeways are known as the Churchill Barriers.

Scapa Flow is empty now. This immense anchorage, which twice in living memory was the home of one great Navy and which also became the graveyard of another, is almost as it was sixty years and two wars ago. Just occasionally a handful of frigates or a couple of destroyers will slip into the Flow to pick up fuel at Lyness, the old base on the island of Hoy, and the familiar grey silhouettes will be seen far out across the water, evoking a surge of memory in those who recall the days when Scapa Flow was in the mainstream of world events. But by the morning they will have sailed away, leaving Scapa to the sea-birds and the little local steamers like the *Hoy Head* and the *Watchful* which chug about between the islands with tourists and the post.

Here and there are relics of the great occupation. There is a litter of concrete gun batteries on the headland overlooking Hoxa Sound. A mile outside the old and lovely town of Stromness more batteries face out towards the open sea, with all the guns gone and the tall range-finder station standing there like a windowless signal-box beside some abandoned railway. In the entrances sealed by the Churchill Barriers and out in Hoy Sound, old block-ships lie rusting, reddish-brown skeletons which are slowly being eaten away by the sea and which take on a bizarre, abstract beauty at sunset or sunrise. On Hoy itself you will see clusters of half-fallen barrack-rooms in lonely fields, with occasionally a dazzlingly white enamelled urinal standing to one side like a slab of megalithic stone. And Lyness itself, with its huts and roads and huge corrugated-iron cinema and handful of people, is a ghost town, the scene of a gold rush long since abandoned, an Orcadian Dawson City.

One wonders what the men and women who served there would think of it if they did go back. Their Scapa Flow was crowded with ships that were anchored in rows like houses on an estate – battleships and carriers and cruisers and destroyers and mine-sweepers – while as many as three hundred drifters shuttled to and fro, carrying supplies and letters and bringing men to new postings or back from leave. So many barrage balloons hung in the sky that one might have imagined that the islands were suspended from them. Three-ton lorries rattled along country roads to where bulled and gleaming guns pointed to the sky or out to sea. The canteens were busy with egg and chips, beer and hot sweet tea and the cinemas ran a succession of films and ENSA concerts at which men starved of normal life whistled and stamped and cheered at Flanagan and Allen, Gracie Fields, Yehudi Menuhin and Evelyn Laye. And now the wind blows through the ruins and the rank grass and the Flow is wiped clean like a slate.

Of course, it is no use regretting it. No one wants those days back. It is better for the Flow to be empty than teeming with warships. Orkney was never so crowded and buzzing with activity but the animation was there for the wrong reason. The litter of concrete and rubble around the islands – fortunately there is not enough of it to spoil their beauty – is better than the smartest and tidiest gun emplacements ever made.

And the Orkney of peacetime is the real Orkney. Its role as a bustling Imperial stronghold was one alien to its character. These remote, unspoilt islands off the north coast of Scotland on the other side of the Pentland Firth are scarcely British at all.

Their flavour is more like that of Scandinavia. Their names – Flotta, Fara, Graemsay, Westray, Shapinsay, Eynhallow and, of course, the name of Scapa Flow itself – have a Nordic ring. There are no highlands and few hills in Orkney, and what hills there are look as if they were shaped and smoothed by Arctic glaciers millions of years ago. Seen in winter under a covering of snow they are more what one would expect to see in Greenland or the Lofoten Isles than within the boundaries of Great Britain. Orkney is essentially a quiet, uncrowded, uncluttered place. It has lonely though well-metalled roads which run with an almost Roman straightness. It has two miniature and attractive towns, Kirkwall and Stromness, where the main streets are narrow and paved with flag-stones and where pedestrians exercise an almost undisputed right of way. It has long stretches of empty undulating land which look ordinary enough in winter but which produce an astounding range of colours in summer from gorse and heather and an abundance of wild flowers. It has isolated grey farm-houses with patchwork fields where seagulls swarm around tractors. It has wide lochs with names like Stenness and Harray where fishers bob about in boats bringing in splendid trout that are subsequently displayed for view in comfortable fishing hotels much loved by gentle Buchanesque men from Perth and Glasgow. Always, at the end of every perspective, is the sea – sometimes beating against huge cliffs as at Yesnaby or Marwick and the coast of Hoy, those mighty western ramparts that contrast strangely with the gentler contours prevailing everywhere else in Orkney; sometimes curving into tiny, sandy beaches littered with sea-wrack as at Skara Brae or Birsay; sometimes boiling in an almost perpetual turmoil as off Cantick Head or in Hoy Sound.

And when one turns inwards away from the North Sea or the Pentland Firth or the Atlantic, there, dominating the scene by its sheer empty vastness, is Scapa Flow.

Perhaps the best way to see the Flow is to go south from Kirkwall towards the Churchill Barriers on one of those evenings in summer when the sky over Hoy is a mixture of clouds and sun. Then every movement in the Flow will be caught by sunlight and the water will become a silvery plasma stretching away for miles, with little, treeless islands dotted here and there, and the long, undulating outline of Hoy will lie silhouetted on the horizon like a sleeping whale. Or cross over to Hoy early one morning – there are boatmen in Stromness who will take you across – and look eastwards from the old H.7 Battery or from the road that rises steeply up from Lyness. From either vantage point you will see a huge panoramic picture of many colours, ranging from the pastel greys and greens and ochres of the islands to the deep blues and astonishing turquoises of the Flow. You will appreciate at once why Scapa is the sort of place that people do not easily forget.

But the Orkney of today, the real, permanent Orkney, is only incidentally our concern. This book is about the Orkney of two short, intense interludes in this century, when thousands of people from the cities, towns and villages of Britain were taken from their ordinary civilian lives and sent northwards to crew the ships and man the defences of Scapa Flow.

2

The 'Jellicoes'

The classic route to Scapa Flow was by train to the north of Scotland and then by boat across the Pentland Firth. Indeed, to go there in your own hammock in your own ship was somehow ordinary and unmemorable. It was not a proper initiation. Only those who had spent twenty-four hours or more in a special troop train and had then been bucketed across the boisterous waters of the Firth, really knew how far Scapa was from home.

In the First War they called the trains the 'Jellicoes', after the Admiral who assumed command of the Grand Fleet in Scapa Flow in August 1914. The name was revived in the Second. No one expects to travel comfortably in wartime, but these trains were worse than most; crammed, cluttered, cold, and interminable. If you started from London, you had seven hundred miles in front of you. If you were a naval rating drafted from Devonport to Scapa you were travelling from one end of Britain to the other. It was a Russian rather than a British experience.

Two of London's famous Victorian terminus stations were the usual launching-points for this dreary trek north. Many servicemen left from King's Cross, travelled to Scotland by the east coast route, and joined the 'Jellicoe' at Perth. But the official 'Jellicoe' – the through train from London to Thurso – started from Euston, striking north-westwards on the old L.N.W.R. line. For its innumerable passengers places like Crewe, Carlisle and Carstairs would always be inextricably entwined with this long journey to war. They were not towns, simply stations, where you woke from an uneasy sleep, and might, with luck, enjoy the incredible relief of a hot cup of tea.

But above all, the north of Scotland was the territory to which the 'Jellicoes' seemed particularly to belong. It was the least known and it was the last part of the journey. North of Perth the Highland Line took you on a slow sweep through the Cairngorms to Inverness and thence along the coast through Invergordon, Tain, and Golspie to Helmsdale. At Helmsdale the line turned inland through the bare, undulating hills of western Caithness and then swung back north-eastwards towards Thurso. Usually it was dawn when the trains came through this final lap. Small wonder that men waking after an uncomfortable, smoky night's sleep and peering through the steamed-up windows felt that they had arrived at the end of nowhere.

If you talk to the men who work the Highland Line today they will speak of the 'Jellicoes' with affection. For those were the great days of the line when night after night, and sometimes twice nightly, the long double-engined trains rumbled north to Thurso. Now diesel engines pull the modern corridor stock of British Rail's Scottish Region through this lonely and under-populated land, the trains are infrequent and half empty, and the little stations with gracious names like Kildonan, Kinbrace and Forsinard have all but closed down.

For countless men service at Scapa really began at Euston or King's Cross. And like everything else associated with Scapa and the Orkneys in time of war, that long journey north was something that left an indelible mark on the memory.

These are the kind of things men thought about their journeys to Scapa over fifty years ago, in the days of the Great War.

¶ A draft of 200 ratings left Portsmouth, August 1914, for Scapa Flow. We were locked in the train for twenty-eight hours, twenty to a carriage.

We had a stop at Carlisle to change driver and take in water. The train was crowded with holiday-makers and a dear old lady spoke to me at the carriage window. She said: 'Don't move – I'll be back', and disappeared into the refreshment bar. Back she came with a wrapped box. A bottle of whisky, I thought, and thanked her. The train pulled out and with eager fingers we opened it. It was a box of Edinburgh rock.[1]

¶ Leaving Devonport late one night we eventually reached Scapa two nights later, having endured a train journey gruelling almost beyond imagination.

Movement in or out of your compartment or along the corridor was comparable to what now might be described as a Commando obstacle course. Men, bags, baggage of all descriptions everywhere, including kitbags and hammocks and the inevitable assortment of 'empties'.

In the afternoon and more particularly at night, the whole train was strewn with 'bodies' trying to sleep. The air was dense with smoke and smelt more like a ship's bilges than a train; but the thought of having a window open, even if one could get to it, was out of the question and asking for trouble. Little or no heat was provided by the train and it was a case of putting up with any discomfort to keep warm.[2]

* * *

¶ At King's Cross, as well as those on draft were many returning from leave in all stages of sobriety (or insobriety). It always seemed a remarkable thing to me to feel one would soon be in the company of strangers, yet after a few minutes one would feel one had known some of them for years. After a few drinks I found myself in such company and we were soon looking for a suitable compartment to travel together.

The compartment into which we piled contained one other passenger, a young lady, but we soon settled down for the journey. It was not long, however, before nature began to assert itself and we realized we were in a non-corridor carriage. As the train did not stop long at any station this soon became an ordeal, then critical. As I was sitting next to the young lady I was given several nudges and whispers which put me in a predicament, but the situation was saved by the young lady herself who, after first telling me she had been travelling all day from France and fully under stood the position, said she would read her news-paper for a few minutes, which she did, and soon everyone was relieved and comfortable.[3]

* * *

¶ The memory I have of the journey north by special train from Portsmouth to Thurso in 1915 was of being confined to the train and living on pies for about three days, with an occasional wash by putting our heads out of the railway carriage window to catch the raindrops.[4]

* * *

¶ We arrived at Thurso at midnight and it was as black as the inside of a coal bag. Our guide told us to catch hold of the man in front and we set off. Arriving at the Town Hall we were given a hot drink and a couple of blankets and bedded down in what appeared to be orange boxes. It must have been close on 1 A.M. when we settled but at 4.30 A.M. we were exhorted to 'Show a Leg' and 'Rise and Shine'. We rose but I don't think we shone very much. Outside were some small wagonettes and we were loaded into these with our bags and hammocks, the drivers jogged the horses and we were on our merry way to Scrabster Harbour.[5]

The journey by 'Jellicoe' was much the same experience in both wars. The trains were, relatively speaking, more comfortable in the second, less likely to have locked doors and more likely to have corridors, so that it was no longer a standing joke that one daren't put one's head out of the window for fear of the spray. But essentially there was no difference, because in both wars men were leaving their homes and their wives and their sweet-hearts and all the consolations of civilization to spend months on end in uncomfortable ships and remote gunsites. In both wars there was the prospect of isolation and hardship and boredom (though there was also the prospect of good companionship and achievement), and some, though they could not know it even if they feared it, would be going to their deaths in a convoy run or a destroyer dog-fight or in some futile military or naval accident.

This is how men saw this first stage of the journey to Scapa in the war of 1939–45.

¶ Those journeys to Stromness are etched deep. The miserable good-byes, the slow progress across London through Underground stations littered with bodies; King's Cross with its hordes of Service personnel – people from the North going South, soldiers from Plymouth heading for Greenock – R.T.O.s, M.P.s, N.A.A.F.I.s – the lot!

You learned quickly in those days. You carried your little suit-case and your gas-mask and tin hat, and you looked pityingly on those loaded with full pack, kit-bag and rifle. When the barrier gate opened, you were through in a flash, while they groaningly tied themselves into webbing. You tore down the length of the train and hurtled into an empty compartment – the corner seats, on that trip, were priceless! In minutes the compartment was full: kit, kit-bags and great-coats piled up, pleasantries were exchanged about the size and manoeuvrability of legs and boots, and then we waited for the train to start.

Eight, ten, twelve hours of it. The blue, dim lighting that made reading impossible; the humped, shadowy figures in ungainly sleep; the snuffles and snores. The sailor's head that lolled on one's shoulder, open mouth blasting out the fumes of that last pint; the fug, the smell of damp uniforms, the acrid taste of tobacco and cigarette smoke. Sometimes a brave soul would lower a window, and the sweet cold night air would roar in – until a snarling, blasphemous, grunting chorus requested that it be closed again.

A short walk became imperative after an hour or so – clambering over enormous boots on sprawling, gaitered legs, squeezing past piled-up mountains in the corridor. Here and there a still, sad, lonely figure at a window, gazing blindly out at an invisible countryside. The firefly glow of a cigarette and the scrape and flare of a match . . .

The train slows down. A station! The static scene is galvanized into passionate life, for a station means TEA! The doors swing perilously before the train has even stopped; a swarm of khaki and two shades of blue converging on the trolleys with their gleaming urns; pint mugs flourishing, waving, thrust out imploringly like beggars' bowls. The warning whistle – the toot from the engine – the unsteady trot with two brimming mugs of scalding tea and a couple of sticky buns, back to a train already slowly moving; the scramble into the doors – any door! – the inevitable couple left behind, racing madly along the platform.

Then again the dim blue darkness. On and on, hopeless, miserable, cramped, sleepless, gritty of eye and foul of mouth from the too-many cigarettes. Faint at first, then louder, the throb of aircraft engines. Clearly audible now – and a little buzz of chatter. Are they ours? Are they Jerries? Can they see us? But the roar dwindles, becomes a distant half-heard hum, vanishes. An airman says, 'God, I wish I was up there with 'em!' A sailor grunts, 'Go ahead, son – more room for us!' and turns his head farther into his collar.

Then, in the grey gloom, we glide at last into Edinburgh. The carriage heaves and turmoils; an unreal fantasy of figures climbs stiffly down and a swelling crocodile surges down the platform. Journey's end for some. Home for some. Just about halfway for us. We find the R.T.O., we enquire about our train – oh, God! Five hours to wait! You can do a lot in five hours. See the town, get a good meal, get drunk – me, I head for a special waiting-room. It's in an odd corner; and it's staffed by W.V.S. It's got a couple of broken-down settees, some beat-up armchairs, some mattresses on the floor, a hand-basin and a bit of a cracked mirror. You queue for a few minutes, then the luxury of a wash and shave. Then you go to the motherly old body and you say, 'One o'clock, Ma, please', and then you collapse on to a settee or into a chair, or on to the floor, and you're out. Asleep. Unconscious. Dead-o.

How they did it I don't know, but there would come a gentle shake on the shoulder, a kindly voice, 'Come awa', sonny – train time!' And a cup of hot sweet tea and a biscuit.

You stumble blearily, sleepily out and find your train. An R.T.O. corporal is calling endlessly, flatly, 'Change at Perth for Thurso. Change at Perth for Thurso.'[6]

* * *

¶ Cold, my goodness it's cold, and a spare blanket of very dubious appearance is at a premium. Snow outside now, but the fellow you've chummed up with has a hip-flask of the best rum in the world and he's pleased for you to have a swig. He's done this trip before, obviously.

What endless purgatory this really is and one's newly married wife is being left farther and farther behind. For how long? Look through the window at the rolling white inhospitable hills of north-east Scotland. This is surely a war on its own.[7]

* * *

¶ I remember the train drawing into Crewe station with every door swinging open so that we could hop out and get a cup of tea, and then just stopping long enough for us not to be able to get one.[8]

* * *

¶ On one winter journey the train was unheated and by the time we reached Carlisle many hours later we were cold and hungry. The brightest prospect for hours had been the excellent meat pies which were usually on sale on the station platform. The window-spaces were jammed with troops of all three services and I was sharing one with a burly, three-stripe sailor, each of us clutching money to buy a pie.

The first thing we saw was a little, wizened old man pushing a barrow and shouting 'Ices'. He was hailed by my friend the matelot in broad Cockney, 'Got any 'ot uns, mite?'[9]

* * *

¶ The one bright oasis to anticipate after the tortuous, slow journey northwards was the entry into a dark and deserted station called Perth, where a stop of some considerable length was made. Always the concerted dash to the temporary wooden building, with no lights to show its purpose, but well lit inside to reveal the welcome long counter, dispensing angels lined up to offer steaming hot tea, coffee or cocoa; a wonderful selection of cakes and sandwiches, sweets and cigarettes. A Forces canteen run by Church organizations, manned by volunteer ladies who waited patiently in the early hours of the morning for this train to come in. How grateful we all were.[10]

* * *

¶ Here it may be appropriate to append a tribute to the Scottish people. In spite of the necessary veil of secrecy regarding troop movements, they seemed to have an uncanny knowledge of our staging stops, which often were in isolated places – and from nowhere, it seemed, would appear tea, coffee, and baked Scottish delicacies, nicely served in spotless china-ware with a precision that would have foxed Rommel himself. And this in spite of the thousand or more troops involved and of the meagre rationing system which was equally applicable to them. This beneficent and welcome gesture was undertaken both by night and by day – even in the small hours.[11]

* * *

¶ I remember passing through Invergordon. At one point the train stopped at a wild remote moor, but beside the track stood members of the W.V.S. with tables full of cakes and sandwiches. We stopped for a meal, then all aboard, leaving them in that lonely place with the crusts and remnants of our meal.[12]

* * *

¶ From the end of 1940 a kitchen car was attached to the train, run by the Salvation Army, and twice during the night – each coach in turn – all could get a jolly good cup of tea and some food. Bless the Salvation Army, who did that magnificent job. I speak for hundreds of thousands who would have had a blessed awful journey but for their efforts.[13]

* * *

¶ On one trip we were held up for four days at Inverness because the preceding train was snowbound. The local authorities gave us a good time. Poor devils in the other train had a bad time from cold and hunger, and I believe a naval Captain died despite a valiant attempt to bring him to safety by sledge. I well remember travelling miles between unbroken walls of snow higher than the train.[14]

* * *

¶ Oh, that long haul from London to Thurso! Hour after hour incarcerated in the train with dreadful thoughts of the limbo to which I was being sent – Scapa Flow. And at Perth being turned out of the compartment which I had shared with two ladies – I was a serviceman and would have to sit elsewhere! Evidently someone thought that this dog-tired young A.C.2 would commit rape and murder on the next stage between Perth and Inverness. Or perhaps they were protecting me from what might be the embarrassing attention of two elderly ladies? 'Hell!' I thought. 'Freedom!' and hauled my pack and kit-bag to the other end of the train.

Another change at Inverness and then the night journey by military train to Thurso. A drunken Norwegian sailor snored like thunder all night and then spewed his heart out with the first streak of a bleak wintry dawn. Others, with army boots off, had added to the foetid atmosphere with the sweat of their feet and I retched inwardly, cowering in a corner despising my companions, despising myself and those who had sent me on this journey to God-knows where.[15]

* * *

¶ Thurso we reached in the early morning. It was a terribly rough day, with enormous waves crashing over the harbour, and after waiting for hours we were told that sailings were cancelled and that we must return next day to see if a crossing would be possible. Thurso, being a small town, was not accustomed to such a sudden increase in population and naturally it could not provide food or accommodation for so many troops. The police station and church halls were packed, so many of us were left out like tramps, but we did find some signs of a transit camp being built near the shore. It was a terrible night trying to rest in such bitter cold and rain, with the winds howling at what we estimated as 'Force 9'. and us curled up in the bare protection of a Nissen hut in its early stage of erection, as yet without any ends built up – a man-made wind tunnel in effect. What a night![16]

* * *

¶ It must have been towards the afternoon that we reached Thurso. We were herded into sheds where we were given what must have been a most unsuitable meal before a sea-trip – tinned herrings in tomato sauce. However, we were young and perennially hungry, so it was eaten.

We were then taken for a terrifying ride on flat lorries, tightly packed so that we had to stand, clumsy with kit-bags, rifles and webbing, over a heart-stopping road which seemed to be on the very edge of precipices with a grey sea beneath. We drove at a shocking speed, and it was with the greatest relief that we stopped at a little harbour.[17]

That harbour, Scrabster – two miles from Thurso on the northern coast of Caithness – became very familiar to the servicemen of both wars. From there the little ferry and supply ships went daily across to the Orkney Islands, which are plainly visible from Thurso in all but the murkiest of weathers. Indeed, there are times when the cliffs and hills of Orkney seem so near that a stranger might almost take them for an extension of the Scottish mainland. On such occasions the channel that runs between Orkney and Caithness – it is a mere six and a half miles wide at its narrowest point – looks beguilingly simple to cross. But two generations of servicemen know otherwise, for this is the Pentland Firth.

3

The Pentland Firth

The Pentland Firth is one of the most notorious stretches of water in the world. Here the North Sea and the Atlantic meet in a confined channel, and the result is an almost permanent turbulence. A calm summer day over Caithness or Orkney is no indication that the Firth is equally calm; a wild day is likely to mean that it is virtually impassable.

Crossing the Firth, like the 'Jellicoe' journey, became an essential part of the Scapa tradition. For a voyage scheduled at under three hours – though bad weather could make it five – it had a remarkably sinister reputation. It was the subject of innumerable jokes and much wry comment. One serviceman suggested that there must be more sea-sick in the Pentland Firth than in any comparable area of water on earth. But though the crossing was something to joke about afterwards it was not much of a joke at the time. It was not usually a dangerous experience, but it had its share of wasteful, unnecessary fatalities. Men sometimes gave up their leave because of it, or tried to beg or buy a seat on one of the few available aircraft going south. If, however, one was going to Scapa by the traditional route that began with the 'Jellicoes', there was no escaping it. Many a serviceman clambering off his three-ton lorry at Scrabster Harbour for the first time, with stories of the Pentland Firth's vindictiveness firmly embedded in his mind by those who knew, must have gone on board his troop-ship in a state of acute apprehension, with more than a casual eye cocked at the weather.

There were two routes to Orkney from Scrabster. Ships bound for the Naval bases of Longhope or Lyness entered Scapa Flow through Switha Sound, the normal gate for the Fleet's destroyers. Ships bound for the Orkney Mainland sailed along the western coast of Hoy, entered the Flow at its north-western gate, Hoy Sound, and berthed at Stromness.

This route in particular could at times take on something of the nature of an agreeable cruise. On sunny calm days – which can happen in January as well as June – it is an exciting experience to watch the great, red-brown cliffs of Hoy move slowly towards you across the turquoise sea. The Old Man of Hoy, a stack of rock as tall as St Paul's Cathedral, stands clear of the coastline like a sergeant at attention in front of his men. Several miles farther on, the cliffs rise to an apex of over eleven hundred feet at St John's Head, which is all the more impressive for being absolutely vertical. Here and there waterfalls find their way over terrifying heights down to the sea.

But this remote and strangely beautiful world can be viciously transformed when the Atlantic turns rough.

¶ The Pentland Firth is well-known by seamen as one of the worst stretches of water in the world. I have seen leave-taking or returning soldiers – and sailors – wallowing in the scuppers in a mess of vomit, or wedged in bunks, or even *tied* to stanchions, for the whole of the trip. That stretch of fast water makes a ship lurch and twist and bucket and bounce as no other that I know of.[1]

* * *

¶ As the stout little steamer heaved its ancient black sides through the crashing waves, skirting the swirls of maelstroms, one would cling to a stanchion and peer through the jagged, slanting rain at the formidable iron-clad heights of Dunnet Head and the gaunt, spray-shrouded cliffs. One felt a ghostly pity for the haggard shades of the Spaniards, fleeing fitfully westwards around the north of Scotland through these terrible seas, hungry, cold and desperate after the defeat of their Armada.[2]

*   *   *

¶ Blackout precautions were strictly enforced – there was even a ban on smoking – as we boarded a requisitioned M.O.W. Transport which was to take us across the Pentland Firth.

The boarding process is worthy of note. For the few – the more orderly method of the hand-railed gangway; for the majority – planks of wood slung from the quay to the side of the ship, with constant admonitions of 'hurry, hurry' – 'get a move on' – come on now – move!' One of our men slipped and fell off an improvised boarding device and, due to the heaving of the ship, was crushed to death between ship and quay. With a full realization as to what had happened and the implications of his action, an officer of the Regiment was lowered, and recovered the body of the crushed soldier.[3]

*   *   *

¶ I remember an occasion when we were crossing the Firth, a young sailor attempted to pass some soldiers talking in the gangway when suddenly he fell into the sea, the gate which was put across the gap in the rails having collapsed. Lifebelts were thrown, and the cry went up 'Man Overboard'. The boat had to travel a considerable distance before it was able to complete a circle to get near the position where he fell. It was of no avail, we couldn't find him.[4]

*   *   *

¶ At Scrabster we boarded an ancient mailboat, and I noticed that several hardened sailors found convenient spots such as boat davits to wedge themselves between the posts and the rails – in a sitting position, feet resting on the rail. Not knowing why, I did likewise.

The old boat left and as it passed Dunnet Head we received the full welcome of the Pentland Firth – not just ordinary waves but hills and valleys of deep green sea – the meeting through thousands of years between the Atlantic Ocean and the North Sea creating a nine- to ten-knot current. One minute we were gazing at the clouds and next minute almost dipping our feet in the

Pentland – hence the importance of being wedged! And that old Labrador – the ship's pet – walked up and down the deck in experienced salt-water style – eyes riveted on the horizon, head held erect, body likewise, legs bending to the angle of the motion.[5]

* * *

¶ What an uncomfortable and, to some, a miserable sea crossing that was. Even in the best of weather the sea carried huge billows which came broadside on, and the ship rolled like a barrel. To the fore of the main deck was the 'saloon' for the lower ranks. This tiny room was always full of khaki- and blue-clad airmen, the air was foul and thick with tobacco smoke, and any who went in because they felt ill would find the conditions added to their misery. Many, like myself, preferred to remain outside whatever the weather, and lean with our backs on the cabins and our feet nearly touching the rail, so narrow was the gangway. I have seen the time when the crossing was really bad, when the ship rolled so much that at one moment we were lying almost horizontally on our backs and the next standing on the rail which was now under us with the swirling waters seemingly only inches from our feet. It was always a relief when land hove in sight and we passed the Old Man of Hoy, a rock jutting out on our starboard side. On occasions when it was very rough, the ship was allowed to pass into the smoother waters of Scapa Flow, and so shorten the worst part of the crossing.[6]

* * *

¶ I was sailing back to Orkney during a south-west gale on the *St Ola* and as we passed St John's Head on Hoy I saw the waterfall over the Head fall upwards. It fell down for a little way, then the force of the wind curved it round and blew it up the cliff again.[7]

* * *

¶ No sooner had the *St Ninian* left the safety of Scrabster Bay than the old girl started bucking and rolling and, with the exception of a handful of young Jack Tars bound for Scapa, we were a miserable sea-sick bunch. How all of us envied these young salts who stood on deck swaying with the movement of the *St Ninian* in best nautical style while we lay groaning. And then it happened. One by one the bold lads made for the rails and they were – each and every one of them – as sick as dogs, and when we reached Scapa they looked a bedraggled lot as they made their way down the gangway. I think most of us felt pleased that even those in a sailor suit could be laid low.

When we did arrive at Stromness I was surprised to see a fleet of ambulances awaiting the arrival of the *St Ninian* but during my short stay in Stromness I soon learned why. The number of 'dead ducks' coming off the *St Ninian* each evening bound for the garrison at Kirkwall (some sixteen miles away) had made the authorities realize that the only way to get personnel back to their quarters was for the ambulance to be laid on as part of a drill.[8]

* * *

¶ I remember on one trip hearing a soldier remark: 'I don't mind someone being seasick on me but when it's someone four places farther along the rail and he missed the three in between, that's what I call bloody bad luck!'[9]

* * *

¶ So you went aboard. Already, in Scrabster Harbour, she heaved gently under your feet; and the motion, and the oil-smell, and the general ship-smell, were a grim augury.

She slipped her moorings and manoeuvred out through the entrance. You walked about the little deck, and hoped – and hoped. But always the Pentland Firth won, and always you surrendered and staggered away to find a place to die in nausea.

And those fiends of hell in khaki or navy blue or light blue would come and find you, and ask you if you fancied kippers and custard, or pork chop with chocolate sauce. Or perhaps an angel, an ugly angel with a cockney twang or a Scottish lilt, would say 'Take a nip – you'll feel better', and the warm glow would slide down and for a minute the day would brighten.

Then, after a century of suffering, you would hear a ragged cheer – and you would guess that you were nearing journey's end. You would find enough strength to totter to the rail and there it was. The Old Man of Hoy. A stark, forbidding, frightening pillar of ancient rock, backed by dark, lowering cliffs. The water, grey even under a summer sun, heaved and crashed at its everlasting foe, and the Old Man just stood and defied it. 'Another hour or so!' someone said. Oh, God, another hour!

But today perhaps the weather would be kind, and in the lee of the island of Hoy it might be calmer.

On up the west side of Hoy, and here, as always, the little miracle. The coastline, rugged and grand and grey, the tearing sea, the tireless gulls, drew and gripped your interest, and you forgot to feel sick, as the *Zet* ploughed its way around the northern tip of Hoy, across the mouth of Burra Sound. Far away we saw, or thought we saw, or pretended we saw, the low grim shapes of England's battle fleet – in Scapa Flow to the south-east.[10]

* * *

¶ I have stood on the quayside at Stromness, waiting to board the *Earl of Zetland* to go on leave, and seen men coming north carried off on stretchers. Wives will never know how we suffered for those ten days at home.[11]

What helped to increase the fearsome reputation of the Pentland Firth was the fact that the ships which crossed it were not built to withstand its violent moods. Returning servicemen today would be pleasantly surprised at the relative ease with which the present ferry steamer copes with it – though there are always a number of occasions each year when she cancels her scheduled sailing, and she has her fair quota of sea-sick passengers. But she was built with the Pentland Firth in mind, and has profited from the experience of her many predecessors.

A roll-call of the ships that shared in the ferrying of men and supplies across the Firth during the two wars would be a substantial one. A sailor of the First War wrote about three of them.

¶ I remember three boats being used at various times in the mail trip across the Pentland: the *Alouette*, the *Flying Kestrel*, and the *Lady Rowena*. The *Alouette* was a small cargo boat and a bad sailing boat. Turtle-backed, she shipped water at the best of times. She showed her worst in a Pentland swell. The *Flying Kestrel* was a Merseyside tender. Built like a tug she was fast but hobbed up and down in the water like a cork. The *Lady Rowena* was a pleasure paddle-steamer from the Clyde. She was a stately lady. She took fair and foul in her stride. She brought me home, and from her aft I had my last view of Scapa.[12]

There was also the *St Ola*,* which continued the regular ferry-service from Scrabster to the Orkney Mainland which was her normal routine in peace-time; but she was mail and civilian boat rather than troop-carrier. Undoubtedly the ships which brought most men to Orkney and were most vividly remembered were the *St Ninian* and the *Earl of Zetland*. They were both, like the *Ola*, vessels of the North of Scotland, Orkney and Shetland Shipping Company, but though these northern seas were their natural home they were no more adept at dealing with them than ships requisitioned from gentler waters. The *St Ninian* indeed, was admitted by expert opinion to have 'some peculiarity in the design of her hull which, while it made her a good boat with a head sea, made her roll miraculously under other conditions'.** Equipped with this fatal flaw, she served throughout both wars, plying regularly between Scrabster and the Flow. Statistics for the Second War showed that she crossed the Firth three thousand times, steaming over 100,000 miles and carrying over 900,000 people. Despite her reputation, she is remembered with affection by men who sailed in her.

---

* The old *St Ola** to the Orcadians. The present Pentland ferry steamer is also called the *St Ola*. There has been a *St Ola* on the Pentland Firth run for three quarters of a century.

** *Northwards by Sea*, by Gordon Donaldson (distributed by John Grant, Booksellers, Ltd, 31 George IV Bridge, Edinburgh, I). We are indebted to this book for a number of the details given in this chapter.

¶ No account of Scapa in wartime would be complete without reference to the old *St Ninian*, the smallish steam packet that helped keep Scapa alive. She was maid of all work. Troop-carrier, mail-boat for the Fleet, provisioner. Many thousands of tons of cargo must have crossed in her smallish hold, and been hoisted out on her old donkey-winch. Hundreds of men must remember her with affection for when she was taking them home on leave, and despairing resignation when taking them back the other way. A real old sea-dog. I wonder what became of her.[13]

The *St Ninian's* active service ended in 1945. She was by then half a century old, and in spite of her reliability and accident-free record, was considered ready for retirement. She lay idle at Aberdeen for some years, and was finally broken up at Rosyth in 1948.

The *Earl of Zetland* was smaller than the *St Ninian* (548 to the *Ninian's* 705 tons), shallow in draught and wide of beam. She carried well over half a million people across the Pentland Firth in the Second War. Known as the *Earl* or the *Zet*, she too had a reputation for rough riding.

¶ One of the Pentland boats was called the *Earl of Zetland* which I understand had a flat bottom. It was said by the troops that it was torpedo-proof because it wasn't in the water long enough. It did everything but loop the loop.'[14]

The *Earl of Zetland* is still in service today, but she is rarely seen in Orkney waters. As befits her name, she circulates among the north isles of Shetland.

There is a story told in Orkney and Thurso which has become, in its way, part of the folklore of the Firth. Early in the Second World War a King's Messenger arrived at Scrabster with des-patches for the Fleet. The sea was at its roughest, and Captain Swanson of the *St Ola* had decided to cancel his scheduled crossing to Stromness. The King's Messenger was angry – it was nonsense that the boat could not sail; the boat *must* sail; it was ridiculous for the Captain to be deterred by a spot of bad weather; and in any case the Messenger was carrying despatches of great urgency. 'All right,' thought Captain Swanson, 'I'll show him what the Pentland Firth is like' – and he agreed to go. The crossing was fierce and the Messenger was soon violently sea-sick. He collapsed on to a cabin bunk, and did not emerge until long after the *St Ola* had arrived at Stromness. As Captain Swanson drily remarked when telling the story afterwards: 'It was only the hope o' deein' that kept him alive!'

4

'A City of Ships'

To most of the 'Jellicoes' passengers the villainous crossing of the Pentland Firth must have seemed the last straw, but there was still one more ordeal to come. Arrival in Scapa Flow was not a comfortable journey's end. For the Army or R.A.F. it usually meant a further wearisome trip to camp in a lurching three tonner. For the Navy men it had not even the attraction of a landfall: somewhere in that great sheet of water a ship was waiting for them. But the first call was the depot ship, the clearing house for all naval personnel posted to the Flow.

In the First War the depot ship was H.M.S. *Imperieuse* ('Imperoose' to the sailors), an old cruiser which had had her engines taken out and a corrugated iron roof built on her. In the Second War the ship which most sailors remembered was the former Union Castle liner *Dunluce Castle*, which came to the Flow early in 1940. 'She was old and pretty rotten,' wrote one of her transit passengers, 'and though thoroughly cleaned to Naval standards and routine, there was an all-pervading sweet smell of mildew and decay.'

But First War or Second, the arrival procedure was the same: the drifters clustering round the depot ship, waiting to claim the travellers for their billets on ship or shore; the heart-stopping leap from deck to deck by men hung about with full equipment, some times in darkness, often still queasy from sea-sickness. It was a rough welcome that Scapa Flow gave them.

¶ On arrival at the Flow, the *Ninian* lay alongside a depot ship with her accompanying drifters. Here began, in my opinion, the hardest task of all – the transporting from the *Ninian* to the appropriate drifter of all one's kit, alone and unaided as everyone else had their own problems. There were often as many as ten drifters lying alongside the depot ship, and if by any chance the one you required to complete your journey was lying well out, you had a nightmare job of transferring a full kit-bag, a hammock, large suitcase, small suitcase, and, if you happened to be a tradesman, a tool-box as well which could weigh a hundredweight or more. In the choppy seas of the Flow those drifters were never still. As one crossed the waist of each successive drifter to reach the one you wanted, with both arms loaded with kit, you poised on the gunwale of one boat, until the gunwale of the adjoining one finished its eight to ten feet rise and fall on the swell, and then quickly jumped for it. This usually meant at least two journeys, sometimes three, from the depot ship to the appropriate drifter. If you took too long you were bellowed at by the Petty Officer of the Gangplank aboard the depot ship.[1]

*   *   *

¶ The packet comes alongside an old liner moored as a base ship. Again the eternal and soul-destroying trek with bag, hammock, tool-box, etc., up the starboard ladder, and down the port one to a waiting drifter (cranes and derricks are not a luxury afforded transit ratings). At last the drifter is away, bound for Scapa Pier (jumping-off place for the Royal Naval Air Station, Hatston, where I was bound), a single stone pier where the eternal portage of gear began again.

At Hatston I am informed that my real destination is County Class cruiser H.M.S. *London*, but she is out on a job so I must kick my heels until she returns.

When that day arrives the whole dismal procedure is repeated. Filled with apprehension at the prospect of setting foot on my first ship. It is Scapa Pier again; over the drifters to the one on Flow duty; her Orcadian skipper informs me he can only land me on the senior ship, which happens to be H.M.S. *Devonshire*. My misgivings increase.

Now takes place one of the most embarrassing yet humorous incidents in my Scapa life. Alongside *Devonshire* with the deck of the drifter some ten to twelve feet lower than the platform of the cruiser's quarter-deck ladder. 'Up you go!' yells the skipper, and I find myself hoisted up to the said platform by two Army Ack-Ack gunners, who then proceed to heave my belongings after me. There I am, perched on an area no more than a yard square, clutching my gear and hanging on for grim life, unable to move, with the drifter chugging merrily away through the Flow heedless of my plight.

Suddenly a bearded face appears over the *Devonshire*'s rail. 'What are we then?' (how many times in the following years am I to hear that fatuous remark). Happily the situation is relieved by the arrival of two side boys, who rescue me, kit and all, and bring me before the bearded one, who turns out to be the officer of the watch.[2]

*   *   *

¶ It's a miserable business, joining a warship, when you're tired, in wartime. You trail around, crouched beneath the slung hammocks, looking for a place to 'sling', dragging your hammock behind you. As the ship's company is swollen with extra hands to man all the guns and with the specialists required to work all the devices, such as radar, every place is taken. Eventually you see a pair of hooks and take a preparatory turn round one with the head-rope of your hammock. A severe face looks over the edge of the nearest hammock. 'You can't,' it says, 'Ginger (or Nobby or Dusty) has slung there ever since we commissioned.' And so you pick up your bed (unlashed now, and awkward) and crawl on.

Eventually I 'slung' in the capstan engine flat, not far from the anchor cable, between a hook and a rack carrying chippy's wood. As the latter was reputed to house rats, I took a cat to bed with me. (One night, at the end of a gunnery exercise, while I was asleep, we came to anchor. I thought it was the end of the world, as the gigantic cable thrashed its way from the chain locker beneath me.)[3]

The usual pattern for the Second World War was for the Navy to travel by the *St Ninian* to Lyness and for the Army and R.A.F. to go by the *Earl of Zetland* to Stromness. But Army men bound for the batteries or anti-aircraft sites on Hoy or Flotta often crossed in the *Ninian* instead; they too were initiated into life at Scapa with the ceremony of ordeal by drifter.

¶ We moved to South Walls, Hoy, in early January 1940, and must therefore have been amongst the earliest of army detachments to reach the Orkneys.

On arrival at Scapa we had to tranship into little drifters for the final leg of the trip to Longhope pier. This was a really fantastic little operation, as it was necessary to climb from the relatively high deck of the *Ninian* down rope ladders carrying every last item of kit, including kit-bags, on to the bobbing and heaving deck of the lighter in a high wind carrying flurries of snow, with the temperature somewhere well below freezing point.

Upon reaching the shore we had a two-mile march (in reality a flounder through snowdrifts) to what was euphemistically described as our camp. This consisted of two unfinished huts, one of which blew clean away during the first night, leaving a bewildered group of soldiery lying on a wooden floor, staring into the night sky and sorting round in the back of their minds for a fresh supply of adjectives.[4]

More frequently, however, the Army had a solid, immobile jetty to land on after the Pentland crossing. Even so, their arrival in Orkney, though less alarming, was often enough no less memorable.

¶ So we arrived at Stromness. At the word of command we gathered our gear and marched down the gang-plank to form in some sort of order on the quay. To receive us stood a little group of officers and senior N.C.O.s holding clipboards. Our escorting officer, who wore black riding hoots, handed us over and, I believe, returned aboard the *Zetland*. What followed then was reminiscent of the Monmouth rebels being sold on arrival at Jamaica or the first Australian convicts at Botany Bay.

'Are there any clerks among you?' asked one of the reception committee. Some of us stepped forward and were eagerly claimed. I and my immediate friends, who had already learned the wisdom of never volunteering for anything, stood fast. But the catechism went on – 'Twenty men who want to keep together' – and twenty men stood forward and were marched away, and so it went on. Some were taken in lorries, one little group went to the quayside into a boat, and disappeared over the waters of Hoy Sound.

At last there were only some twenty-five of us left. 'Another ten men. . . .' We consulted, decided, and stepped out. We were looked over briefly, formed into column and marched off, to the commands of a Sergeant whom we were to come to know very well in the next few days.

We did not have very far to go, for the Company, of which we were now members, was sent to North End Camp, Stromness, just outside the town.

North End Camp was then a collection of Nissen huts, more or less floating in a bed of mud. Floundering and slipping, we were marched to an empty hut and there we thankfully took off our webbing and sank on the concrete floor.[5]

The marathon journey was over. The soldier was in his iron hut or wooden barrack room, the sailor trying to find his bearings in the tortuous interior of an unfamiliar cruiser or battleship.

But for many, there was another way to reach Scapa Flow. For countless sailors of both wars, getting to Scapa meant simply sailing there in one's own ship.

¶ My first sight of the Flow was on an April evening in 1940. We arrived in H.M.S. *Glorious* straight from the Mediterranean as a cool sun dipped behind the dark shapes of the desolate islands that surrounded us as soon as the ship entered Hoxa Sound.

These had been the islands of the Norsemen, and the eerie shadows of anchored ships were suggestive of a maritime Valhalla. Their ghostlike shadows seemed frozen in a crystal silence, and the leaden waves were the only things that stirred.

The contrast with the Mediterranean could not have been greater. Only the occasional cottage of some hardy crofter and a handful of scraggy sheep braved the windswept slopes of these Pictish Isles. At Malta blue waters had sparkled invitingly in the sunshine, but here dark tides surged sullenly between iron-bound shores where only seabirds ventured.[6]

For every serviceman or servicewoman who came to Scapa Flow there was always that first occasion when the new arrival saw in the clear light of day the reason for being there – the Fleet lying at anchor and the enormous sheet of water in which it lay.

J. W. Beardsley first saw the Flow in July 1915, and found it unforgettable.

¶ The following day I had the opportunity of looking round that natural harbour, Scapa Flow, from the decks of H.M.S. *Hercules*. The scene filled me with pride; the mighty array of the Grand Fleet gave me a sense of security. Squadrons lay in lines with the flagship heading each line. Almost in the centre of the Flow lay the formidable *Iron Duke*, flagship of the C.-in-C., Jellicoe; in the distance behind the C.-in-C. lay the *Lion*, Beatty's flagship of the advance guard of the Fleet, the battle-cruiser squadron. The flotillas of destroyers lay in groups around the Flow.[7]

R. C. V. Ross came to Scapa in September 1917, when Beatty had succeeded Jellicoe as C.-in-C. and the famous *Iron Duke* had yielded her role as flagship.

¶ What a sight it was: that great landlocked sheet of water with line upon line of huge warships moored a quarter of a mile apart. After fifty years I need no book of reference to reel them off: *Revenge, Ramillies, Royal Sovereign, Resolution, Royal Oak, Emperor of India, Benbow, Marlborough, Iron Duke, Hercules, Collingwood, Neptune, St Vincent, Colossus, Superb, Bellerephon, Temeraire, King George V, Ajax, Centurion, Erin, Orion, Monarch, Conqueror, Thunderer*. And of course, our own proud Fifth Battle Squadron, *Barham, Malaya, Valiant, Warspite* – and the Fleet Flagship, the *Queen Elizabeth* herself.[8]

A generation later the sight of the Flow with the Home Fleet in occupation was equally remarkable – only this time there were young women in uniform to see it, as well as young men.

¶ I shall never forget my first sight of Scapa – on the wide flat expanse of water, ringed with hills, sat the quiet grey shapes of the battle fleet, their silhouettes sharply defined against the paler background. All sizes and shapes, they ranged from the huge battle cruisers and aircraft carriers down to corvettes and destroyers. In the weeks following we visited ships in the Flow regularly and used to climb the hills behind our Wrennery to a place where we could look down on to Scapa and see which ships were in – but I shall never forget my first sight.[9]

It is not a sight that is likely to be seen again. The Fleet at anchor in Scapa Flow is as much part of British past history as Nelson's great Fleet of 1805 waiting off Cadiz. It was, as one sailor put it, a 'veritable city of ships' – even if, at times, it was a city that could disintegrate like a mirage.

¶ At the height of the war and when the American Fleet joined us, it was an inspiring sight to see the vast array of ships in Scapa, each class forming its own line, the six battle squadrons, the armoured cruisers, rows of destroyers and submarines all gleaming in their freshness and ship-shape tidiness. When the Fleet sailed on exercise or to battle as in the case of Jutland, the Flow seemed a vast expanse of sea, a wilderness with just one guard ship remaining.[10]

* * *

¶ Scapa Flow itself was a constant awesome sight for me. One morning it would be stiff with warships, destroyers, submarines and every conceivable craft that you could name. They'd be there at dusk but come the following morning there would be not even a rowboat to be seen – they would have vanished as if they were drawings rubbed off the water.[11]

THE FIRST
WORLD WAR

SCAPA FLOW
(A Hymn of Hate)

Have you ever heard the story of how Scapa got its name?
If you haven't then you're slow, because it's earned a world–wide fame.
It has caused a lot of howling amongst our tars at sea,
So I'll tell to you the story as a sailor told it me:

Sure a little bit of wastage fell from out the sky one day,
And it fell into the ocean in a spot up Scotland way.
And when the Sea Lords saw it, sure! it looked so bleak and bare
They said, 'Suppose we start to build a Naval Base up there.'

So they dotted it with colliers, to provide the tars with work,
With provision boats and oilers, that they dared not dodge or shirk.
Then they sprinkled it with raindrops, with sleet and hail and snow,
And when they had it finished, sure, they called it Scapa Flow.

Now the Navy's been at Scapa ever since we've been at war,
And whenever it is over, they won't want to see it more.
But for years and years to come, whenever sailors congregate
You may bet your life you may hear them sing that Scapa hymn of hate.

5

Setting up the Base

Nearly a hundred years went by before Scapa Flow was put to the use for which the Maritime Surveyor, Graeme Spence, had recommended it in 1812, as a roadstead for a fleet of line-of-battle ships in time of war; but it was not quite forgotten by the Navy. For one correspondent who remembered a boyhood at Longhope on Hoy in the early years of the century Scapa was always closely linked with the Fleet.

¶ Looking backwards to about 1908 and on to the outbreak of war in 1914, I remember that Scapa Flow was used for gunnery practice and the annual Naval regattas and sports. Those large battleships sailed regularly into these waters and Scapa would be full of ships lying at anchor and at night there would be thousands of sparkling portholes in the darkness.[1]

In Kirkwall, according to the local press, such visits of His Majesty's ships seem to have given a considerable boost to the social whirl.

The Captain and Officers, 2nd Destroyer Flotilla, held an At Home in the Town Hall, Kirkwall, on 29th September 1909. It was one of the best dances ever held in Kirkwall. Those in charge of the At Home, not to be dependent on the local arrangements for lighting the hall, had it lit by electricity. Two destroyers – the *Exe* and the *Jed* – were moored alongside the pier and cables laid from them across the Peerie Sea to the Hall. The several electric lamps being at various distances in the hall, were very effective. The whole of the lighting arrangements were carried through without a hitch, and reflect great credit on those in charge.*

On the smaller islands, however, they were made of sterner stuff. The newspaper's Flotta correspondent struck a rather waspish note:

The first destroyers have taken things very easy since they first arrived in Orkney waters. At least so it appeared to us. The day after that on which they came was Saturday – a holiday. Sunday, of course, 'counted off'. Monday, on account of Queen Mary's birthday, a 'holiday'. Friday and Saturday last – 'holidays'. So that, although vessels have been here for ten days they seem to have been idle, or comparatively so, for the greater part of the time. And yet, when the Flotilla comes to leave, we expect to read of the hard work the men put in while in the North – of the rest they are needing after their strenuous labours in 'Scapper Flo'.*

But these halcyon days were coming to an end and Flotta was soon to have a very different view of the Fleet.

The British Home Fleet came to its war station in Scapa Flow in the last days of July 1914.

¶ I was an Ordinary Seaman in H.M.S. *Hindustan*, 3rd Battle Squadron – known as the 'Wobbly Eight' as they were bad steering ships. In July 1914 my ship was in Weymouth. On Sunday, 26 July, the newspapers said in heavy print: 'A great war cloud hanging over Europe'. On Monday we began to think it was more serious. Tuesday evening we heard the 1st Fleet was leaving harbour next morning. Naval patrols were sent ashore to collect up local men on leave. All leave expired at 10 P.M. Next morning, Wednesday, 29 July, hands were called earlier. We hoisted in boats and secured 'ship for sea'.

---

* We are grateful to Lieutenant-Commander G. S. Corlett for providing these extracts taken from his father's scrapbook.

At 9 A.M. we left harbour, consisting of the 1st Battle Fleet and cruisers. We steamed at moderate speed, in line ahead. In the Channel we turned east. After dark we increased speed, without navigating lights. Ships were completely darkened. Our ship almost hit a merchant ship and I heard them shout from their bridge: 'Where's your bloody lights?' All next day we were steaming off the north-east coast but not knowing our destination. Ships changed to 'War Routine'. My job was to help screw fuses in our lyddite shells (our shells weighed a ton each). In the afternoon of Friday, 31 July, land ahead was sighted and within two hours we anchored in Scapa Flow.

Saturday and Sunday were busy days. We cleaned ship. We painted out our white recognition bands around the funnels. At twelve o'clock on Sunday, when we were about to go to dinner, a signal came from the Flagship that we were to dismantle two twelve-pounder guns from our ship and take them ashore with a supply of ammunition, fifty Marines and a number of seamen. At 1.00 P.M. they were away, with food and one blanket each. Our Commander was in charge. These guns weighed twelve hundredweight each and had to be got up the side of a hill and mounted for firing across the harbour entrance.

My job that Sunday was to go aboard the Fleet's repair ship, H.M.S. *Assistance*, and help to bore holes in metal plates for the guns' mounting. On Monday, 3 August, my job was to help in beaching what boats we could do without (less fire risk if in action). I even remember a decent piano being ditched. We steamed out of harbour next morning so were at sea as war was declared. Returned to harbour next morning, took in coal, then straight out. Tents and soldiers were near our guns on the hill. A few days later we came across some German trawlers, brought the crews aboard with their belongings, and the fish, and sunk the trawlers.

One job worth noting, we had the job of chipping our polished enamel paint off the ship inboard, to prevent danger of poison if it got in wounds.[2]

* * *

¶ On 4 August, our Captain, A. C. Scott, R.N., cleared lower deck and informed us he had some important news: 'As from midnight tonight we are at war with Germany. Should it be our fortune to meet the enemy, I shall use the ship until she ceases to float. Then it will be every man for himself and God for us all! Coal ship.'

At daybreak we sailed, the whole Grand Fleet in company. For ten days we steamed to and fro, sinking everything that floated, amongst which were a number of German fishing boats and trawlers. The crews were taken prisoner, who on being captured said they didn't know of hostilities. But some boats had *fresh* meat aboard. On our first cruise we took forty-nine prisoners.[3]

The Commander-in-Chief of the Home Fleet when it sailed into Scapa in the summer of 1914 was the veteran Admiral Sir George Callaghan. His period of command was due to end in December of that year, but with war on the horizon the Admiralty decided to retire him at once and install his already nominated successor. This was Admiral Sir John Jellicoe, the thoughtful, supremely professional sailor who had always been intended by that energetic First Sea Lord, Admiral of the Fleet Lord Fisher,* to be 'Admiralissimo when Armageddon comes'. On 2 August Jellicoe travelled north from London by the railway line which was to make his name its special possession. He was met at Wick by the light cruiser *Boadicea* and ferried across to the Flow. At 8.30 A.M., on 4 August – a matter of hours before the official proclamation of war – he took over command from Callaghan and raised his flag in the battleship *Iron Duke*. In his letter of appointment, which he had carried with him in a sealed envelope and which he finally opened on Admiralty instruction in the early morning of that memorable 4 August, he read that his title was to be the new one of 'Commander-in-Chief of the Grand Fleet'.

---

* Lord Fisher of Kilverstone, First Sea Lord from 1904 to 1910 and from October 1914 to May 1915.

So the Grand Fleet, the greatest Fleet that Britain has ever assembled, came into being. Its enemy, based across the North Sea at Wilhelmshaven, was the High Seas Fleet of Kaiser Wilhelm's Germany. In the contest that was to follow, the Grand Fleet, heir to a reputation that had been undisputed since Trafalgar, was the champion; the newly created High Seas Fleet was the challenger.

The fleet based on Scapa Flow during the Great War existed for three main purposes: to maintain Britain's mastery of the seas and protect her coasts and shipping; to hasten Germany's defeat by an effective blockade; and to bring the High Seas Fleet to decisive action. It was the third purpose, inevitably, that kindled the enthusiasm of the Royal Navy and of the British public. What the whole nation wanted, and expected, was a second Trafalgar – a resounding assurance that nothing had changed, that the spirit of Nelson lived on, that Britannia was still the ruler of the waves.

In the first months of war the Grand Fleet moved massively to and fro in the North Sea like an army marching and counter-marching outside the camp of an enemy. But the Germans replied with a weapon which baffled and enraged their British opponents – inaction. The British, it is true, scored a dramatic success with a surprise attack into the Heligoland Bight in August in which three German cruisers were sunk within shooting distance of their own shores. But this victory produced almost the opposite effect from what was expected. Far from provoking the High Seas Fleet to come out and avenge the injury, it persuaded it to retire into harbour and pull down the shutters. The Kaiser ordered Admiral Pohl to avoid any further loss of ships. Admiral von Tirpitz protested at this 'muzzling policy' but the muzzling continued. As Churchill put it, 'Apart from movement by individual submarines and minelayers, not a dog stirred from August till November'. In September, Jellicoe's whole Fleet swept boldly towards the Heligoland Bight in the hope of repeating its August success but not a single enemy ship was sighted. Sir David Beatty, the energetic and popular

Vice-Admiral whose battle-cruisers* had covered themselves with glory in the previous month, expressed the general mood when he commented bitterly: 'I fear the rascals will never come out. It really is very disappointing and looks as if we should go through the war without ever coming to grips with them. Such a thought is more than I can bear.'

Although the enemy's main force lay impotently at Wilhelmshaven, the British Fleet was not the confident mistress of the seas that she seemed. There were two new and unknown weapons in this war which had not troubled the tacticians of any previous one – the mine, and even more disturbing, the submarine. In addition, Scapa Flow was far from being the secure, attack-proof anchorage which Jellicoe craved for his ships.

When the Grand Fleet arrived in the Flow on the eve of war there were practically no defences whatever on any of the islands, with the exception of the twelve-pounder naval guns landed by the first arrivals. There were no booms or obstructions across the numerous entrances for anti-submarine protection. After its sorties in the North Sea, taunting the enemy, the Fleet had to have a safe anchorage to return to and it was only too clear to those in command that it had nothing of the kind. Penny-pinching by the Treasury and neglect by the Admiralty had left the base wide open to attack. Fortunately, the Germans considered such a situation beyond the bounds of credibility. As late as January 1915 Admiral Jellicoe wrote to Lord Fisher: 'If you would only just compare the orders for the protection of the High Seas Fleet . . . with the arrangements here you would be horrified. *I wonder I can ever sleep at all.* Thank goodness the Germans imagine we have proper defences. At least so I imagine – otherwise there would be no Grand Fleet left now.'

---

* The battle-cruisers – a product of Lord Fisher's period at the Admiralty – were supposed to carry out the reconnaissance and scouting duties of a cruiser but to pack something of the punch of a battleship. Since speed was essential to their concept, they were less well-endowed than the great Dreadnoughts with heavy protective armour. *Lion* – Beatty's flagship – *Tiger* and the other battle-cruisers of Beatty's squadron were the Navy's beautiful 'Cats'; but, as Churchill put it, they were cats with thin skins. The battle-cruiser played a part-heroic, part-tragic role in both wars.

This state of unpreparedness was brought to a crisis point on 17 October 1914, when there was a reported sighting of a submarine in the Flow. It was never discovered whether it was in fact a German submarine or a false alarm from a nervous lookout, but Jellicoe did not hesitate. He refused to hazard the Fleet in those unprotected waters. He took it to Lough Swilly in the north of Ireland. On the same day Beatty, on board H.M.S. *Lion*, wrote to the First Lord of the Admiralty, Winston Churchill: '. . .The feeling is gradually possessing the Fleet that all is not right somewhere. The menace of mines and submarines is proving larger every day and adequate means to meet or combat them are not forthcoming and we are gradually being pushed out of the North Sea, and off our own particular perch.'

Within a week Churchill addressed a peremptory minute to the First Sea Lord, the Third Sea Lord, the Fourth Sea Lord and the Naval Secretary.

24 October 1914

Every nerve must be strained to reconcile the Fleet to Scapa. Successive lines of submarine defences should be prepared, reinforced by electric-contact mines as proposed by the Commander-in-Chief. Nothing should stand in the way of the equipment of this anchorage with every possible means of security. The First Lord and the First Sea Lord will receive a report of progress every third day until the work is completed and the Commander-in-Chief satisfied.

W.S.C.

Churchill described these anxious times in his history of the war:

Everything depended upon the Fleet, and during these months of October and November the Fleet was disquieted about the very foundations of its being. There lay the mighty ships: every man, from stoker to Admiral, was ready to die at his duty at any moment. Still, at the summit from which we watched, one could feel a new and heart-breaking sensation. The Grand Fleet was uneasy. She could not find a resting place except at sea.*

* Winston S. Churchill, *World Crisis 1911–1918*.

So Jellicoe's Fleet moved unhappily here and there, taking shelter in Scottish and Irish bases, not daring to linger long in the Flow. An ex-sailor summed up this stage of the war as he experienced it.

¶ And so it went on – week by week, month by month. Out of harbour at dawn, days at sea, to Scapa Flow again at dusk, coal and provision and away by dawn. As the winter months drew on, the rain, wind and snow added to the discomforts and difficulties that had to be encountered. The only real pleasure that entered our lives at this very trying period was the letter from home which helped to make our lot a little more endurable.[4]

By the beginning of 1915 sunken blockships were placed across the narrower channels, boom-defence drifters were stationed across the larger ones and various 4-inch and 6-inch batteries were erected to command these entrances. The anchorage was moved from the north end of the Flow off Scapa Pier to the southwest side under the lee of the long, whale-backed island of Hoy. The base ships were anchored off the little village of Longhope while the Grand Fleet itself lay on the north side of the island of Flotta. The auxiliaries, the colliers, oilers, store and ammunition ships, lay between Longhope and Hoy Sound. Gradually Scapa became the haven for which the Fleet longed and which both ships and sailors sorely needed.

¶ A trip on a drifter to do some routine job while a nasty nor'easter was blowing did not increase my love for Scapa Flow. But I was rebuffed by a three-badge A.B. of the minesweepers who, when I moaned to him about Scapa, pulled me up and said: 'Scapa is like a mothering hen to us; once inside those enfolding cliffs we can eat and clean in comfort.'[5]

6

'No World Outside the Ship'

For most of the Great War Scapa Flow was the main base of the Grand Fleet. Usually one of the battle-squadrons with its attendant destroyers lay anchored off Invergordon in the Cromarty Firth. Rosyth in the Firth of Forth became the home of Beatty's battle-cruisers and was increasingly used as an alternative base after 1916. However, for the vast majority of the sailors of the Grand Fleet Scapa was the place where they lived out their war. More often than not that great 'city of ships' was at anchor far out in the Flow. But it was a city of its own, cut off from outside contacts. For the sailor of the Grand Fleet in Scapa Flow (without a bustling dockyard town at the end of the gangplank or a libertyboat's trip away, as in the great naval ports farther south) his ship was his home, his life, his world.

It was a world of countless complex activities and rituals and codes. It was also very crowded. With a complement of thirteen or fourteen hundred men, a great battleship could be as full of strangers and separate communities as a teeming suburb. It was not, of course, a way of life peculiar to Scapa, except that in Scapa they were perhaps more obsessively conscious of it than they would have been anywhere else in home waters. Scapa made each ship an isolated world in itself.

¶ There was no Tannoy system and all orders were transmitted by the Bosun's Mates and the Side Boys. Some of the latter had very thin, reedy voices and sometimes they would get a bit mixed when they had to pipe an order like 'Starboard and Turret Watches for exercise fall in to work main derrick'. Smoking was strictly forbidden below decks and after dark it was only permissible in the after superstructure which was lit by faint blue police lights.

Trading was carried on by various ratings to augment their incomes. There were snobbing firms (cobblers), jewing firms (tailors), dhobi firms (laundry) and usually a couple of barbers. These were all tucked away in various odd corners as they had no official standing. In the After Medical Station we had a bearded A.B. who owned a hand sewing-machine, and he could be found every evening, seated beneath the ladder, his machine always in action. He would interview customers, measure them up, instruct them how much serge to purchase from the Slop Room, and would then run up a seaman's jumper and trousers and sew on the necessary badges as neatly as any professional tailor. Of course, the snobbing firm had to find a spot where the hammering did not disturb the watch keepers, but they made a very good job of their shoe repairing. The dhobi firms usually had a stoker to assist as it was essential to have someone who could hang the washing in the engine room when he went on watch, and take it down again, all dry, when he came off.[1]

* * *

¶ The routine aboard H.M.S. *Hercules* was interesting enough and in spite of a thousand hands aboard, the space provided for each fighting unit did not under the circumstances seem inadequate. All of us were well fed, plenty of fresh veg, butter, meat, our own bakery, distilled water, a good comfortable hammock, complete with warm blankets; in fact, we were really comfortable whilst lying in the Flow. However, we were subject to what was known as *eighteen at one** – in other words we had to be able to raise steam for 18 knots at one hour's notice.[2]

---

* Usually the Fleet was at four hours' notice for sea. Towards the end of the war the time was often considerably reduced.

* * *

¶ Food in the Fleet was plentiful compared with what the civil population got. Each man was allowed half a pound of meat and a pound of potatoes a day, and lashings of dried peas, haricot and butter beans, cheese (known as bunghole), salt fish (toerag), and eggs (grenades). Pea soup which the digestion failed to disperse resulted in many unmusical nights on the mess-decks. Fruit was very scarce and many men developed blotches and mild scurvy. Bread soon became dry and wooden but the supply was plentiful. The daily issue of rum kept the majority happy.[3]

* * *

¶ At Scapa, although the Navy did its best, we found it necessary to augment our diet by the nearest available form of livestock – the seagull. These were catapulted from the masthead, skinned and jointed, and made into what was called *gosh*, a stew which tasted like fishy chicken, but which was pleasant, firm-fleshed and certainly edible.[4]

* * *

¶ It was a regulation that all divers had a monthly dip, when each one had to do a certain amount of time on the bottom. In Scapa the bottom was very sandy which meant visibility was good, so a diver would take with him the mess 'spud net' – a strong net bag for cooking potatoes in. If the spot happened to be a good one, the diver would pass his time catching scallops. These shell-fish were very tasty but to catch them one had to be in the right position. The scallops propelled themselves along the bottom by opening and closing their shells, always moving back wards. This meant one had to be behind to make a catch, other wise they would move too quickly, so disturbing the sand and disappearing into a small cloud.[5]

* * *

¶ On commencing to weigh anchor one day to proceed on exercise our capstan engine broke down and ship's company were ordered 'Weigh anchor by hand'. Only those on watch were excused and for three hours, to the beat of the Ship's Marine Band playing hornpipes and gay airs, about fifty men at a time, relieved 'on the run' every ten minutes, manned the capstan bars, hopping occasionally like kangaroos to clear the many obstacles in the path of the capstan. I wouldn't have missed that unique event for anything.[6]

*   *   *

¶ I was a boy seaman aged 16¾. Life was not easy for us boys. We were the hand-rags. Under an exacting Commander there was much holystoning of decks which commenced at 6 A.M. We were compelled to kneel on the deck which had been hosed with sea water and sprinkled with sand and coarse grit. We were barefooted with trousers rolled up to the thighs. This, in bitterly cold weather after a couple of hours left us numb with cold, our knees painfully sore. In harbour, duck suits were worn during the working day by all seamen, however cold the weather.

Various exercises were carried out and one which we dreaded was weighing anchor by hand, in which the capstan was worked by seamen pushing on capstan bars. I recall an occasion when a scream stopped the men pushing. The Commander, demanding to know the reason, was informed that a boy was in danger of being crushed. His reply was: 'Carry on, it's only a boy.'

At sea some boys kept all-night watches with the older seamen at their gun positions and from 7 P.M., when the last meal of the day was eaten, there was nothing more in the way of refreshment until 8 A.M.[7]

*   *   *

¶ Although the practice of bullying junior Midshipmen in gunrooms had nearly died out, it still survived in the *Vanguard*, but to be fair, I believe it was done to sharpen our wits. It took different forms of which a straightforward beating with a stick was the least offensive, as, after that, we were always left alone for a few hours.

What was gall and wormwood to us was never being allowed to sit down in the gun room except for meals, on Sunday afternoons, or when at sea. Life was all the more irksome when we found that our term-mates in other ships were being treated reasonably. However, as there was nothing we could do to improve our lot, we just had to look forward to the end of our first twelve months at sea, when we would become senior Midshipmen.[8]

*   *   *

¶ In *Colossus*, Captain Pound, in order to provide some pastime for the officers in the evenings, besides cards, billiards, etc. (we had a billiard-table!) had the idea of persuading the gun room officers to give short lectures on famous men. He asked me as Instructor-Lieutenant to prepare a list of great men or women whose biographies could be obtained in cheap editions and to present this list to the Midshipmen with instructions that each of them was to give a talk of twenty minutes in the Admiral's cabin to the other officers on Tuesday evenings after dinner. Naturally, they did not receive this message with unqualified acquiescence and they asked if they were obliged to choose a subject from the list. I said no! they could choose anyone they liked, and by way of mild protest, every one of them chose a great German![9]

*   *   *

¶ There were different bugle calls for everything – calling out the watch on deck, or part of the watch – different boats' crews – cooks to the galleys – action stations – and many many others.

One young seaman was before the C.O. for not mustering. The C.O. asked did he hear the bugle call, and he answered 'Yes, sir, but I did not know the tune.' The C.O.: 'Fourteen days No. 10. By that time you will know the tune for defaulters.' For No. 10 punishment you turned out at 4.30 A.M. and worked until 9 P.M. Half hour for meals. Usually you were on your hands and knees with a bible (holystone) in each hand holystoning some part of the deck. Not so good in winter.

There were also cells on board for severe offences. Anything from three days to fourteen days. First three days on low diet – twelve ounces dog biscuits and a basin of water. You also had to pick a couple of pounds of oakum a day. Easy when you know how. For anything over fourteen days you left the ship and went to detention barracks at one of the naval ports – Portsmouth, Chatham, Devonport, where they tamed lions.[10]

* * *

¶ There was not much crime, though there was a murder in one of the battleships during my time. A Ship's Corporal was stabbed in his hammock, at least it was intended for a Ship's Corporal, but he swapped billets and the wrong bloke was murdered.

What little theft there was never reached the authorities, but was dealt with by the thief's messmates; and it was remarkable how little there was considering the circumstances. You could leave a handful of silver or a watch on the mess shelf for days and it wouldn't be touched until an inspection was due to take place – and then it would be looked after for you by somebody in the mess who took good care to advertize the fact that he had it.

The biggest crime of all was to thieve somebody else's tot. That was unforgivable! If for some reason a man was away from the ship at tot time; it was put on a shelf and there it would stay – nobody would touch it. Rum was only issued to a man over eighteen years old, and if he preferred not to draw it he could have it put to his credit in the ship's book – a halfpenny one day, and a farthing the next – but not many did that as the tot was worth much more in the way of barter, and it also served as an expression of thanks for help.

For example, a stranger might give one a lift with a heavy box up a ladder. You not only thanked him but suggested 'Sippers' the next day – and sure enough at tot time the stranger would turn up, and during a quarter of an hour's yarning both of you would take 'Sips' at your tot. This went on all the time, as in a crew of 1,400 men one might not see a chum for some weeks, but when you did see him – 'Sippers'.[11]

There was one unavoidable problem of naval life in Scapa – time. There was too much of it. Jellicoe put his ships through a rigorous schedule of practice and exercise, so that even when they were confined to the Flow they were never idle; but the ordinary sailor still had many off-duty hours which somehow had to be filled. What made the situation worse was that in winter the night came down as early as half past three or four in the afternoon, driving men into the bowels of their ships to make do as best they could. Summer restored the balance somewhat by giving them their decks to walk on until late at night, and even at more inhospitable times there was the occasional compensation of a dazzling display of Northern Lights – the 'Merry Dancers' as they are called in Orkney – or an Orkney sunset. But most of the time they were driven hard back on their own resources. Many of their activities were simple, almost domestic; others had to be concealed deftly from the eyes of authority. Some men coped best in company; others managed best on their own.

¶ Calm-natured men took life philosophically and passed their time reading anything that came to hand, even the ship's notices; restless ones paced any small space of deck available. There were a few who had a musical bent – some were professional, while others thought they would improve as time passed. An accomplished accordion player would always be in demand.[12]

*   *   *

¶ A popular pastime with the energetic was a brisk walk when off duty, usually in pairs, backwards and forwards some twenty to twenty-five yards on fo'c'sle or quarter-deck, either in bright sunshine or pressing 'forward' against a howling gale and leaning back on it on the return journey.[13]

*   *   *

¶ Leisure time was occupied in a number of ways. Some read, some wrote, some played cards – there was usually a lot of gambling, especially at 'Crown and Anchor', which was illegal but went on with the aid of look-outs (and a man could pick up quite a respectable income by being taken on as one of the latter). A lot of chaps made wool, rope and serge mats; some did embroidery or knitting; while some just 'spun a yarn' – they could always get an audience. There wasn't a great deal of interest in politics although a political argument would always attract a crowd and would invariably end in a free-for-all.

We got newspapers occasionally through the ship's canteen and *John Bull* went round every mess-deck every week. Bottomley was very popular amongst the troops although everybody knew he was the biggest rogue unhung.

Some men set themselves up as money-lenders. They were illegal, but one could always see a notice on the board, 'One for Twenty-five. 18 Mess', which meant that someone in 18 Mess was prepared to lend a pound for twenty-five bob at the end of the month; the only security required was your name.[14]

*   *   *

¶ Gambling of any sort (with the exception of organized betting at Fleet Regattas) was strictly forbidden and therefore flourished. The Crown and Anchor Board was a popular favourite. The Board was invariably a piece of canvas (so that it could be quickly rolled up and put away) on which were painted six squares. The top middle square contained a crown and the bottom middle square an anchor. The remaining squares were taken up by the Aces of Hearts, Diamonds, Clubs and Spades. The man running the Board had three dice with the above symbols on each and the players put their money on any symbol they fancied. If the dice came up with their symbol their money was doubled.

The patter of the Operator was often very amusing and went like this:

'Here you are, me lads, the Old Firm. Where you like and where you fancy. The more you put down the more you pick up. Speculation is the art of accumulation. If you don't speculate you don't accumulate. Come here in a wheelbarrow and go away in a motor-car. Come here in a rowing boat and go away in a Flagship. Smack it down thick and heavy, me lads. Who says a little bit on the sausage (anchor)? All down, all backed? Up she comes again and it's the name of the game and the Stoker's Friend' (a crown, an anchor, and a spade).

Some time after the war, I met an old shipmate who used to run a board in the ship and I asked him how he got on. He told me that after paying his scouts and a couple of the Ship's Corporals (Ship's Police) and also the mess bills of his messmates to compensate for the inconvenience he put them to, he had managed to clear £870 in the three years he was in the ship.[15]

*   *   *

¶ We had plenty of exercise, running round the upper deck whilst the band played rollicking music – twice a day, morning and evening. All officers as well as the men.

We also had dances twice a week on the upper deck. The band used to play for an hour, from 6 to 7 P.M. One sailor had to be the lady and we used to do the barn dance, valeta, two step and lancers. There was always a lot of ribald remarks from the onlooking matelots, all in good fun but – unprintable.[16]

Such dances became a regular pastime in this world without women. 'To see sailors with beards,' wrote one serviceman, 'tripping the light fantastic with the top half of their overalls hanging over their belts was a sight that can never be forgotten.' In the same way, fancy dress – often the product of a quite incredible ingenuity – was an accepted, almost a necessary, feature of life on board ship; and always it was the 'women' who were the most popular figures. 'Women' were also an essential for any of the numerous ships' concert-parties that sprang into existence. An illusion of femininity was a good deal better than no femininity at all.

¶ To meet the problem of boredom Captain Grant and the Flag-Lieutenant (father and son if I remember rightly), having noticed the men dancing together when suitable music was being played by the Marine Band outside the ward-room during dinner (a Thursday night event, this), conceived the idea of organizing a fancy-dress ball. Costumes were to be made from materials available in ship's stores – a chit describing requirements and signed by the officer-of-the-watch secured their issue.

The event was a complete success. There were Cavaliers, Roundheads; characters from Dickens in Mr Pickwick, a recognizable Pecksniff, and of course Uriah Heep; a Harlequin (but no Columbine – an understandable omission!); Hamlet and Shylock, a witch and two jesters – altogether a good hundred or more.

The First Prize went to a really magnificent Queen Elizabeth I (an R.N.V.R. yeoman of signals with a striking resemblance to the Virgin Queen – hooked nose included!). His 'jewel'-encrusted crown; his ruff-like neck ornament (a wire frame covered with white bunting) decorated with more jewels (broad beans, peas, haricot beans – plain and coloured); the shaped bodice with its mass of pearls (more haricot beans and even rice gummed or sewn on); and finally his wide crinoline-type skirt (a wire framework covered with white and yellow bunting and lavishly decorated with 'jewels') – all these were marvels of ingenuity showing keen imagination and a praiseworthy measure of patience. He was a very popular First Prize-winner.

Second Prize went to a young stoker impersonating a V.A.D. nurse. His nursing uniform was a clever copy of the real thing, but his figure (reminiscent of Nell Gwyn) was what caught everyone's eye and caused a minor sensation, for the bust was suitably and generously padded, as were the hips. My own little effort was an impersonation of Mephisto – the costume a creation principally of black and red target canvas and bunting of the same two colours; covered head to toe in red (face red-ochred), close-fitting black head-dress with pheasant's tail-feather from the ward-room galley, black cape with red lining, cutlass-belt and fencing foil and finally medieval-type pointed footwear. An upward-tilted moustache and small imperial beard completed a presentable 'devil' – and won me Third Prize.[17]

*　*　*

¶ Entertainment, apart from the flickering bioscope shows rather amateurishly presented, was provided by ships' concert-parties.

A merchant ship had had her holds gutted to form a floating theatre, and any ship with a concert-party could provide a show there – the exigencies of war permitting. Some were good, others – usually too ambitious – had best be forgotten. But the satirists of today had nothing on us when it came to taking the micky out of Royal Naval Authority.[18]

There were two ships in the Flow whose sole function was to improve the morale and the well-being of the Fleet. There was the S.S. *Borodino*, the Junior Army and Navy Stores-Ship, where officers and men could buy 'anything from an elephant to a shirt-button' from white-coated shop assistants behind impeccably laid-out counters. There was also the immensely popular S.S. *Gourko*. This was the floating theatre where the concert-parties performed, with stage and auditorium like any theatre on shore, with lighting effects as good as those of Shaftesbury Avenue, and even, for the most ambitious productions, wigs and costumes hired from the West End. The *Gourko* would moor alongside any warship wishing to stage an entertainment; if the Fleet were called to sea she would simply slip her wires and let her warship go. The psychological effect of these two non-combatant vessels was considerable. The *Gourko*, in particular, was always in demand. She provided a transitory but vivid reminder of the glamour that still existed in the world.

¶ I was a professional violinist in civil life and to be put in the gunners' party hauling up small ammo all day, I nearly went crazy, so I went and saw the regulating officer, and he thought, oh! what, another one! Soon after this we started to give concerts on the old *Gourko* – she would tie up alongside and all the ship's company would be invited aboard. This gave me my chance. I got a fiddle up from London (it got cracked in transit) and played at the concert. I was lucky, I had a good pianist, a G.D. like myself. Admiral Beatty and Admiral Sir Charles Madden were at these concerts, and Sir Charles came and spoke to me as I came off the stage, much to the disgust of most of the company.[19]

Beyond the ship, there was only the Flow and the other ships – each with its huge complement of men. Even on the next vessel in line the sailors moving about the decks were no more than miniature figures across the intervening expanse of water. Their nearness and at the same time their utter remoteness only served to emphasize the isolation in which each ship's company was set. The sea-birds were about the only creatures that came near enough to be worth watching. Observing their energetic routines helped to reconcile at least one sailor to a Scapa which at first sight he had found depressing.

¶ As time went on and the better weather arrived and the sun grew stronger, nature made the Flow a little more interesting. Gulls, those scavengers of the sea, became more numerous. Shags came and showed off their diving abilities, and I am sure I saw more than one gannet drop from the sky, disappear, and then back to the heavens again. But it was the shags whose movements I followed most. They would bob up from nowhere, swim or rest a while, and 'hey presto' they were gone. Watching them, and seeing them dive, one would suddenly become aware of a turbulence in the water in a certain area just like a deluge of rain. It was the shags chasing a shoal of coalfish or saithe who were trying to escape from their winged enemy. I have seen these coalfish in their thousands swimming near to the ship for safety when being chased by the shags.[20]

It was a hard, unnatural life, enclosed in steel and bounded by water. There is something very moving in one old sailor's recollection of reaching out towards the lost world of life ashore and the gentler aspects of nature from which the war had made them all exiles.

¶ I found a young blackbird and brought it back and put it in a cage in the superstructure. In some way it seemed to provide a link with the world outside, for we had no world outside the ship.[21]

7

'Hands Coal Ship!'

Provided the British serviceman is convinced of the fundamental justice of the war in which he is engaged, he will put up with almost any amount of hardship and deprivation. A basic resilience laced with wit, good humour and companionship, will somehow allow him to endure.

There was, however, one recurring experience of naval life in the First World War to which the British sailor never became reconciled. It had a nightmarish quality about it that no amount of jibes or ribaldry could shrug off. It happened with such dreary and predictable regularity that it was never far from the minds of the men who took part in it. It was an experience from which there was no escape, unless you were sick, on watch, a Wireless Rating, a Cook, or the Captain. *All* the ship's company, officers and men, were reduced to a scurrying, miserable, back-broken, black-faced mass by the process of coaling ship.*

The canvas navy of the nineteenth century had its own rigours and squalor, but coaling ship made the old sailors bitterly nostalgic for the days of sail. For the ratings of the new generation, coaling was as basic to naval life as gunnery drill or seamanship. When, as the war went on, the first oil-burning battleships joined

---

* Wireless Ratings were exempted on the grounds that this heavy work might endanger the sensitivity of their touch or their hearing.

the Fleet, the sailors in the coal-burners regarded the crews of the new arrivals with a resentful envy.

What made coaling more objectionable was that it was the inevitable postscript to every visit to sea. The moment a warship limped back into Scapa after an exhausting bout of patrol duty or a sweep across the North Sea the colliers would bear down on her ready to replenish her with hundreds of tons of coal. There was no rest, no relaxation until this task was over. An uncoaled ship was a useless ship, a dead thing in Jellicoe's hands. A coaled ship was an effective fighting unit ready to wage war.

For many sailors, inevitably, 'coal ship' was the first thing they did on arrival in Scapa Flow. It was the first act of the Fleet on reaching Scapa in August 1914.

¶ The squadron entered Scapa Flow at dusk. While it was coming to its anchorage, the collier fleet was under way in readiness to coal the battle-cruisers.

The shrill whistle of the bos'n's pipe, followed by 'Port watch out torpedo defence nets, starboard watch prepare coal ship'. The ship's company sprang into action about their respective duties. The ship had barely dropped anchor when the collier *Mercedes* came alongside and was made fast. Again the bos'n's pipe – 'Hands to supper and clean into coaling rig. Coal ship in half an hour's time.' Away we hurried to scramble to eat and change into that most hateful rig of all time.

The bugler sounded 'The General Assembly, at the double'. We doubled to fall in. As soon as the watches were reported present the Commander gave his orders. 'The country is now at war. We have to take in 2,500 tons of coal with utmost speed. The squadron gets under way at dawn. Hands coal ship! Carry on!'

Away we doubled to the sound of 'The Charge' on the bugle. The competitive spirit to try and get the first hoist inboard made us work like slaves. Each hoist consisted of ten bags, each containing two hundredweight. The hold gangs began shovelling furiously to get the bags filled. Soon the winches began to work and up went the first hoist. For the next few hours the winches did not stop. Throughout the night the shovels were working and the winches rattling away, whilst the inboard gangs were clearing the dumps at the double to have the coal tipped into the bunkers. Those poor devils in the bowels of the ship were trimming the bunkers as the coal shot into them. The stokers were enshrouded by an indescribable cloud of dust, which got right into the lungs, and they had only a Davy safety lamp to guide them – it is doubtful if a miner at the coal face endured conditions worse than these.

Within minutes the ship was enveloped in a fog of coal dust, which became encrusted on the skin by perspiration. A thick layer formed around the eyelids which became very troublesome. Supply parties prepared and distributed corned beef sandwiches and provided hot cocoa and lime juice to sustain energy. No rest was given or expected until the last hoist was inboard.

Meanwhile the squadron was very vulnerable to torpedo attacks by submarines as the boom defences were not as yet prepared. A sharp look-out had to be maintained from the bridge, whilst at the entrances to the Flow a continuous patrol of T.B.D.s had to be maintained. The crews of these small vessels had a very hectic time. Thrown about by a relentless sea they maintained a steady watch, patrolling as it were like shadows. No signs of lights of any description were to be seen as they watched the dark waters for the hidden foe, ready to drop depth-charges should occasion arise, and to warn the Admiral if an attack was being made.

At length the 'Cease fire' sounded on the bugle and a tired and dusty ship's company downed tools and had a breather. Not for long, however. Soon came the pipe 'Clear collier', followed by 'Stand by to cast off collier'. Shovels and coal bags were hoisted across, the collier's holds covered and a tired crew climbed inboard.

'Duty sub cast off collier. Duty watch in torpedo nets. Non-duty watch clean ship. Special sea duty men to your stations. Fo'c'slemen of the duty sub on the fo'c'sle. Duty guns' crews close up.' It was dawn and the squadron was under way and ready to search the sea for the enemy.[1]

There were one or two elements in coaling ship that afforded a measure of light relief. One was that the ships of the Fleet often turned the operation into a race and there was some satisfaction in beating the other members of your squadron. Another was that ships were occasionally coaled to music. At times it would be the ship's band that would thump away encouragingly while the coalers slogged on. At others an impromptu male-voice choir of hundreds of black-faced, dusty-throated men would sing the traditional coaling hymn, to the tune of 'Holy, holy, holy' –

> *Coaling, coaling, coaling,*
> *Always —ing well coaling.*

And to finish off the whole grim procedure there was the slightly more enjoyable business of hosing the ship down – an operation which could lead to a certain amount of comedy and horseplay. But in the main coaling is remembered as a thoroughly unpleasant and loathed necessity.

¶ Apart from minor discomforts life wasn't so bad sheltered in the Flow except for one special day – 'Coal Ship'. We coaled ship each time we came back from convoy or from one of those false alarms that the German High Seas Fleet was coming out to challenge us. The journey we had completed determined the amount of coal needed to fill our bunkers. Usually it varied from 100 to 600 tons – after Jutland it was 1,200 tons.

Everyone fit took part in this grim pantomime except those actually on duty and the range-takers. No protective clothing was issued (hadn't been heard of in those days). In summer and winter sweat was the order of the day. One could wear anything, rugger and soccer shirts, long shorts, short shorts, hard hats, felt hats, knickerbockers; and if it was hot many were in the 'buff' wearing nothing more than what we would now term an outsize 'G-string'. The whole scene always reminded me of a fancy-dress ball.

The collier tied up alongside *Hercules* and the Bo'sun would pipe 'Hands coal ship'. The men rushed to their respective stations, the collier parties with shovels (and sometimes their bare hands) filling bags which were hoisted in by derricks, sluiced on to barrows of the station-porter type, rushed to the manholes and tipped, so that the coal roared down into the stokeholds in the bowels of the ship. No elevenses, nothing at all until all was finished.

As the coal in the collier got lower so the dust got thicker and those tipping in the manholes got blacker. Dust in your eyes, in yonr nose, dust everywhere. But the worst was to follow, getting your body clean. In the bathroom was plenty of hot and cold, but only two shallow bath tins which served as bath. Eighty 'Blue and Red' marines, crowded to sardine capacity, competing with the Black Hole of Calcutta! There was only one way in and one way out. Those who were cleansed had to fight their way out amidst the uncleansed. The goal? A piping hot meal waiting in the galley to be served to the mess when they were ready. It was always a special meal cooked perfectly.[2]

*   *   *

¶ If there is any more uncomfortable place to be in than a battle-ship during coaling, I've yet to find it. We took in around 1,000 tons and everywhere was a fog of very fine coal dust. All food from the galley carried a fine film of it and it penetrated every-where. As soon as the coal was in, the shutes were unshipped, the deck plates put back and the 'Water Carnival' commenced. Hoses, scrubbers and deck cloths were the order of the day and the mess decks were soon alive with shouting, singing men. I've yet to see a funnier sight than a big, brawny A.B. wielding a hose whilst clad in nothing but a cap and a pair of sea boots. And this whole performance took place every time we came in from sea.[3]

*   *   *

¶ The routine was six days at sea and then in to take in 2,000 tons of coal and out to sea again. I can see those beastly coal-lighters now – lying waiting to lie alongside – one either side as soon as we had dropped anchor. At 6 A.M. the following morning all hands assisted in the loading process: only a very exceptional few ever were excused, from the Commander downward. After coaling the ship was always hosed down and the mess-deck cleared of as much dust as possible, but nevertheless the first salvo in gun practice always brought down showers of coal dust. That is probably why they say the old sailors were full of 'grit'.[4]

*   *   *

¶ On one occasion before coaling on H.M.S. *Agincourt* the deck Commander had the whole crew on the quarterdeck and read from *The Daily Mail* an announcement that the German *Von der Tann* had reached the world record for coaling, 394 tons per hour. The Kaiser was so pleased that he ordered each man of the crew to be given a piece of German sausage. Our Commander informed us that we required 1,600 tons and had to beat the *Von der Tann*. We got down to it to the accompaniment of the ship's Marine Band and finished in four hours. After scrubbing down decks and our bodies we sat down to a meal, and at each place there was a typed card: 'With the Commander's compliments on obtaining the coaling record, 400 tons an hour – a bit of German sausage.'[5]

Undoubtedly the worst spot to be during coaling was in the bunkers below deck, under the manholes through which the avalanche of coal came roaring down. One sailor of the Second World War wrote on behalf of his father, a sailor of the First World War:

¶ As the coal came down through the manholes, my father would have to start shovelling the coal into the far corners of the bunker, and build it up until it was about a foot from the deck-head. The dust-covered lamps gave poor light. When these lamps became obscured by the increasing bank of coal, an oil-lamp would be handed down through a manhole.

If they stopped for a meal, the Stokers would simply wash their hands and mouths, and sitting round the table they looked exactly like the Black and White Minstrels.

It was hot and hard work keeping the fires going when at sea, especially when sailing at a fast speed when up to twelve tons of coal would be consumed in a single hour. Trolleys were filled with coal and taken to the fires and in this respect the roll of the ship assisted a great deal and it was just a question of guiding the trolley as it ran 'downhill'.

The heat was tremendous and because clothing soon became uncomfortable, the men usually worked completely naked except for wooden clogs which were a necessity on the hot metal decks. Occasionally, boiling hot water dripped down on them from the pipes above.[6]

'We never got the coal dust out of our eyes,' wrote one sailor who was on the *Black Prince*, an armoured cruiser of the 1st Cruiser Squadron. In the months before the Battle of Jutland, *Black Prince* was constantly on patrol in the North Sea. It was an unvarying routine of 'four days on patrol, then back to harbour and coal ship (750 tons), then out again'.

This sailor was fortunate. Four days before Jutland, he was sent south for a gunnery course. *Black Prince* was sunk at Jutland with the loss of all hands.

8

Guarding the Fleet

It was a tough life outside the Flow on the ceaseless patrols among the mines and submarines of the North Sea, but it was in many ways tougher still for those inside the Flow, or for those manning its 'gates'.

Jellicoe had the highest praise for the hardy men who crewed the trawlers on the booms. 'These trawlers,' he wrote, 'were moored in positions in which they were exposed to the whole fury of northerly and southerly gales; in many cases they were within a few yards of a rocky coast, heavy seas breaking over them and bringing on board tons of water.'

These tiny ships were never off watch, since no one could tell at what hour an enemy submarine might strike. Theirs could also be a dangerous duty. One sailor recalled how on a very dark night the trawler responsible for opening the 'gate' in the submarine nets got in the way of the armoured cruiser H.M.S. *Shannon* and was sliced in two.

Also exposed to the weather and enduring considerable hardship were the Royal Marine Pensioners who manned the gun defences of the Flow, and the men responsible for the searchlight and signal stations and – later in the war – the minefields. For them life at Scapa was uncompromisingly harsh and monotonous. Their watchfulness could never be relaxed but was seldom rewarded by any excitement. They knew they had, in Jellicoe's words, to 'stick it out for the safety of the Fleet'.

¶ The boom defences consisted of long lines of drifters or trawlers across the entrances to Scapa, with submarine nets slung between them. As we were moored or anchored fore and aft, and the nets secured either side amidships, we had the full effects of Scapa's weather whichever way it came.

I was drafted to a drifter which bore the grand name of H.M.D. *Buces* – formerly a fishing boat of Buckie in the Moray Firth.

The ship's company or crew comprised a Skipper, Mate, Driver or Engineer, one Stoker, and four Deckhands. At the formation of the boom defences, the crews were all semi-civilians serving under Naval T124 or T124Z branch of the R.N., but at my time of joining, some of the crews were being replaced by Naval ratings.

We drew stores from the storeship *Zaria* berthed in Longhope, and for other stores two men from each drifter were taken by tender once a week to St Margaret's Hope – a small village at the other end of the Flow. It was about an hour's run to get there, but the couple of hours on shore was worth it; and that was the only occasion we ever were ashore.

The Skipper was a real character. He had been fishing all his life and I believe was actually the Skipper of the *Buces* when she was fishing out of Buckie. He knew Scapa like the back of his hand, and sometimes if the weather eased, we would put the small boat out and go fishing. Before setting out, he would ask us what kind of fish we wanted. Then he would take us to a certain spot in the Flow, shoot out lines and then drift for about thirty minutes; then haul in and there would be the kind of fish we asked for and plenty of it.

On the whole it was rather monotonous on the boom-defence vessels, work being mainly maintenance and keeping a constant watch on the nets and operating gear day and night.

The Fleet, on putting to sea, was always impressive, and as they had to go through the 'gates' in the nets, they passed very close to us and we always had a grandstand view – *and* their wash, which was often considerable.[1]

*   *   *

¶ As a corporal in the Royal Marines I was sent, along with two other privates, to the signal station on Flotta Island. We landed on Flotta in appalling weather on 1 January 1915. At that time the only place for us was a mud hut, with planks across the top, covered by turf to keep out the rain. In the hut was a box with all the flags and pennants jumbled up, three berths, a telephone and a cracked combustion stove. This stove had to be used for all heating and cooking. The fuel used was peat. For the first few months we had to even sleep with all our clothes on (plus greatcoats) in an effort to keep warm. The turf did not keep out very much of the rain and so in addition to being cold, we were wet through for most of the time.

About half a mile away from the hut was a well. Some crofters lent us a small barrel and a wheelbarrow so that we could get our water supply from the well up the hill to the hut.

Later on, in June, Admiral Lord Stanley went ashore and was horrified when he saw the conditions under which we men were working and living. He gave orders for food and extra clothing to be given to us straight away, and not long afterwards carpenters arrived and built a hut with comfortable bunks, etc.[2]

* * *

¶ In 1916 I was with a few other ratings manning two searchlights on the tiny uninhabited island called Switha at the entrance to Scapa Flow.

Life was pretty grim on that lonely island outpost. There was no harbour or even a jetty. In stormy weather you were reduced to 'iron rations' because the provision boat couldn't get in. Oil fuel for the searchlights had to be floated ashore attached to ropes.

One dark night when it was snowing hard and blowing a blizzard, Tom Bowlin, a Royal Naval Volunteer Reserve man, set off across the island to relieve the man on the searchlight there at the other end. The man he was to relieve, Lomax, had been on the first watch, from 4 P.M. to midnight.

Half an hour later came a phone call from Lomax to say Tom had not yet arrived. It was after midnight, so our small party set out, strung along a rope to which each man was secured so there would be no disappearing in drifts. In this way, each carrying a hurricane lantern we combed the length and breadth of the island, but without result.

Next morning he was found in a huddled heap on a rock at the bottom of the high and almost perpendicular cliff. Tom must have walked straight over the cliff edge in the snow, and only a few yards from his destination. When picked up he was dead from injuries and exposure.[3]

* * *

¶ I was a Royal Marine Corporal stationed on a shore battery situated on top of a hill named Houton Head which gave us a good view of the 'fairway' from the Atlantic into Scapa Flow. We were in charge of a minefield. Below us to the left the Royal Naval Air Service were camped with their seaplanes anchored off shore. Down in the valley from our camp we had two search-lights housed in two camouflaged huts in which we had to do duty from dusk until dawn. We had to make our own electricity to service both the mines and the lights. The mines were 'non-contact' and had to be exploded either by a switch or by moving a vernier telescope over a copper stripped table. The table was for surface ships and the switch for undersea vessels.

To pinpoint a submarine, attached to the centre of the mine field were microphones with wires leading up to the look-out hut, in a special compartment of which a man sat for four hours with earphones clasped over his head. Facing him was a 'tell-tale', an instrument that could let you know when any vessel was directly over the minefield.[4]

As well as its defences on dry land, the Fleet had its defences in the air. Air-warfare was in its infancy, and Scapa was the scene of some of its first experiments. As early as October 1914, the old 20,000-ton Cunarder *Campania* had been bought by the Admiralty, reconstructed to take ten or eleven seaplanes, and given a 120-foot flight-deck above the forecastle. She carried out her trials in the Flow, and served with the Grand Fleet for the greater part of the war.

Houton, on the north shore of the Flow, became the main land seaplane base, but there were more than seaplanes at Scapa.

There were flying-boats, airships, even kite-balloons. Originally these latter were flown from a number of specially adapted vessels, but later they were stored on shore and transferred to the Fleet as required, where their purpose was to spot submarines and to direct firing – crows' nests on strings rising from the decks of their ships like monsters out of Jules Verne.

Later in the war, the aeroplane took over from the seaplane as the principal aircraft used by the Navy. In August 1917 the first successful deck-landing was made on the flight-deck of the new aircraft-carrier *Furious* in Scapa Flow. By this time too the technique of flying off aircraft from the turrets of fighting ships had been successfully developed.

Even in four years there was considerable progress. Yet few of those who shared in these early experiments – which to many sailors of the older school must have seemed little more than a side-show – could have imagined that these flying machines darting skywards from the turrets of Dreadnoughts or the decks of carriers were ultimately to lead to so radical a revolution in the techniques of sea war that some of the great pitched battles of a quarter of a century later – such as the Battle of the Philippine Sea in 1944 – were to be fought almost exclusively with aircraft and bombs rather than guns.

¶ In September 1914 I proceeded in a cattle transport vessel to Scapa Flow with two seaplanes for the air base established for the protection of the Grand Fleet against submarine attack. When the Fleet was at anchor, the principal duty of the base was to carry out patrols at dusk and dawn, to see if any hostile submarines were in the vicinity of the harbour: and when the Fleet was leaving or entering harbour, to carry out a wide sweep of the sea near the approach entrance.

The armament available for attacking any enemy who might be encountered consisted of two sixteen-pound bombs which lay, or rolled about, on the floor of the cockpit. These it was hoped to drop by hand on any enemy craft. The dusk patrols were the most important and also the most risky, for it was clear that in case of a forced landing away from the vicinity of the base no rescue search would be possible after dark, owing to the closing of the harbour entrance boom defence and the necessity for the Fleet to be screened by total blackout.

These anti-submarine patrols did provide the Fleet with some measure of security, for although our ability to attack any hostile craft was of a primitive nature and we had no means of communicating with the Fleet until we got back to base, the dropping of a bomb – however wide of the mark – would have immediately alerted the anti-submarine surface vessels to action. We also had an extensive range of vision for reconnaissance.

With such a large population afloat in Scapa Flow it was inevitable that someone would throw overboard during the night floating objects such as tin cans or bottles, with the result that in the dim light of early dawn a look-out in one of the capital ships would mistake one of these objects for the lens of a submarine periscope and alert the anti-submarine gun crews to action, and the colliers to take up their position of screening the flag-ship, *Iron Duke*, from attack.

This would usually happen when we were preparing to leave Kirkwall to launch the dawn air patrol, the sound of gunfire accelerating our departure. By the time we arrived at Scapa all suspicious floating objects in the eighty square miles of water had been sunk and we would proceed with the routine patrol.[5]

* * *

¶ The function of the seaplane station was to locate and harass enemy ships, mainly submarines, in the North Sea. It was equipped with 'Short' seaplanes and flying-boats with twin Rolls 'Eagle 8' engines. The flying-boats carried a crew of four, made up of pilot, navigator, wireless operator and flight engineer.

Ours was a busy corner of Orkney. Together with the adjacent Kite Balloon Station, administered by H.M.S. *Canning* anchored offshore, we numbered some eight hundred officers and men. In addition, there were some two hundred civilians employed by contractors erecting hangars, concreting etc.

Our parades would have delighted lovers of comic opera. The other ranks would line up facing about twenty officers, no two being dressed alike. These were early days in the life of the Royal Air Force, and uniforms varied from the light blue of the

Commanding Officer, through the khaki uniform of the Foot Guards (Adjutant) to the dark blue of the Royal Navy and every combination one could think of, not forgetting the Royal Flying Corps with forage cap. The men must have looked an equally disorderly assembly. Except for the shoulder flash I could have been in the Royal Field Artillery, with splendid riding breeches and puttees done up cavalry style.

The worst aspect of the climatic conditions were the severe gales, when all hands turned out to keep the aircraft and their cradles head to wind and hold them down. I recall one terrible night with gusts up to ninety-five m.p.h. when about forty of us were lifted with the flying-boat off the cradle and several feet into the air. It then crashed down on the tarmac, smashing a great hole in the hull. When the storm abated there was hardly a sound aircraft left.[6]

* * *

¶ I was posted to a Kite Balloon Station at Caldale, a camp with a dozen officers and about a hundred men, two miles west of Kirkwall. The purpose of this station was to supply balloons to the drifters for submarine-spotting, and when balloons were ordered all hands were required at the hangars for man-handling these awkward monsters, in attaching them to the winch on the old Maudsley solid-tyred lorries. The balloons were then let up by the winch on the steel cable to a height of about 500 feet and the lorry drove off with its lofty attachment, rather light on the rear wheels.

When a gale was blowing, much excitement was aroused in Kirkwall when the cable wrapped itself around chimneys and brought them crashing to the ground. One gusty day a balloon broke free. The last unfortunate man to hold on to his guy rope was carried up thirty feet and fell, injuring his spine.

I was ordered to chase the balloon on my motor-cycle to report where it went to. This I did with gusto at full throttle and managed to keep it in sight to the north end of the Island, until my exhaust valve burnt out and I could only report that it was heading due north and making excellent progress.[7]

* * *

¶ Several of the battle-cruisers flew off planes as early as 1917 though of course they could not land aboard ship again. They usually flew back to Turnhouse Aerodrome near Edinburgh and were returned to their ships on a lighter. Ours on *Indomitable* was a Sopwith Pup and was stowed on a wooden platform built on to one of the midship 12-inch gun turrets. When it was proposed to fly off, a runway of wood planks was laid on top of, and clamped to, the barrels of the guns, the turret trained a couple of points over the bow, the ship steamed full speed into the wind and when the plane was revved up sufficiently the holding-down gear was released – and off she went.

One thing was important, though. Before he was allowed to take off, there had to be either a destroyer or a motor launch stationed on our quarter to pick him up if he did not fly. On one occasion while we were exercising in the Flow, the motor launch didn't turn up. The pilot, whose name was Lieutenant Bird (universally known as Dicky, of course) apparently persuaded the Old Man that, as he had previously done the trick successfully so many times, he should let him go. Of course on this occasion the plane just rolled off the end of the runway into the water with the ship steaming at twenty-seven knots! What a panic there was as the ship steamed in a wide circle and came up to him again.

My recollection is that there was far more effort made to salvage the engine than there was to rescue poor old Dicky Bird. I can see him now, sitting on the tail smoking a Woodbine.[8]

Fear of the submarine dominated the thoughts of the British commanders in Scapa Flow, and imaginary sightings were frequent in the early months of war. Yet there was legitimate cause for their apprehension for in both wars it was the U-boat rather than Germany's surface warships that threatened Allied domination of the seas. Watching out for submarines was a priority task that involved not only the boom-defence vessels and the air arm but also a substantial number of highly mobile 'small' ships which were constantly prowling the waters outside the Flow – many of them crewed not by the regular seamen of the

Navy but by either fishermen enrolled in the R.N.R. or 'hostilities only' sailors fresh from 'Civvy Street'.

¶ The small patrol boats, mostly trawlers and drifters on which I had intermittent spells, were fully employed watching for U-boats, mines and any suspicious-looking vessels. Such hardships as cold weather, mountainous seas, cook unable to keep galley fire alight, extended days at sea, risk of going for shelter and getting out of control too near rocky coasts were a regular part of our life. At night, no lights. One tiny illumination over the binnacle in the wheel house. All these hazards were cheerfully borne by the crew who cursed roundly at any frustration of their efforts in the course of duty.

I never heard the war mentioned once but the one thing that was absolutely not tolerated was anyone leaving the teapot empty on the stove in the fo'c'sle. In one four-day session I never saw the pot emptied once. Fresh tea was added each time to the existing contents according to the requirements of the individuals.[9]

*   *   *

¶ I became one of the crew of a motor launch on active service as a submarine chaser. Our first skipper – an Australian – had been thinking things over and announced to the occupants of the bridge – the sub-lieutenant, coxswain and myself (signalman) – that 'This is a small boat, made of wood. We carry 5,000 gallons of petrol, plenty of paraffin, a magazine crammed with explosives, depth charges full of T.N.T. A cigarette end or an absent-minded cook could easily start a fire and what would be left of us? And who would know? So I've decided that we must train ourselves to perfection in the most necessary thing of all – I mean abandoning ship. I've drawn up a list of the positions each man, from myself downwards, will take and he is to become proficient in this so that some day at sea, when the siren sounds four blasts for abandon ship there will be no panic, no questions asked – just quick action.' Well, we did as we were told and managed our allotted tasks to perfection.

Then one nasty day we were doing a patrol on our own in a remote spot and the four blasts went. Everything went along perfectly; life-jackets issued, emergency rations, water, ship's papers, signalling code book – dinghy lowered – all in a few minutes. We were all in the dinghy – it was only a test drill. The skipper said: 'Splendid! We'll just row about forty yards from the ship and then we'll return and call it a day.' *But* – something went wrong! We were about twenty yards from the launch when suddenly the gap between the two boats started widening rapidly. We had entered a different current and were moving swiftly away from our floating home – our life – our existence! No help from any source. We took turns at the oars but everything was in vain. The launch was getting farther away. 'Seems like another *Marie Celeste*,' said the undiplomatic Sub-Lieutenant. 'Shut up!' roared the skipper. The engineer, who had religious leanings, said: 'Man proposes, God disposes.' 'You go to hell,' roared the skipper. 'We're on the way,' murmured the coxswain. Then the miracle happened. Apparently we had entered the edge of a very large whirlpool and were behaving like a roundabout at a fair – we were rushing back to the launch. With skilful manoeuvring the dinghy was steered out of the current as we approached the launch, which we reached with great relief. Very little was said afterwards about abandoning ship – but fire precautions were intensified.

After the British naval attack on Zeebrugge in April 1918 the authorities had information of an enemy plan to attack the boom defences of Scapa Flow with a fleet of small craft, the idea being to render the booms useless and thereby let in a powerful force of submarines to play havoc with the Grand Fleet. All motor launches around the Orkneys – thirteen in all – were called in by the Extended Defence Officer and given instruction to form up into two columns, one of seven boats and one of six (our boat being senior) and to pick their own time particularly in inclement weather and at night-time with ships all blacked out to make a mock attack on the boom without warning.

Our skipper kept them waiting, then one dirty night with a favourable tide at about 1.30 A.M. he organized by dimmed torch code the whole thirteen boats to drift via the swift Pentland to the North Sea. Then, with dimmed stern lights to guide the following boat, the attack was made. As signalman with the searchlight I was to point out with the beam the opening which we were to attack.

As we approached the boom I opened up the 'shutter' and fastened the ray on to the required spot. The southern Orkneys, hitherto quiet, suddenly sprang to life with a hundred search lights and seemingly – by the infernal noise – a thousand guns (firing blank shot). I looked back at the following launches smashing ahead through driving rain and spray, in perfect line ahead. Experienced naval strategists and long-service sailors manning them? Not on your Nellie! Ninety-eight per cent of them were 'hostilities-only'. Take our boat: skipper – dentist; second-in-command – bank clerk; two petty officers – motor mechanics; coxswain – a butcher; myself – a cinema projectionist; cook – a clerk; first seaman – overlooker in Lancashire mill; second seaman – an inshore fisherman![10]

9

Libertymen

'In from out' was the phrase the Navy used when they sailed back into Scapa Flow from patrol or convoy and dropped anchor in the shelter of that security which the big guns and the small ships maintained for them. Ceaseless vigilance secured a place for the Fleet to rest in, but once in harbour the natural desire of everyone was to go ashore. The trouble was, there was really no shore worth going to. Sport and games were necessary for the maintenance of morale and fitness and the Navy did what it could. Sailing and rowing regattas were arranged and there was keen competition between ships and squadrons. Every year there was a Grand Fleet Boxing Championship outside the Y.M.C.A. hut on Flotta, which was sometimes witnessed by as many as 10,000 men. Football was played all the year round, and after a spell at sea the men would stretch their legs in a cross-country run.

¶ The Fleet used Flotta Island for most recreation purposes as it contained the only level strip of land thereabouts. Often we had to play games in deep snow and with soccer this wasn't easy. A gale was usually blowing too but to a man who had been cooped up in an ironclad for several weeks it was an elixir to last him for days.[1]

* * *

¶ Most of the big ships were able to run ten or twelve football teams which played against each other when circumstances permitted: thus there would be teams from the wardroom, gun-room, seamen starboard watch, seamen port watch, stokers, Marines, signalmen etc., forming a small league in each battleship.[2]

* * *

¶ So life went on, in Scapa to 'coal' and out to 'patrol'. The cycle of events got so monotonous that it was decided we needed some relaxation. So we were landed on Flotta Island for cross-country running.

After running for a while my pal and I spotted a small track. We followed it, and it eventually led us to a crofter's cottage. The dear old lady inside made us tea, hot scones, and boiled eggs. We left with little doubt which had benefited us most, the run or the food. We left with our stomachs full and our hearts content, with a prayer for our safety from the dear old lady.[3]

Even at these simple recreations they were not wholly safe from danger.

¶ I remember the ratings from a battleship coming ashore in a pinnace for a game of football. The inward run was all right, but on returning the weather turned foul and all the twenty-odd men were drowned. Next day all flags on the Fleet flew at half mast.[4]

Some of the Naval men didn't bother to go ashore at all for months at a time. They felt it wasn't worth it to visit the one canteen on Flotta.

¶ At one period I did not set foot on dry land for seven months and that was not unusual. Boys were not allowed ashore except in organized parties no matter where you were, though after I was 'rated' I did pay a few visits to the wet canteen. But it was scarcely worth the trouble.

Apart from the fact that it meant a long trip in a drifter, as the one boat called at a number of ships on her way, there was only the one canteen (where one guzzled a large amount of beer, usually roaring out ribald songs that one couldn't sing anywhere else) but the place closed at 8.30 P.M. (invariably ending with a fight or two), and then there was the job of picking out your own drifter from the many at the pier, the long trip back to the ship, and having to pass the Officer of the Watch before you got back 'home' to your own mess.[5]

For the officers Flotta had a little more to offer. A golf course was laid out there and Admiral Jellicoe could often be seen having a hurried round when he could spare a little time from his work on board the *Iron Duke*. This golf course left one rating with an unhappy memory.

¶ We were not allowed to land at Kirkwall but only on the island of Flotta where there wasn't even a tree. The only amenity there was a tiny hut where one could obtain a cup of tea and a bun. There was a small golf course laid out for the use of the Officers of the Fleet.

The Surgeon Commander came to the Bay (I was a Sick Berth Attendant) and asked if one of us would caddy for him. I volunteered. The Liberty Boat was called away and the only people going ashore were the Surgeon Commander, the Engineer Commander, the Engineer's Writer, two ratings and myself. The Engineer's Writer was caddying for the Engineer Commander.

After the two officers finished the game we were rewarded with 2s. each and told to get a cup of tea. In the tea hut we found the two ratings who had come ashore with us. We all four strolled down to the jetty in time to catch the boat on the half hour. Alas! The officers were aboard and the boat had left. We waited half an hour and then begged a passage on the *Conqueror's* boat. Arriving at our ship *Thunderer* we clambered on board and were met with the curt order 'Fall in on the quarter deck'. Our protestations that we had been on the jetty in good time fell on deaf ears. 'Commander's Report', we were told.

The following morning 'Defaulters' sounded off and I duly fell in with my fellow-criminals convinced that the Commander would listen to our plea. No such luck. We found ourselves in dire trouble for the Commander would not deal with us as our offence was so serious, and we were committed to the 'Captain's Report'. Again we loomed up on the quarter-deck. Our names were called. 'Off caps'. 'Did remain absent over leave thirty minutes etc. etc.' We received a dressing down and then the two libertymen were sentenced to loss of one day's pay and six months' stoppage of leave. The other caddy and myself were put down as having gone ashore on duty, so we were not fined the day's pay but had to undergo the six months' leave stoppage.

I think the Surgeon Commander felt somewhat guilty about it all, because he sent me ashore to Kirkwall on duty, ostensibly to purchase some thermometers.[6]

For all libertymen the true Mecca was Kirkwall, the capital of Orkney, on the mainland. This little town of some four or five thousand inhabitants with a narrow main street 'where two wheelbarrows tremble when they meet' (as someone wrote at the time) had to meet the needs of a floating population of about 100,000 men, not all of whom, fortunately, came ashore to visit it. Some ships' companies were confined to Flotta or Longhope for their shore leave. For the favoured few a chance to visit Kirkwall usually meant a long trip by drifter from their berth to Scapa Pier, at the north end of the Flow. Then there was a two-mile walk into the town. What they found there wasn't exactly a substitute for Portsmouth, Devonport or Chatham but it compared very favourably with the bare, sparsely-inhabited islands which were all they could see from their ships at anchor.

¶ After several months aboard, a place like Kirkwall seemed to be the hub of civilization. Its ancient cathedral, its little shops and neat villas, its quayside and its friendly inhabitants with their soft, northern speech, served as a refreshing reminder of the wider world to which we hoped one day to return.[7]

*   *   *

¶ One Sunday I wangled a trip in a drifter to Kirkwall. I visited the little St Magnus' Cathedral, built of red sandstone eight hundred years ago. I was able to explore this most interesting edifice thoroughly, under the guidance of a kindly verger. There had been a heavy snowfall the day before and this Sunday was a sparkling day of wonderful visibility. So, in my rubber knee boots, I walked to the summit of Wideford Hill to see the view. It was amazing! It looked as if one could throw a stone across the Pentland Firth into Caithness. To the north I could see the Shetland Islands* and to the south I could see a tall obelisk which I had noticed in Sutherland, at least forty miles distant, on my journeys to and from Scapa Flow.[8]

* * *

¶ Flotta was the only island the ratings were allowed ashore on. There were no pubs on it, only a miserable canteen that sold tea and biscuits. What the hell good was that for thirsty young sailors?

Occasionally individual ships would anchor on the far side of the Flow near to Kirkwall on the main island. Officers and P.Os were allowed to go ashore to Kirkwall. There were pubs but no spirits were sold, only port wine and beer. I believe you couldn't get any spirits north of Inverness in the First World War. I managed to get to Kirkwall once. We went ashore to get sand for holystoning the decks, so we hurried on with the job and away we went to Kirkwall for a binge. The only one I ever had at Scapa.[9]

* * *

¶ As a rest and change from Fleet routine it was customary to send the ships, in turn, for a few days to the north shore of the Flow, where normal duties were performed until noon, after which a 'make and mend' was granted. Then there was the choice of sailing, picnicking, bathing, walking across the country, visiting the Kirkwall shops, or enjoying a little trout-fishing.

---

* The Shetland Islands cannot be seen from Orkney, but Fair Isle can on a very clear day.

How well I remember delights of 'bangers' fried over a drift-wood fire, and washed down with a little sloe gin.[10]

* * *

¶ When I was Admiral's skiffman I used to go ashore with the Admiral. His barge used to tow me close in and then I would pull the Admiral ashore. He would go bird-nesting, looking for eggs not birds and he would be away about two hours so I used to go lobster-hunting. There were several pots around so I would haul them up and occasionally find a succulent lobster. Somebody told me I should have put two bob in the pot, but as I never seemed to have two bob I used to say to myself 'My need is greater than yours, chum – thanks a lot'.[11]

It all sounds idyllic but you had to pick your weather for jaunts ashore. Scapa in winter was not to be trifled with.

¶ In December 1917 – a week before Christmas – the air had a freezing bite in it and our winter wear was used in earnest. On the day prior to our off-duty day a cruel blizzard struck the Orkneys. It finished early next morning and everywhere things looked grim. Being our 'day off' someone suggested a walk ashore for the experience. The 'walk' around the bay at Longhope is roughly seven miles and with snow level with the eaves of the cottages it was very difficult going. After a couple of miles on the road – or rather the site of it – we noticed that the tide was going out so we found the walking much easier on the beach. The days are very short in winter and darkness was approaching as we completed our walk; we shouted ourselves hoarse but nobody responded from the launch, almost a quarter of a mile away.

Being hungry we entered the small grocery store near-by. We all felt very warm after the exercise. We wore thick woollen Balaclava helmets, heavy overcoats and thick woollen mittens. The proprietor, for his own and his family's protection, would not serve us with anything they would need as they were completely isolated. But he did offer us a large tin of peaches which we accepted. He opened the tin and offered a dessert spoon.

Our hands had never felt the cold, yet when the first man attempted to remove his right-hand mitten with his left the left hand was completely inactive. He tried to pick up the spoon; he stretched his arms – both hands hung limply from the wrists. The same thing happened to the rest of us. I made a bold attempt to grip the tin with my wrists but only succeeded in emptying the contents over my face and overcoat.

Now the darkness had set in. We shouted again to the launch – still no response. A few hundred yards away was a small farm. We kicked on the door (we couldn't knock) and the door opened. We pleaded for a hot drink. We were immediately invited inside into the large sitting-room – flag-stone floor, walls adorned with oriental straw-like pictures, crossed violins and bows, and in the centre of the room a large well-polished heating stove. All the furniture was carved, especially the handsome massive circular mahogany table. Our kind-hearted host said: 'Make yourselves at home, we'll get you some tea.'

While they prepared the meal the circulation began to return to our hands – and our feet – and our hosts discreetly kept out of the room whilst four members of the Royal Navy, trained for the annihilation of U-boats, fought hard to keep the tears back whilst experiencing the excruciating pain. We were soon returned to normality and were treated to a handsome tea of home-made bread, home-made butter and jam and scones. Our hosts flatly refused to accept payment but were not in time to beat me to it as I pounced on a beautifully carved child's money box.[12]

To be a libertyman ashore in Scapa in the Great War was, for many, often slightly more unpleasant than actually being on duty. It was better, perhaps, to hang on until one could disembark at last on that dry land beyond the Pentland Firth over which the 'Jellicoes' pounded for 700 odd miles.

In the meantime, perhaps this was the ultimate answer to the problem of exercising on small islands.

¶ When I was in the crew of the Captain's boat we often called for his friend, Captain Keyes (later Admiral Sir Roger Keyes) of H.M.S. *Centurion*. They used to take boomerangs ashore.'[13]

10

Jutland

As the war dragged on, the frustrating pattern established in its early weeks continued. There were occasional sweeps by the Grand Fleet, more constant sweeps by the cruisers. The Germans emerged, but only to bombard a few British coastal towns – to break windows and kill civilians. Naval forces under Admirals Warrender and Beatty raced to attack the marauding German battle-cruisers, but they escaped in the thick weather of a winter storm, leaving the British commanders groping forlornly for their enemy in heavy seas and torrential rain.

In any case this abortive non-engagement was too far south to involve the squadrons based on Scapa. Similarly the Battle of the Dogger Bank early in 1915 was an encounter with which men from Scapa were only marginally concerned. True, the Grand Fleet hurried down the North Sea at the possibility of a round with the Germans; but the action was fought by forces from Rosyth and Harwich and was over before Jellicoe could arrive on the scene.

These diversions apart, Jellicoe's squadrons saw more and more of Scapa and less and less of the North Sea. An elaborate programme of rehearsal and preparation kept the Fleet fit and ready. The Flow was big enough for gunnery practice with guns up to 6-inch calibre and for torpedo work. Jellicoe wrote: 'Ships were firing, running torpedoes, practising fire-control exercises, carrying out experiments and exercises in dealing with destroyers, day after day, from daylight until dark.' But all this was not winning the war.

The months slipped by. The High Seas Fleet refused to put itself at risk. Jellicoe still worked for that crucial encounter which would reaffirm Britain's mastery of the waves. But he too, like the Germans, was not anxious for any death-or-glory battle simply to fill the world's headlines. He knew that there was one vital proviso in all he did – namely that he could not, in any circumstances, risk being beaten. A victory at sea would not win the war, though it would be an enormous stride forward; but a defeat could lose it. Jellicoe's aim was to engage the High Seas Fleet with forces so superior that such a defeat was impossible.

It was not until the last day of May 1916 that the long-expected meeting of the Grand Fleet and the High Seas Fleet took place. The main Fleets were only engaged for a few minutes at a time, and the whole fragmentary action was over by the first light of the following morning; but the controversy over this battle, which involved 250 ships and twenty-five admirals and killed more than eight thousand men, is not finished yet.

The Battle of Jutland was fought because it had become psychologically necessary. Neither Navy was enjoying itself; each felt guilt at standing by in comparative idleness as the tide of war rolled bloodily to and fro in Flanders. But the Grand Fleet could not atone for its enforced inactivity until the High Seas Fleet decided to emerge from the safety of its harbours. The spring of 1916 made that decision inevitable. The battle of Verdun had just been fought with huge casualties and little result. The stalemate on land created the demand for some crucial gesture at sea. Moreover, the High Seas Fleet was now led by new commanders – Admirals Scheer and von Hipper – who were more aggressively-minded than their predecessors and who realized that the best way to cure the rising sense of frustration among their men (and among the people of Germany at large) was to accept England's challenge.

The Grand Fleet left Scapa on 30 May after Jellicoe had learnt from the Admiralty that the High Seas Fleet was almost certainly putting to sea. Simultaneously, the 2nd Battle Squadron sailed from Invergordon, and Beatty and his battle-cruisers, together with the 5th Battle Squadron, sailed from Rosyth. The Scapa and Invergordon sections combined, and the whole gigantic force steamed towards the Jutland coast with Beatty out ahead by some sixty-five miles. Their German opponents were also in two main sections, with Admiral von Hipper's scouting group of battle-cruisers about sixty miles ahead of the High Seas Fleet proper under Admiral Scheer.

Beatty and Hipper clashed first, on the afternoon of 31 May. Subsequently, as Scheer's main force appeared on the horizon, Beatty turned northwards hoping to run the Germans on to the guns of Jellicoe's advancing Grand Fleet. But the main Fleet action never became the set-piece battle which everyone expected. The big ships exchanged fierce fire for two or three minutes; then the Germans, in a manoeuvre that was quite unorthodox according to the text-book theories of the time, turned abruptly through 180 degrees and disappeared into the smoke and mist, while their destroyer flotillas went in with a torpedo attack from which Jellicoe turned away. Some time later in the gathering dusk the two Fleets, virtually by accident, met again, but again Scheer turned about and took his High Seas Fleet out of ambush, while Hipper and his scouting force charged the British in what became known as Hipper's 'death-ride' and the destroyers again caused the Grand Fleet to turn away with a torpedo attack.

No night action was attempted by the Grand Fleet, though there was a series of violent clashes mainly between the lighter units of the two Fleets during the hours of darkness. Dawn found Jellicoe convinced that he still stood between the enemy and his base, whereas in fact Scheer had broken through astern of the British battle-squadrons and was already out of danger. The seas were empty of Germans and there was only a solitary Zeppelin to arouse the hostility of the British guns.

The Royal Navy had gone into action a firm favourite, but Jutland was not the clear-cut victory that the British public and the British sailor wanted. The Germans, indeed, sank more ships than the British, who had the bitter experience of watching three of their prized battle-cruisers blown up with appalling loss of life. The Germans proved superior in the accuracy of their firing and the effectiveness of their shells, and crucially superior in the protection given by their armour. Their punishment, too, was considerable, but in terms of sailors killed they lost 2,551 to the Royal Navy's 6,097. And yet there is on the other side the incontrovertible fact that the ships of the High Seas Fleet scarcely showed their noses in the North Sea again. Jutland gave a tremendous fillip to the German people, but it removed their much-vaunted Fleet from effective participation in the war. After Jutland, Germany went underwater; the U-boat was her main maritime weapon from then onwards.

This is not the place to enter into the controversy as to who was responsible for failing to make Jutland the exhilarating victory everyone wanted. The sailors who wrote of it in their reminiscences were not concerned to discuss its overall strategy. They simply described what they saw – if indeed they saw anything of the battle at all. For the vast majority of the participants in this holocaust in the North Sea were below decks at their action stations, and their memories were of sudden rumours and hurried orders and the thunder of guns and explosions, with, if they were lucky, a few moments on deck in the calmer moments of the action.

The Fleet had often sailed from Scapa in similar circumstances to those of the end of May 1916, but there was, as one sailor recalls, something memorable and ominous about this occasion.

¶ The eve of Jutland I always remember – blazing red and orange colouring caused by storm clouds, indeed very wonderful and beautiful; a sky which seemed a foreboding of something dreadful about to happen![1]

Arthur Sneesby was a Boy Seaman on *Conqueror*, battleship of the 2nd Battle Squadron which sailed from Invergordon.

¶ Often in the night in that month of May we were alerted to sea, with everybody out.

The anchor would start to be hauled up, the ship would get under way – and then from the bridge the Captain would sing out, 'Stand by to re-moor ship'. This meant going out to sea, turning round and coming in again so as to berth in our allotted positions, and by the time we had finished dawn had come.

But after these false alarms, at the end of May we did not turn back but went straight on towards the Jutland coast, everybody keyed up.

All I could feel as the *Conqueror* and her sister-ships steamed at full speed ahead with black smoke and grit coming out of the funnels was the blood tingling in my veins and what we were going to meet.

It was about late afternoon on 31 May when I heard over the voice pipe, 'All 13.5 guns stand-by, range so many yards, deflection so much, *fire*!' The shock of those ten big guns, the flash and smoke over the side of the ship was terrific.

After this the night action. The way those destroyers fought firing their small guns to the last! Although we could hardly see them the explosions of ships blowing up were very visible, *Black Prince, Defence, Warrior*.

I saw H.M.S. *Marlborough*, 5th Battle Squadron, turn sixteen points of the compass with a hole in her side from a torpedo.

H.M.S. *Tiger* had her funnels shot off. H.M.S. *Queen Mary* was blown up. My cousin was on her and lost his life.

I know that the Jutland battle has never been solved by the critics. What I know – and this is my answer – they fled back to their base in the night; we waited for them in daylight. First of June, they would not come out; we waited till nearly noon and then we returned home, we were ready for sea again on 2 June after coaling and renewing ammunition.[2]

Charles Gifford was a Signalman on *Castor*, light cruiser, which Jellicoe had made 'flagship' of the destroyer flotillas, with Commodore J. Hawksley as Commodore (F).

¶ H.M.S. *Castor*, on which I was a signal and wireless rating, led all the destroyers out from Scapa – there must have been about forty of them. We went far ahead of the Fleet, then spread out and formed an inverted U as a screen.

Then certain orders were given to our gunnery and torpedo men and the rumour spread that the German Navy was out.

Some said they will have returned to Kiel by the time we get anywhere near them. We had no knowledge then as to what the battle-cruiser Fleet under Admiral Beatty was up to or even if it was at sea. It was in the late afternoon of 31 May that we found out what was afoot.

We saw the explosion of the battle-cruiser H.M.S. *Invincible* and before everything from her had fallen down we had passed close to her. There was nothing to be seen, she must have burst open and sunk in seconds. Anyway, our time had come and the enemy were now trying to get us and the destroyers behind us. Shells were falling just ahead and astern as I stood alongside the Commodore on the bridge. Our defence against shrapnel bursts was a well-painted canvas screen and many times I dodged up or down behind it. My thoughts at the time were – I hope I will not be wounded.

Then the order was made, torpedo attack, and we swooped towards the enemy on a long and large curve and fired our tubes. I was very occupied at this time having to make many flag signals to be passed on down the destroyer line, and so did not have the opportunity of watching for results from this attack of ours. I do know that the enemy guessed what we were up to and turned away from us, making very small targets for us to fire at. But what a sight it was to see about twenty destroyers like dogs tearing at their leash, following us round in a great arc at full speed, their sharp bows cutting through the sea!

The attack over we found ourselves out of touch with the enemy and twilight had set in. It was soon dark, and at this stage of the action it was very tricky – all our faith and trust lay in the Commodore, who like myself never left the bridge afternoon, evening or night. We did know that we were between the enemy and their base and that perhaps they would try to force their way through our lines during the night. Now and again we saw flashes of heavy gunfire ahead or on our beam. This was very dangerous business where one could fire on one's own fleet.

About 9 or 10 P.M. I found the Commodore alongside me on the starboard side of the bridge. To me it seemed he wanted someone to talk to, and I said to him it was a wonderful operation he had carried out earlier in the evening. He said, 'Thank you Gifford, but tonight is more tricky [he did not use the word dangerous] than ever.' He said, 'Are you well versed in the silhouettes of the German Navy?' and I said, 'Yes sir'. 'Well, be sure of yourself and keep a very sharp look-out on your starboard bow.' 'Very good sir,' I replied.

It was about half an hour later that I spotted the mast of a ship coming towards me. I shouted the alarm. I told the Commodore where it was, but none of them could see it, they had not been trained for night-spotting like I had. But the Commodore took no chances and ordered his gunnery officer to train the guns on the bearing I had given. Then I saw two more cruisers following up behind. To me they seemed less than half a mile away and they were definitely German cruisers that had crossed the line ahead of us and were steaming home as fast as they could.

Our guns fired their first salvo into the German control tower and bridge which flashed up like an explosion, then the second and third ship started to fire on us. We were now steaming at full speed firing our guns and torpedoes at them and the destroyers behind us were firing their torpedoes. It was all over in about fifteen minutes but it seemed an hour to us. I had not realized that we had been badly hit because I had been so occupied until a fire broke out on the port side. It was the Commodore's pinnace on fire. The Commodore calmly called out, 'Call the fire party', and it was put out in a few minutes. The boat was badly damaged because an enemy shell had gone through it. This shell could not have been ten feet behind us all on the bridge.

During the action a squeaky voice kept calling through a voice pipe near me, 'Giffy, Giffy, what's happening, are we all right, have we been in action, what's going on up there? For God's sake keep in touch with me.' At the end of it all the Officer of the Watch told me to go down and calm the owner of the terrified voice, as he called it. On my way down I had to pass by many dead and wounded men all being tended by our doctor and his orderlies. It was not until then that I realized that we had been badly hit.

I carried on to complete my mission of comfort and found that the voice was a very young cockney wireless boy locked in the aft emergency wireless receiving station. When I showed up he looked as if he wanted to faint with relief. After half a minute or so he gave me a smile and said how glad he was to see me. I told him that we had been in action and that I believed there were some wounded, but it was now all over and we were on our way home and there was no more danger.[3]

J. C. Marsh was a Sick Berth Attendant on *Thunderer*, like *Conqueror* a battleship of the 2nd Battle Squadron.

¶ I was awakened at about 2 A.M. by the sudden jerking of the ship right aft which we always felt when she was heaving in the anchor. This, plus the working of the propellers at intervals, denoted that we were preparing for sea. A little later the bosun's mate was piping 'Navigating party muster at your stations', and then, 'Four-inch guns crews and part starboard watch for night defence, close up'.

When we were roused at 6.30 A.M. we were well out at sea and steaming for all we were worth. We had no idea what was happening but we knew it was something out of the ordinary as the ship was vibrating with the speed we were making. However, later in the day the bugle sounded off 'Action stations', and every one scurried away to his appropriate part of the ship. My particular spot was the 'Forward Medical Distributing Station' with the Chief Petty Officer and the Surgeon Commander.

At 6.20 P.M. approximately *Thunderer* went into action, firing some forty rounds of 13·5-inch shell. Of course, like so many of the ship's company, we could see nothing and hear nothing beyond the thump of our own guns. Once we thought a shell had come in aft, and the people aft thought it had come in forward, but apparently the whole Fleet had felt it and it must have been due to some underwater explosion. We remained at our stations throughout the night and about midnight I asked the Chief if I could go up top for a breather. When I arrived on deck I found there were lots of others up there including a crowd of stokers who were as black as tinkers. There was a sudden outbreak of firing between what appeared to be a cruiser and some destroyers and then the bugle sounded 'action' again and we all dived for the hatches.

About dawn on 1 June, a chum of mine popped his head up through the hatch and then signalled down to me. I went over and he whispered, 'Zeppelin sighted. Orders to load with shrapnel.' I again asked the Chief if I might go up top. He agreed and I climbed up into the blacksmith's shop in the after-structure. I failed to sight the Zeppelin but there was a gunnery officer up there and I asked him. 'There – away astern.' I looked and saw a tiny cigar-shaped object in the sky a long way off.

The Fleet altered course and this brought the Zepp on the beam and all the heavy guns were trained in her direction. It was my impression that they were simply indulging in aiming practice when suddenly the whole world seemed to erupt as the Fleet let go broadsides. My hat disappeared and I sat down suddenly on the deck. I was shaking like a leaf when I got up. The Zepp shot downwards and then flattened out. I don't know if the sudden shock upset her instruments but she certainly seemed out of control for a while. It was pretty obvious that the Zeppelin could see both Fleets although we could not see one another, and she was evidently guiding the German ships out of danger.

The remainder of that day was a rather melancholy period as we steamed back over the battle ground and saw numbers of bodies floating by. All had life jackets on but they had died of exposure during the night. On our return journey there was a general signal to say that H.M.S. *Malaya* would break formation and draw out of line to bury her dead.[4]

S. T. Dent was a Signalman on *Marlborough*, flagship of the 1st Battle Squadron. *Marlborough* was the first of Jellicoe's great battleships to open fire in the main fleet action; she was soon to be badly damaged, but nevertheless contrived to play her full part in the battle.

¶ In the opening stages of the action, my own ship *Marlborough* was struck almost amidships on the starboard side by two torpedoes, slowly heeled over to an acute and dangerous angle – and there stuck. Her ten 13·5 guns were now at extreme elevation and she was rolling sluggishly, but (whilst the single line of battleships sped swiftly by at full speed) *Marlborough* was repeatedly scoring hits on her allotted opposite number, the German battleship *Seydlitz*. An outstanding display of gunlaying skill.

In the early hours of 1 June the stricken *Marlborough*, engines now silent and ship's company snatching what sleep they could in odd places, lay wallowing gently not far from where she had been attacked, when H.M.S. *Fearless*, scout flotilla-leader attached to 1st Battle Squadron, came alongside, took aboard the Admiral and his staff – and myself – and transferred us to *Revenge*. By this time the main action had been broken off and the German Fleet had hurried back to the safety of harbour leaving us once more mistress of the seas.

Marlborough limped back to harbour with a surrounding escort of Hull and Grimsby fishing trawlers – ready in emergency to take off the entire ship's company. She reached Hull eventually and was patched up, then went to Newcastle for permanent repairs and later rejoined the Grand Fleet.[5]

For the sailors of the Royal Navy, Jutland was to become a proud but disappointing memory. The death roll was so high, the losses unbelievably savage, and yet there was none of the expected elation of victory to compensate for these bitter blows. The Grand Fleet watched in vain for the enemy to come out, then slipped sadly home.

¶ We on the lower deck had no means of telling the outcome of the Jutland Battle, and we were quite confident that the German Fleet had been sent to the bottom. In the early morning light, on 1 June, we saw much floating debris as we swept over the scene of the fray, but, save for a solitary airship, there was no sign of the enemy. The previous night we had clashed with what we had imagined to be a ghostly remnant of Scheer's Fleet, and were sure that our victory was complete. But now, back at Scapa, amidst the bustle of re-fuelling, reports were fluttering through that the honours were with the Germans and that we had suffered a moral defeat. It was beyond belief; and we concluded that the news was German-inspired; but it did have a somewhat chilling effect upon our self-confidence.[6]

*   *   *

¶ Our battery was placed right on the point of the island of Flotta. I was on duty when the Fleet came in from the Battle of Jutland. It was about 4 A.M. It was a sad sight. No flags flying, no bands playing, but some battleships with their 12-inch guns cocked up in the air. Some of them with covers over the places where they had been hit. Especially the cruisers and destroyers, who I believe had many dead aboard.[7]

*   *   *

¶ My first and most poignant recollection of Scapa is of the departure from the Flow of the entire Fleet of warships, destroyers etc. towards the end of May 1916; of rumours of a big battle; and of working all through one night making coffins. The entire dockyard staff, of all trades, was engaged upon this gruesome task. The Fleet returned next day, with their dead, who were buried on the island of Hoy.[8]

*   *   *

¶ After returning from Jutland the Flow seemed to welcome us with open arms; this was when it was a real haven. After coaling ship for two days we landed ashore to bury our dead. Jellicoe and Beatty were there with bowed heads to say good-bye. The Flow was calm that day for the lads we lost who would never again enter its sheltered waters, but as night came the Flow was full of angry waves battering the ships' sides.[9]

11

The Hampshire *Disaster*

Within a few days of the Battle of Jutland, the Army and the nation suffered a shock which displaced the Navy on the front pages of the newspapers, even while they were still trying to decide whether Jutland had been a victory or a defeat. Scapa was only a springboard for the tragedy, but the names of Lord Kitchener and the cruiser *Hampshire* will always be linked with Orkney, and they are still held in bitter memory among the Orcadians.

Lord Kitchener came to Scapa Flow in early June 1916, the head of a military mission bound for Russia. Russia's war effort, after a flying start in 1914, had been running down steadily as confidence in the Tsar and his advisers declined and massive incompetence in the organization of the war left the army short of supplies. As an ally Russia was becoming dangerously weak and the British Government decided that a visit by Kitchener, the War Minister, to Petrograd, could stiffen Russian morale and supply some valuable advice where it was badly needed.

It was Kitchener's own idea to go to Scapa Flow to embark on the cruiser which was to take him to Archangel. He wanted to visit the Grand Fleet at its base. The party left London on 4 June. By the time they arrived at Thurso next morning the weather had sharply deteriorated. On the flagship *Iron Duke*, Jellicoe waited to welcome his distinguished guest for luncheon.

H.M.S. *Oak* arrived alongside from Thurso and Lord Kitchener at once impressed upon Jellicoe the necessity for not losing so much as a day of his timetable. There was to be no question of waiting for more favourable weather.

The original plan had been for the *Hampshire* to sail up the eastern side of Orkney, a route which was regularly searched by minesweepers as a routine measure. However, as the eastern coast was getting the worst of the weather, and as there was no possibility of mine-sweeping in such a heavy swell, Jellicoe decided to route the *Hampshire* along the western and lee side of the islands. This would also give the escorting destroyers a chance of keeping up with the cruiser, an impossibility in the heavy seas on the eastern side.

H.M.S. *Hampshire*, an eleven-year-old cruiser of the County class, had played her part at Jutland a few days previously under the command of Captain Savill, and had been lucky enough to escape without damage or a single casualty. On return to the Flow after the battle, orders were received to provision ship immediately. The following day, 4 June, came a signal to anchor close to the *Iron Duke*. Although Lord Kitchener's visit to the Flow and his destination were top secret, the crew of the *Hampshire* were well aware that they were going to take aboard some very important person. The preparations on board ship and the extra special clean-up gave that away. The news travelled around to other ships and other eyes were watching when Kitchener boarded the pinnace which was to take him across to the *Hampshire*. A Yeoman of Signals on H.M.S. *Marlborough* remembers the moment.

¶ I watched *Hampshire's* picket boat visit *Iron Duke* (to collect Kitchener presumably) and later return; then in the gathering darkness I saw the dimly-outlined cruiser leave her berth and head for the open sea.[1]

Within half an hour of the party going aboard, *Hampshire* was under way. It was 4.45 P.M. and the storm still raged. Even the sheltered waters of the Flow were agitated. A Royal Marine on H.M.S. *Hercules* was surprised to see the cruiser leaving her buoy on such a night.

¶ The night the *Hampshire* left Scapa seas were running high. The Flow had mountainous waves. We were shipping seas on deck and it was the dirtiest night we had seen at Scapa. Yet the *Hampshire* weighed anchor and proceeded on her journey.[2]

The searchlight outpost on the island of Switha had been alerted.

¶ We were informed by heliograph and semaphore signalling the time of Kitchener's departure aboard H.M.S. *Hampshire*. Members of our crew were standing on a rock to wave as the ship steamed out through the raised booms at the harbour entrance towards the open sea. A gale-force wind was blowing and heavy seas were running.

Through our binoculars we could see where ten miles away the mountainous waves were dashing against the Pentland Skerries rock.[3]

An hour or so earlier the escorting destroyers, *Unity* and *Victor*, had left to search the waters along the route which the cruiser was to follow. At 5.45 P.M. they picked up the *Hampshire* and the convoy proceeded along the western coast of Orkney. Soon, however, Captain Savill had to make a decision between speed and destroyer protection. The *Hampshire* was making eighteen knots. A slower speed would make her an easier target for submarines. The destroyers could only produce a maximum speed of fifteen knots in the tremendous seas which were running. Gradually, this speed was reduced even further. At 6.20 P.M. Captain Savill ordered the lagging destroyers back to base and the *Hampshire* nearer to the coast where there might be a little protection from the violence of the gale for the comfort of his distinguished passenger.

At 7.30 P.M. the cruiser was about one and a half miles from the shore between Marwick Head and the Brough of Birsay. The western coastline of the Mainland of Orkney, along which she was now steaming, is formed by beetling cliffs and jagged rocks. Sometime between 7.45 P.M. and 8. 00 P.M. the *Hampshire* struck a mine. Within fifteen minutes she sank.

Lord Kitchener seems to have been last seen standing on the bridge, without a greatcoat. Some two hundred men are estimated to have got clear of the ship on rafts and boats, but they had little chance in those raging seas. Some of the rafts were cast on to the cliffs but the men had no hope of reaching the top and died of exposure. However, miraculously, twelve men did manage to get ashore and make their way inland where they were looked after by local crofters.

An Army look-out post, manned by Orkney territorials, saw the disaster but it was some time before the incredible news reached the flagship in Scapa Flow.

¶ I was a boy telegraphist on the *Iron Duke*. Before he set off on that fateful journey Kitchener came down and inspected our wireless-telegraph office. I was very impressed by his stature and bearing.

The weather was very bad that day, even in the shelter of Scapa. The last I saw of K was when he climbed aboard the *Hampshire*, which had tied up to the next buoy to ours.

Attached to our main wireless-telegraph office was a small cabinet which was always tuned in to the Admiralty, who sent out signals at certain hours. That night, I had the first watch and went to read what was coming in, mainly for experience. After a while the Admiralty started transmitting and by the call and procedure signs I realized it was for the *Hampshire*. The first few lines were in code and the remainder in cypher. We decoded the first part and found it was for Lieutenant-Colonel Fitzgerald (K's aide-de camp). Different types of ships had certain wave lengths and in the Fleet certain ships listened on those wave lengths (guardships) and passed on anything they received. After a while the guardship reported she couldn't contact *Hampshire*. Neither could we – not even the destroyer escort. But the next morning our attendant destroyer came alongside with the body of K's aide aboard.[4]

The rescue ships which hastened to the spot found only dead bodies.

¶ Late that evening a message was received to close the flagship with all despatch. Having done this a picket boat drew up alongside, a hasty conference was held and we then moved off out through Hoxa Sound, word being passed around the ship that a good look-out must be kept for 'black objects'.

The night wore on until around four o'clock, just as dawn was breaking, the P.O. of the watch was heard to shout from the upper deck: 'Black object on the port side, sir'. Almost immediately we were surrounded by floating bodies and it was realized they were from H.M.S. *Hampshire*. Boats were lowered – the main objective being the search for Lord Kitchener. Messages were passed to base, and soon tugs, trawlers and auxiliary craft were on the scene. As for the destroyer itself the quarter-deck was soon strewn with bodies, including that of the junior officer on staff – a Surgeon Lieutenant. His wrist watch had stopped about ten minutes past eleven.

The quarter-deck being occupied, further bodies were brought forward and placed on the iron deck, and I recall seeing the body of a Chief Petty Officer who, having drowned with his arms folded over his chest, gradually thawed and opened them out due to the heat from the stokehold deck.[5]

*   *   *

¶ The next morning a note on the ship's notice-board informed us that *Hampshire* had foundered, feared loss of all hands. The lower deck took a dim view of the *Hampshire* being allowed to leave Scapa under such weather conditions. The question was, had the Admiralty insisted on her proceeding that night, or could it be that Kitchener would not wait for better weather? The sinking of the *Hampshire* remains a mystery.[6]

The whole story of the circumstances surrounding Kitchener's mission to Russia and the fate of the *Hampshire* does in fact contain elements of mystery. There are hints of sabotage and treason; theories of an Irish plot to avenge the crushing by England of the Easter Rising in Dublin only a few weeks earlier; other theories that news of Kitchener's highly confidential assignment had been leaked to the Germans. Excessive secrecy on the part of the Admiralty helped to foster an atmosphere of intrigue and suspicion. Years afterwards questions were still being raised in Parliament about a so-called 'secret report' on the disaster that was alleged to carry a different story from that of the official White Paper.* In Orkney a strong tradition still survives that local people were prevented by the authorities from approaching the coast to search the cliffs for possible survivors and that the Stromness lifeboat was forbidden to be launched. The fact that no trace of Lord Kitchener's body was ever found even gave rise to legends that he was not dead at all. Perhaps the most bizarre theory of all was submitted by one of our correspondents who claimed that Kitchener survived the disaster to emerge later in Soviet Russia under the pseudonym of Joseph Stalin.

A few miles along the coast from Scapa Flow, on a bare headland overlooking the place where the *Hampshire* disappeared, the Orcadians erected by public subscription the Kitchener Memorial, a stark tower of castellated stone. One can climb up the grassy slopes and stand there looking out at that watery grave, knowing that this craggy cliff was the last sight in the eyes of so many drowning men; that the sea has never given back to the land the legendary soldier whom it drew down into its depths more than half a century ago.

---

* There is no place in this book for these speculations but the whole affair has been dealt with at length and in fascinating detail in *The Mystery of Lord Kitchener's Death* by Donald McCormick.

12

The Vanguard *Disaster*

Death is never so terrible as when it strikes without warning and in the dark, and in a place where man believes himself to be safe from harm. Twice this happened in Scapa Flow – once in each war – and the waters of the Flow are the only known grave of nearly two thousand men. The great anchorage, the haven of the Fleet, lost two capital ships within its protective shores.

The night of 9 July 1917, is still remembered with grief by the people of the islands. H.M.S. *Vanguard* blew up at anchor on that summer night with the loss of over 700 men. The unimaginable horror of those few seconds when a mighty battleship ceased to exist seems to have remained vivid after more than half a century in the minds of those who saw it.

It had been a happy day. A member of *Boadicea's* crew recalls that the Fleet was having its inter-squadron regatta – 'like a Derby Day afloat'. *Boadicea* was anchored beside *Vanguard* and *Vanguard's* stokers had challenged *Boadicea's* stokers to a cutters' race. There was quite a lot of money laid by both ships. It was a very keen race and *Boadicea's* stokers won by twelve strokes. After the day's sport *Vanguard* returned to her Fleet position. At 10 P.M. it was 'out pipes' and everyone turned in – though a score of Vanguard officers were enjoying a night out in the theatre ship *Gourko*, which was lying alongside a battleship of another squadron, the *Royal Oak*. At about 11.20 P.M. a Leading Mechanic at the seaplane base at Houton on the north shore of the Flow glanced towards the anchored lines of ships between himself and Flotta.

¶ I was looking across at the Fleet when I observed that one of the ships appeared to lose its true outline and quiver. It then appeared to lift up in the middle and from this point there rose a vast column of orange-brown and slate-grey smoke. This immediately burst into a flickering pillar of fire which cast a crimson glow over the whole anchorage. Up to this point, the silence of the Flow was unbroken, though a slight tremor had run through the earth. The pillar of fire mushroomed out and in its light debris could be seen travelling upward. This spectacle lasted four or five more seconds, then the silence was shattered by the sound of a terrific explosion. The ship was about five miles distant but the shock wave, which had taken about eleven seconds to reach me, was heavy enough to momentarily stop my breath. I realized that a battleship had blown up, but it was not until morning that we learned that it was H.M.S. *Vanguard*. I often wonder if anyone else saw this disaster taking place and felt the loss as I did.[1]

* * *

¶ I was coming along the upper deck when there were three tremendous flashes which seemed to reach the sky. Simultaneously three terrible explosions. Under the impact *Collingwood* heeled over temporarily, then debris began to fall like hail – mostly pieces of steel. I tried to run for shelter but my legs would not work and I thought myself a cheap little coward. The Fleet was practically obliterated with a tremendous pall of smoke which took a long time to lift. Pandemonium broke out, boats were lowered for survivors but alas, only mutilated bodies were picked up. The big question came next. Which ship had gone up? No one knew until the C.-in-C. made the recognition signal (which must be answered instantly). All answered except H.M.S. *Vanguard*.[2]

* * *

¶ I went and turned in at 'out pipes' (10 P.M.). Something disturbed my sleep – two more quick bangs and out I jumped. The Quarter Master was calling 'Away all boats' crews – ship blown up'. Stuff on fire was still falling when I ran along the middle to the upper deck (I was 2nd Coxswain of a steamboat) down the ladder and got right away. Awful smell of burning material and floating oil. Amid the silence an officer was calling 'Save all books' – no doubt signal books, in case the lead-weighted cover had been blown off them.[3]

* * *

¶ I had a sleepy impression of a shock on the ship's stern and felt the ship rolling, which was uncanny in harbour. I went on deck to find that *Vanguard*, the next ship but one in the line, had blown up. There was a huge black cloud of thick smoke above her position and the searchlights of the ships of the Grand Fleet were playing on the spot. It was an awe-inspiring scene of warships, searchlights, smoke, little pools of oil burning on the water, and the heather burning on Flotta. Picket boats and drifters were moving about in the half-light, looking for survivors.[4]

* * *

¶ I was serving aboard H.M.S. *Malaya* up in Scapa Flow in the summer of 1917. Prince Albert, known to us as 'P.A.' (later to become King George VI) was officer of my division.

On the night the *Vanguard* blew up I was bos'n's mate on the first watch – on the upper deck.

A few minutes later, having been relieved by the middle watch, I went for'ard and turned into my hammock to get what rest I could before my next duty. The Commander, who was organizing the sending out of boats to search for survivors, was standing beside my hammock, when Prince Albert came up to him and said, 'May I take charge of the second picket boat, sir?' The Commander answered rather sharply, 'Certainly not!' I have never forgotten how quick our future king was to volunteer to go to the aid of others, regardless of the danger.[5]

Captain R. F. Nichols was a Midshipman on H.M.S. *Vanguard*. He escaped death that night by one of those chances which set a man shivering years afterwards.

¶ Each evening that week the concert-party of the new battle-ship *Royal Oak* was to entertain the personnel of the Fleet in the theatre ship *Gourko* lying alongside her. Monday night (the night of the explosion) was officers' night and several of the *Vanguard's* officers planned to go. I had the morning watch next day which for us Midshipmen meant turning out at 5.45 A.M., so, guessing the concert would not end till late, I decided not to go. The morning watch was the worst of the lot too; far easier to get into trouble as there were so many things to be remembered, so an early night was advisable.

One of the Sub-Lieutenants had been invited to dine in the *Royal Oak* prior to attending the concert, and he picked on me to act as his 'valet' while he bathed and put on his best uniform. I had to take all his bathroom accessories to the bathroom, run his bath, present his toothbrush suitably daubed with paste, and hand him his towel and each garment at the appropriate moment. Small wonder that after this long drawn out affair I was b—y-minded. So when a signal suddenly came from my great friend and term-mate Baxter-Tyrie – a wild but charming Australian – suggesting meeting on board the *Royal Oak,* I gladly accepted.

Save for the haunting thought of the morning watch, the concert was excellent and lasted much longer than was intended. At 11.15 P.M., when we were already due back in the *Vanguard,* the show was still in full swing. Then, just as the 'Goodnight' song was being sung, we were heavily shaken by two terrific explosions at no great distance from us. All the same, the 'Goodnight' song was finished and the National Anthem sung; then we streamed on deck to find out what had happened. In spite of the darkness of the night, a heavy cloud of smoke could be seen against the starlit sky; and amidst the tense atmosphere that prevailed, no one could say just where the explosion had occurred. Fully an hour passed before the *Vanguard's* officers were summoned to the quarter-deck to be told the fate of our ship – that she had blown up and sunk in a matter of seconds.

We were shocked, sickened and horrified. Captain Dick and all those other fine men, including two of my term-mates – all must have been blown to bits. But for the concert, and in my own case Baxter-Tyrie's signal, we should have been amongst them – by such thin threads do our lives hang.

Everybody spoke in hushed tones and treated us almost with reverence. On boarding our picket boat the coxswain, who was passing the ship when it happened, tried to confirm the disaster by showing me a chart he had taken from the water, as if to prove his words. We just had to believe the incredible.[6]

The hopeless search for survivors continued all night. Only one officer and two ratings were picked up, and the officer was too injured to live. For days afterwards men were put ashore to comb the debris for confidential material – a ghoulish task, especially for the younger men.

¶ All hands were called on our ship and every boat was lowered to see if there were any survivors. I was in the cutter's crew and we were detailed to go ashore on Flotta Island. All the heather and gorse had been set alight by debris blown ashore from the *Vanguard* and we had to beat out the fire with single sticks. Whilst going ashore we were going through masses of thick oil, clothing, sailors' ditty boxes, arms and legs, but no survivors.[7]

* * *

¶ A general signal was made to the Fleet to 'Raise steam for full speed with all despatch and report when ready to proceed'. Ships were then placed at a minute's notice to proceed. 'Action stations' were taken up and a sweep of the anchorage was conducted but without result. As soon as it became daylight men were landed on the foreshore to search for bodies. Divers were sent down to examine the wreck and one young diver, performing his first 'professional dip' was so overcome when a body approached him as he made his way along the sea bed that he pulled his emergency line and was quickly hauled up and the cause of the movement explained to him.[8]

* * *

¶ From daybreak the activity on board H.M.S. *Victorious* was the constant tap, tap as the dockyard men made coffins for the bodies washed ashore.[9]

* * *

¶ Next forenoon, about 10 A.M., I went ashore. There was a lot of stuff on the beach – 150-pound bags of flour were three-quarters of a mile inland (about a mile and a half from where the ship had been anchored) and looked as if a knife had cut them dead centre.[10]

* * *

¶ I was a wireless operator in H.M.S. *Emperor of India* and the real shock of the event to me came when I was standing on deck next day and watched a picket boat towing a piece of the main wireless cabin of the ill-fated *Vanguard* with some of the instruments still attached. I thought of the wireless operator sitting quietly in the cabin as I had done so often and then – oblivion.[11]

* * *

¶ One of the divers from the *Indomitable* did some salvage work in *Vanguard* and described to me the scene on her mess-decks. In some places bodies were still lying in hammocks – 'fleabags' we called them – just as if nothing had happened.

Of course there was a panic after that and Jerry subs were continually being sighted inside the Flow. I remember on one occasion all the colliers and store-ships were brought out from Longhope and anchored round the Fleet for our protection. We didn't hear the last of that from the merchant seamen for years.[12]

Almost certainly the cause of the explosion was the spontaneous combustion of cordite in the ship's magazine. The difficulty of storing cordite safely on board ship was very great in those days and there are five other instances of ships exploding at anchor in which cordite was believed to be the cause. This, therefore, was an ever-present hazard, which would be forcibly brought to men's minds when such a disaster occurred. H.M.S. *Vanguard* took with her not only the lives of her crew but the peace of mind of their comrades throughout the Fleet. When rumours of sabotage got about, the authorities allowed them to spread – it was better for the men's morale.

¶ It was a terrible shock to everyone and all hands were on edge. The old battleship *Bulwark* and the minelayer *Princess Irene* had blown up down south and we saw the remains of the armed cruiser *Natal* every time we visited Invergordon.

The evening after the *Vanguard* went, the pipe to 'Darken Ship' had gone but we had not heard it in the sick bay. Along came the party carrying out the order and they let go the steel hatch above the sick bay flat. We were sitting at the mess table when the hatch dropped but we all came near to going through the deck head we were so strung up.[13]

'It is wonderful how the sailors put these things out of their minds almost immediately,' wrote Beatty to his wife a few days after the catastrophe. 'We were under the shadow of a great calamity one minute and it is almost forgotten the next. The sailors are full of heart, but, like children, forget at once.'

Perhaps that is how it seemed from the quarter-deck of the flagship, but evidently he was wrong.

13

'Waiting for Them
to Come Out'

The sudden extinction of the *Vanguard* would perhaps have been less demoralizing if it had happened at a time when the Grand Fleet was in constant action. But it occurred in that long doldrum period after Jutland when the battle squadrons were lying impotently at anchor, and their commanders were wondering if they would ever see the High Seas Fleet again. To the sailors in Scapa there was a bitter irony in the fact that a 20,000-ton Dreadnought had blown up when the nearest enemy battleship was hundreds of miles away and tethered to her buoy.

This was the most trying period of the war for the Navy. Jellicoe had become First Sea Lord now, and Beatty was Commander-in-Chief flying his flag, after several weeks in *Iron Duke*, in the more modern *Queen Elizabeth*. Beatty was desperately anxious to keep the competence and the morale of the Fleet at a high pitch, and rehearsed and exhorted it in every way he could. 'All acknowledge,' he wrote, 'that we are advancing in efficiency day by day . . . until our great day comes to prove that it has not been all wasted effort. The fly in the ointment is the dread that that day will never come!'

It was a common sight to see Beatty at the concerts in Scapa's theatre-ship *Gourko*, and at the end of the performance he would rise and address the men. Always he spoke of their invisible enemy, the High Seas Fleet, and always his message was the same: 'Soon they will have to come out, and there is only one thing for us to do. Annihilate them.

But the game of 'waiting for them to come out' was to continue to the Armistice. There was to be no opportunity to stage a revised version of Jutland. For the great battleships the war was as good as over. The submarine counted now, and the destroyer, and the tireless light cruiser, and that revolutionary concept which became a practical reality in the spring of 1917 – the convoy. These were the really vital factors in the struggle for the seas. The huge floating gun-platforms anchored in Scapa or Wilhelmshaven, on which two great nations had lavished their money and pride, were to assume the role of passive spectators of the central drama. It was not a role that appealed to the sailors who manned them.

There was still, for the British at any rate, the occasional sweep to sea. There was still the hope of an encounter. There was some convoy work to be done. But for too much of the time the battle squadrons of the Grand Fleet were simply swinging round the buoy.

The mood of this forlorn period of the war impressed itself deeply on the men who endured it. Inevitably it gave rise to discontent, but to counterbalance this there was a full awareness that the soldiers in France were having a far worse time of it. Indeed, in the last year of hostilities, it was influenza that threatened the Fleet rather than German guns.

¶ The atmosphere was always one of monotony and frustration at not being involved in the exciting things that were happening in other spheres of the war. The Fleet had just come through the Battle of Jutland and the feeling was that the authorities were not going to risk that again and consequently were going to keep us out of harm's way for the rest of the war. There were always plenty of people putting in for a draft to destroyers, submarines etc. In fact towards the end of 1917 the buzz went round that anybody who was prepared to volunteer for transfer to the Infantry could do so, though whether anybody actually did I don't know. We did spend a fair time at sea, usually on a sweep as far as the Norwegian coast, but after four or five days we returned either to Scapa, or to Rosyth (which we much preferred).[1]

*   *   *

¶ Towards the end of the war the Army and Navy exchanged parties. Our people always came back full of admiration for the Army and what it was enduring. By contrast the Army probably thought we had a pretty comfortable life, and so, on the whole, we had. We had none of the mud and blood. Our main enemy was boredom. Each time we went on a sweep we hoped we'd meet the Germans. We were, I suppose, buoyed up by the knowledge that without us the Army wouldn't be in France at all. But it was depressing to hear that sailors had been booed ashore after Jutland.[2]

*   *   *

¶ I think the worst part of being in Scapa was the monotony of it. Swinging round the anchor day after day. It was amazing how healthy everyone kept, except when the Flu attacked the Fleet – and put it out of action. We had about three hundred out of our crew of twelve hundred officers and men down with it. Part of the battery deck forward and other parts of the ship were set aside to sling hammocks. Nine died. Every evening when the temperatures were taken the high temperatures all got a tot of brandy.[3]

*   *   *

¶ There was always trouble. Men got bored, waiting for the great day which never came. There was a fight almost every day on some mess-deck, and a stampede of men to get to see it.

There was also unrest owing to bad conditions. My pay was 9*d*. a day, my wife and one child got 16*s*. 6*d*. a week. Any extra food you had to buy.[4]

*   *   *

¶ Throughout the Service there was always a certain amount of grievance and one remembers that it was at Scapa that the Grand Fleet Fund originated and from that the Royal Naval Benevolent Trust which thrives today. It was there also that the resurgence of the Lower Deck Societies began, which eventually, in the 1920s and 1930s became the driving force of the Lower Deck Welfare Conference. Although recognized as Friendly Societies, it was illegal to really discuss lower deck grievances. Yet it was done, even so far as Lower Deck Joint Committees being formed in each main port. These no doubt acted as safety valves, the gases escaping to those in authority so they knew what was going on.[5]

The smaller ships – the light cruisers, the destroyers, the sloops – were still in the thick of the war. They were ideally suited for convoy work, and there was still the ceaseless duty of patrolling the approaches to the North Sea and enforcing blockade. There were hardships to be faced, and even on occasions laurels to be won. The sailors on these ships were too busy to be bored and their morale could be remarkably high.

¶ Life was hard at the best of times in a destroyer. In wartime and in northern waters – with endless days and nights at sea, on patrol or escort duties – sea-sick – everything sticky and wet. The smell of oil fuel and fear of floating mines at night, made it hell at times. Yet I doubt if any one of the crew would want to leave for the greater ease and security of a 'big ship'.

Almost everyone in a small ship gets to feel he is someone in time; with a greater sense of responsibility and the need of self-discipline to the advantage of many in later years.[6]

* * *

¶ I was a Wireless Operator on board the cruiser H.M.S. *Achilles* and in March 1917 while on the northern patrol we encountered a ship about two hundred miles north of the Shetlands. She had *Rena-Norge* painted on her sides, but turned out to be a German raider. With the help of our boarding steamer H.M.S. *Dundee* we had action and she was eventually sunk, with no survivors. Instead of returning to our base in the Shetlands, we received a wireless message to proceed to Scapa Flow to recuperate – and I suppose to get a cheer from the Fleet, because at the time it was thought that we had got the German raider *Moewe*.

On entering Scapa we proceeded through the lines of ships for a welcome by the crews and their bands.

One band was playing 'Any Old Iron' (the *Achilles* being an old four-funnel cruiser). Without any hesitation our own band struck up 'And the Green Grass grew all around my Boys' – referring of course to the fact that the other ships never went to sea.[7]

Sailors on the big battleships must often have watched with envy while the smaller warships slipped their moorings and headed away from the Fleet anchorage towards the open sea. But the opportunity to sail in one of them could lead to a chastening experience – particularly if the 'small ship' concerned was very small indeed.

¶ Of great interest to bored signalmen on battleships was the development of the Northern Approaches defence system in view of the growing U-boat menace. Patrol vessels in increasing numbers were required for duty between the Shetland Islands and Iceland and as there were not enough destroyers available for this purpose, fishing drifters were called into service and manned by naval reserve crews with an experienced signalman on each boat – lent by the Grand Fleet.

When my turn came I welcomed the change from swinging at anchor in Scapa Flow and carrying out futile, and I thought time-wasting, Fleet signal exercises (at which *Marlborough* was a recognized expert and often champion!). But I changed my mind during the trip which lasted three or perhaps four days. It was interesting of course to experience the easy-going life aboard a fishing vessel with nothing to do but keep a sharp look-out for submarines; thrilling too to see for the first time the northern lights on a quiet night off Iceland, their long streamers of light extending from just above the horizon to high in the sky above and stretching from port to starboard across the breadth of the northern heavens – the whole display gently undulating like a huge proscenium curtain disturbed by a wind from one side of the stage.

But when a force 8 gale struck us later, the d—n ship did everything except turn right over; the antics of a bucking bronco at a rodeo were nothing compared with the acrobatics of that drifter. I was sick of course, violently, and wished in my misery the ship would sink. I struggled below, reached my bunk in the fo'c'sle, and after being pitched out once jammed myself in. The place was a shambles; tins of condensed milk on the deck below the tiny mess-table rolled backwards and forwards in the sea water with dismal regularity; a burst bag of sugar and another of flour lay on the table with a broken basin and a leaking sauce bottle. The ship's cat came in stepping daintily but unsteadily through the water and sprang on to the table, found nothing to its liking, then leapt towards an empty bunk opposite mine. The boat heeled over and the cat missed its footing, fell to the deck in the swirling water, then charged through the door spitting and shrieking like a thing demented.

Back in harbour I decided 'never again'; if ever it fell to my lot to be chosen for this duty in the future I would refuse and take the consequences. It was my last and only trip for which I was duly thankful, but it taught me a new respect for the fishermen and their way of life.[8]

Quite late in the war Beatty was able to spare a division of battle-ships to help in the escorting of convoys. It made the men of the big ships appreciate the unending work of the destroyers, and it also improved their opinion of Scapa Flow.

¶ Convoying was rough business. It meant action stations directly we left the Flow. It also meant reducing speed to the slowest vessels in convoy, sometimes reducing to ten or eight knots. Submarines were our chief menace; thank heaven for our 'guardian angels', those wonderful little vessels our destroyers.

The Flow was our haven of rest and as the number of convoys increased so we began to realize what it meant to us, breathing a sigh of relief when within the safety of its shores.[9]

Yet even within Scapa Flow there were occasional moments of danger and high drama. Nothing occurred remotely comparable to the tragedy of the *Vanguard*, but in 1916 there was an incident that could easily have taken the lives of many men. It happened while one of the Grand Fleet's battleships was proceeding to, and another was returning from, the night-firing area in the Flow. Commander, later Captain, Geoffrey H. Freyberg, R.N. was a crucial witness.

¶ In mid-August 1916 (2½ months after Jutland) there was a disastrous collision at night between Jellicoe's two latest twenty-five-knot battleships, *Valiant* and *Warspite*, which resulted in the near-sinking of both ships and the court-martial of both captains. The utmost secrecy was maintained in respect of the collision and no leakage ever appeared in the Press at the time.

The collision took place on a dark, clear August night, both ships being without lights as a Zeppelin attack was expected. I was Commander on the bridge, close to Captain Woollcombe. We weighed anchor at 9.45 P.M. and the Captain turned the ship to the south-east, ready to replace *Warspite* for sub-calibre night firing within the large eastern confines of the Flow. The Captain then said to me, 'Slow ahead both engines', and as we gathered way I caught sight of *Warspite* bearing down on us on our port bow. I called to the Chief Yeoman of Signals: 'Switch on navigation lights full brilliance', and added to Captain Woollcombe: '*Warspite* on port bow – full astern both engines, sir?' He hesitated and said to the Officer of the Watch: 'Mr Glenny, can you see *Warspite*?' 'No, sir.' 'Port look-out, can you see *Warspite*?' 'No, sir.' I stamped my foot and exclaimed: 'If you don't go astern you will sink her, sir.' Then – 'Full astern both engines!' As the LB. telegraphs clanged I picked up the LB. telephone and said to the Engineer-Commander: 'For God's sake, give her every ounce of steam you can – we are in grave danger!'

Within two minutes came the noise of the crash, which was like the sound of ten thousand tin kettles falling on a stone floor. *Warspite* went on, almost colliding with H.M.S. *Erin* in outer end of D line, and then anchored as did *Valiant* to inspect the enormous damage inflicted.

Valiant, with her bows cut away for thirty feet, struggled down to Invergordon floating dock where complete new bows were welded on in the incredibly short period of six weeks. *Warspite*, with two 6-inch guns knocked clean overboard and a huge gaping hole under the starboard side of her forebridge, was escorted with much difficulty to Rosyth dockyard for repairs lasting three months. A Court of Inquiry presided over by Captain W. C. M. Nicholson was all the action desired by the C.-in-C. (Sir John Jellicoe), who felt that two or more Courts-Martial might undermine the morale of the Grand Fleet. However, under unrelenting pressure by the Admiralty he eventually was forced to give way and the two Courts-Martial – at both of which I was the principal witness and as such subjected to the most intense hostile cross-examination by the prosecution – were held in Scapa Flow in late October, 1916. Both Captains were found guilty of hazarding their ships and sentenced to be severely reprimanded, but neither Captain was relieved of his command.[10]

Outside the Flow, though at no great distance from its entrances, a terrible fate overtook two of the Grand Fleet's destroyers early in 1918. It was a tragedy that remained all the more vivid in the mind of one man who remembered it because of its remarkable prelude.

¶ In January 1918 we witnessed one of the finest displays of the Aurora Borealis ever to have been seen at Orkney, and it was an unforgettable spectacle. A brilliant arc rose from behind the Orkney Mainland, and from it great dazzling electric shafts continuously shot forth that set the sky ablaze, while high overhead the heavens were festooned with lines of golden draperies. It was incomparably lovely, and no man-made pyrotechnics could hope to vie with this extraordinary phenomenon. Ships and shore stood out clear and stark in the eerie light.

An ageing C.P.O., who had seen many years of service at sea, observed: 'I have oftentimes seen the Aurora in these waters; but never quite like this. It means we are in for some rough stuff; you mark my words.' And he was right.

Two nights later we set out on our usual patrol, just as the sun was setting in Turner-like pageantry, and the calm air gave promise of a smooth passage. We on *Boadicea* contacted our two destroyers, and headed eastwards into the night. After we had been sailing for probably an hour, the weather began to change violently, and suddenly we drove into the teeth of a blizzard. The sea became furiously turbulent, and a howling wind beat upon us with tremendous force. Then came the snow; stinging, blinding, and smothering, reducing visibility to zero. The wallowing destroyers dropped astern, and a searchlight was employed as a stern-light, but even this could scarcely suffice to penetrate the swirling mass.

At length, finding it increasingly difficult to navigate, the destroyers requested permission to return to base. The request was granted, and thus their fate was sealed. They must have completely lost direction, and the last message we received from one of them read: 'On rocks; breaking up; position unknown.'

Nothing more was seen or heard of the two ships, and so the terrible tempest accounted for the loss of over three hundred lives. We did hear that one man was eventually picked up on an outlying island; but whether alive or dead we never knew.[11]

The two destroyers wrecked battling their way back to Scapa were *Narborough* and *Opal*. One man did survive – he was picked up by the Fleet's search parties after having spent two nights on a cliff-ledge. He was apparently none the worse for his experience, though it was feared that others might have struggled ashore only to perish in the snow. 'It is very hard on them to have such a terrible end,' wrote Beatty of his lost men, 'especially during war, when they might have died fighting.'

Incidents of this kind are scarcely worth a footnote in the official histories. They are the side-shows of war, with no bearing on the ultimate outcome. Yet they are as much part of the reality of war as the great actions which affect the destiny of nations. Scapa and her surrounding seas, perhaps inevitably, had a fair share of such episodes. Always there was the same routine – the telegrams to the next of kin, the published casualty lists, and, for survivors, the long journey south by the 'Jellicoe' route to Chatham or Portsmouth or Devonport for re-kitting and re-drafting.

One Marine, whose ship, *King Edward VII*, was sunk by a mine in the Pentland Firth – though miraculously without loss of life – recalls such a journey in 1916.

137

¶ We were taken into Scapa Flow by destroyers and eventually put ashore at Scrabster. We were wearing all sorts of rigs – some wearing heavy sea boots and very few in a complete uniform. We marched to Thurso railway station. In the train the carriages were crowded so we arranged periods on the seats, on the floor and in the luggage racks.

On the train journey to Chatham, as we passed slowly through the level-crossing at Gillingham, there was a large crowd of women in the road – doubtless mostly service wives and mothers. The rumour had apparently got around that the ship's company of H.M.S. *King Edward VII* – a Chatham-manned ship – was coming in to the R.N. barracks and they guessed the reason for kitting up and feeding preparations on a Sunday afternoon. We Royal Marines were in the last few carriages of the second train. One woman was reaching over from the top of the level-crossing gate and calling the name of a Chief Petty Officer. She appeared exhausted and distracted. I recognized the name and called out: 'Yes, he is safe and well – coming later!' She brightened up at once but still appeared doubtful so I shouted: 'Tall – Chief Gunner's Mate.' She immediately recognized my description and slid back into the arms of friends.[12]

In the last weeks of 1917 a battle squadron of the United States Navy joined the Grand Fleet in the Flow. Admiral Hugh Rodman, the 'Kentucky Admiral' as he was known, realizing that the British 'had had three years of actual warfare and knew the game from the ground-floor up', put himself unreservedly at the disposal of Admiral Beatty. It was to be a remarkably happy collaboration at all levels.

When the Americans arrived, the British commanders prepared to greet them with due solemnity. But the British sailor does not take it too kindly when naval formalities are sprung upon him without warning.

¶ We had just sat down to breakfast one morning when the order came: 'Clear lower-deck. Hands cheer ship.' With a lot of moaning all hands lined the rail all round the ship and as each American drew abreast of us, a very pompous old Commander announced through his megaphone: 'Three cheers for U.S.S. *Delaware*. Hip hip . . .' and as we all waved our hats in the regulation manner the reply came: 'Hurray –' followed by a four-letter word. The Commander nearly threw a fit, and ordered two Lieutenants to apprehend the culprits and put them on a charge. The Lieutenants were frantically running from one side of the ship to the other but of course they never found out who it was – the four-letter word always came from where they were not![13]

The Americans became the Sixth Battle Squadron of the Grand Fleet, and took their turn with the British in escorting convoys and supporting cruiser operations.

But the war was moving away from Scapa. Beatty preferred Rosyth and from April 1918 he made it his main base. It was from Rosyth that the Fleet sailed on its last attempt to cross swords with the German battleships, when later in that same month Scheer took the High Seas Fleet on a sortie towards Norway to intercept an important convoy. Scheer missed the convoy, and Beatty, to his intense disappointment, missed Scheer. The Germans returned to base before he could catch them. They did not emerge again.

There was still round-the-clock activity in the Flow as the smaller ships came and went from convoy and patrol, and the Battle Fleet paid its occasional majestic visits, but the real drama was far off. The months of 1918 slipped by, and November came.

¶ Armistice night, 11 November 1918! The American battle-cruiser *Arkansas*, with whose crew we on the *Southampton* had struck up a strange, ill-assorted but nonetheless warm friendship, coming alongside, ship's band at full blast. . . . Some of their officers being invited aboard, complete with bottles, to join our celebrations, which were already well under way . . . The 'massed bands' (our small one and their large one) trying to play each other's music. . . . The complete abandonment, for a few wild hours, of all semblance of routine![14]

* * *

¶ Armistice Day was one of high drama at the seaplane base at Houton. The wireless chaps had passed the joyous news down the line soon after 11.00 A.M. None of the men expected to do any more work on this day of all days. After dinner, several hundred of us crowded into the hut nearest to the canteen, taking the piano with us. At 1.15 P.M. a bugler sounded the 'Fall in', as usual. The sound reached us faintly above the din made by our singing. Those that did hear pretended not to and spontaneously all decided to disregard it. The next we knew was officers bursting in with drawn revolvers, the bugle call was sounded again and we paraded dejectedly. There had been no official pronouncement about the Armistice prior to the parade and what was said at it I do not remember, but none will have forgotten that afternoon when we had two or three hours' hard labour carrying gas cylinders between the hangars and the quayside several hundred yards away.'[15]

* * *

¶ Some of us on *Victorious* were due for early demobilization under the condition of interrupted studies. However, when we applied to the Captain for release, he explained to us that, whilst he appreciated our wishes, if he could maintain his ship's company at full strength a little longer he would retire with the rank of Rear-Admiral, but should his ship's company be reduced he would retire as Captain, and this would make a difference to his pension. Naturally, we acquiesced to his request; he had been a very good Captain to us.[16]

Strangers in the Flow

Under the terms of the Armistice, the German Fleet was to be rendered immediately harmless until such time as the Allied Powers could decide upon its final disposition. Article 23 read: 'The warships of the German High Seas Fleet indicated by the Allies and the U.S.A. will at once be dismantled and then interned in neutral ports, or in default, in ports of the Allied Powers.' In the event, no neutral port wanted the responsibility or the burden of surveillance and it was decided that the ships should be interned in the traditional haven of the British Fleet – Scapa Flow.

At noon on 19 November 1918, the High Seas Fleet put to sea on its heartbreaking voyage, led by the battle-cruisers *Seydlitz, Moltke, Derfflinger, Hindenburg* and *Von der Tann*. Rendezvous was 8.00 A.M., 21 November, May Island off the Firth of Forth.

It was 'Operation ZZ' to the British, and the order paper circulated to the Fleet carried the instruction: 'To meet and escort to an anchorage on the Firth of Forth the ships of the German High Seas Fleet, which are to be handed over to the Grand Fleet for internment.' 240 British ships went out, in one line as far as open water and then in two lines six miles apart. The last in line was Sir David Beatty's flagship H.M.S. *Queen Elizabeth*, flying the flag he had worn at Jutland in *Lion*. The Fleet was cleared for action. There was still fear of last-minute treachery by the Germans.

The German Fleet was to be led by the flagship *Fredrich der Gross*; with Admiral von Meurer in command. The 6th Light

Cruiser Squadron, led by its flagship *Cardiff*, was detailed to meet the Germans and lead them to the rendezvous. As a recognition signal, and to indicate the ship which the foremost German ship should follow, *Cardiff* was to break a Blue Ensign at her foremast-head.

¶ As the appointed hour approached, the expected smoke on the horizon appeared – dead on time! *Cardiff* then signalled to us that she was detaching herself and steaming ahead at full speed – all as arranged. In due course we saw a huge Blue Ensign broken and shaken free!

Cardiff then turned about, 'marked time' as the German ship approached, took station on her and then the great trek to captivity started. The remaining four ships of our squadron steamed on past the German battleships and battle-cruisers until we came abreast of the light cruisers. We then turned about, took station on a pre-selected enemy ship, trained all we had on her and commenced the job of escort. As we were still very much at war, all gun and torpedo crews were closed up and trained continuously on the enemy ship being escorted – in our case, the *Königsberg*.[1]

Admiral Rodman of the United States Navy said that the sight of the *Cardiff* reminded him of the old farm in Kentucky, where many times he had seen a little child leading by the nose a herd of fearsome bullocks.

Beatty had turned the Fleet 180°. This beautifully executed manoeuvre had placed him abeam of the German flagship and in the lead of the procession back to the Firth of Forth. Now the British could take a long, slow look at the ships whose outlines they had been studying in books during those long years of waiting.

¶ We were allowed up one at a time from our action stations, and we could not believe our eyes – it was like a wild dream, just miles of ships. That day of course all leave was stopped. Officers and Petty Officers all got tight, and the crews got hold of anything that would make a noise and just bashed it to hell.[2]

* * *

¶ We brought the enemy in and anchored them off Inchkeith – how dirty and bedraggled they all looked. I had a grandstand view of the whole operation, working a Dumaresque instrument on the 6-inch fighting top of the foremast – a crew of eight, including Major Rendell of the Marines. He made a profound remark to us during the surrender – 'It just needs a shot from either side to start the whole show again!' However, after our boarding parties examined the enemy ships it was confirmed that our conditions had been kept – all the breech blocks had duly been removed.[3]

At 3.00 P.M. the ships anchored in the Firth of Forth. Beatty sent a signal to the Grand Fleet: 'It is my intention to hold a service of thanksgiving at 6.00 P.M. today, for the victory which Almighty God has vouchsafed to His Majesty's arms, and every ship is recommended to do the same.' At the ceremony of Sunset on the flagship, three rousing cheers were given for the Commander-in-Chief. Beatty acknowledged them with the words: 'Thank you – I always told you they would have to come out.'

To the German Fleet Beatty sent the following signal: 'The German Flag will be hauled down at sunset today, Thursday, and will not be hoisted again without permission.'

The first units of the High Seas Fleet arrived in Scapa Flow on Saturday, 23 November and over the next four days the melancholy procession continued. Eventually all seventy-one warships were brought to their assigned moorings, strung out between Lyness and the north-west corner of the Flow. They would never put to sea again.

From a shore battery at Houton, a Marine corporal saw the Germans arrive.

¶ They came in one long line and as they came nearer I could hear their bands playing lively music, which I thought was very funny. They must have been just as pleased as we were that all was over. They all dropped anchor more towards Hoy but near enough to see quite plain with the naked eye. As each ship was put in place the bulwarks were soon crowded with men fishing.

It was very comical, but they might have been hungry. After a few days big liners began to arrive and took the crews off the ships and back to Germany.[4]

As laid down by the terms of the Armistice, only skeleton crews were left aboard the humiliated ships.

Now began a hard and bitter winter. The British sailors had found the rigours of the climate and the daily hardships harsh enough, but the Germans carried the additional burden of defeat, and the knowledge that their homeland was in political chaos and near to starvation. The British did nothing to lighten their lot.

¶ After the German ships had been berthed at Scapa Flow we moved up there from the Firth of Forth to do our one month guard duty. It was Christmas, 1918.

The *Seydlitz*, being the largest German ship, carried the whole of the stores and supplies for all the Fleet and it was the custom to collect one German rating from each ship or group and take them to the *Seydlitz* to draw stores and rations etc. Being the Christmas period, they drew extra fare, including Christmas crackers, streamers, hats and tinsel etc. The meat they drew was in awful condition. I knew they were our late enemies but they were God-fearing men of the sea and mostly Christians and my heart softened to them as they, like us, were in a god-forsaken place, but were trying to make the most of the first 'Peace on earth, goodwill to men' Christmas of 1918 in terrible conditions.

Later, to supplement their meat rations they carried out a few raids ashore and slaughtered a few sheep, much to the crofters' concern.[5]

The restrictions placed upon the beleaguered Germans were almost inhuman. Not only were they not permitted to go ashore at all, but they were not even allowed to visit each other's ships, and any contact with the British sailors was absolutely forbidden. F. W. Tuckwell was an armourer in H.M.S. *Royal Oak* which was based in the Flow from May 1918 until August 1919. He acquired some German inter-Fleet communications which give some idea of the strictness of the surveillance.

From . . . The Senior Officer British Destroyers
To . . . The Senior Officer German Destroyers

At 0630 today (Saturday) the Guard trawler, Lieutenant Dring H.M.S. *Royal Sovereign* in command, saw that G.104 had a boat down astern of her. He reported this to the Guard Destroyer, who ordered him to arrest her. On going back to do so he found that the boat had been manned and was pulling back to G.104, evidently having visited another Destroyer – G103.

The boat has been confiscated and the Rating found in her is being sent to you to be dealt with.

I must point out to you that a repetition of this kind of thing will bring about considerable changes in the privileges now enjoyed.

Signed: Colin Maclean
Senior Officer of Flotillas

How the Germans accommodated themselves to their internment is described by Vice-Admiral Friedrich Ruge, who was then in command of one of the destroyers.

¶ We had to get all our food from Germany – it was not very much and not very good. So we started fishing and trying to get seagulls – the fish were good and the seagulls not. And we were not allowed to go ashore or to visit the other ships so we were thrown entirely upon our own resources. And we started lessons in languages and in geography and in mathematics. And when the weather got better we sat on deck and I had a guitar and we sang old songs, and then we even played tag round the funnels and the bridges – a destroyer is quite good for playing tag.

Officially we were not allowed to have any contacts with the British but of course in seven months that couldn't quite be carried out. We ourselves had quite a lot of contact with the crews of drifters. They were not only on guard, they carried mail around and our provisions, and the doctor, the purser and so on. And we were in need of tobacco, soap particularly, our stuff from the war was awful and the drifters were well stocked so we tried to find things to barter. We hadn't much alcohol – the big ships had a lot – so we furnished medals and ribbons and badges and so on as souvenirs. We invented most wonderful new Orders and so on and everybody was happy about it.[6]

This illicit trading was frowned upon by the senior German officers – disciplinarians who could not countenance slack behaviour among their ratings.

From: Senior Naval Officer
         of the German torpedo boat
         B.Rr . . . 2114

To: The Senior Naval Officer of the British destroyers at Scapa, on board H.M.S. *Spenser*

During the last few days it has been observed from here and has also been reported to me by separate groups that the picket *Pendoran* remains alongside certain groups for hours on end during the day, without having been detailed to do so from here and without there being any apparent reason for her remaining alongside. She was seen today alongside buoy J/2; on 13 June by buoy P/3 and 25, on 12 June by buoy P/3 and P/4 and on other days by buoy P/1 and 26.

During the whole time that she lay alongside, no work on the buoys or the chains was observed. On the other hand, reports have reached me that she was spending her time there to exploit to her advantage the torpedo boat crew's lack of smoking requisites and was engaging in brisk bartering.

In spite of constant supervision by officers and in spite of frequent admonition, prohibition and punishment, it cannot be prevented that often valuable State property on the torpedo boats is used in the bartering.

I ask you, for your part, to take steps, by giving suitable directions to the picket, which would help to back up my authority.

Signed: Cordes
Korvetten Kapitan

The situation of the German ships was, in fact, a peculiar one. They were not prisoners, although treated as such. They were merely *interned* while the terms of a possible peace treaty with Germany were being thrashed out by the Allied Governments in Paris. Technically, though she was hardly in a position to do so, Germany could refuse terms which she considered unacceptable and recommence hostilities. This was the view held by

Vice- Admiral van Reuter, in command of the High Seas Fleet in Scapa Flow.

Van Reuter was in a difficult position. His discipline was undermined by revolutionary elements among the crews, who had formed themselves into Sailors' Councils, modelled on the Soldiers' and Sailors' Soviets set up in Russia in 1917. He was given no official information from any source. Admiral Fremantle, the British Commander at Scapa, had only the most formal dealings with him. The only news van Reuter had was from English newspapers, several days old. All mail from Germany had to go through British censors in London, which meant a delay of three or four weeks. He tried to improve his situation by having the trouble-makers repatriated in batches to Germany. His officers welcomed the rule against communication between the ships as it kept in check the spread of revolutionary propaganda and made it easier to keep discipline, although they considered the ban on shore-going inhuman.

On 25 March van Reuter changed his flagship from the *Friedrich der Grosse* to the *Emden*, where he was sure of a loyal crew. He needed men he could rely on, for he had a plan which required secrecy and complete obedience for its success. Van Reuter knew that the fate of the High Seas Fleet rested in his hands.

In 1914 the Kaiser had issued a standing order to the Fleet: 'All ships put out of action must never fall into enemy hands.' This was the order which van Reuter was planning to obey. Had the German Fleet been interned in a neutral port, the situation would not have arisen, but now it lay in the grasp of one of the combatants and if hostilities recommenced it would be all over before it began as far as the German Fleet was concerned. So van Reuter made his preparations for the most dramatic sight which Scapa Flow was ever to witness.

It was an unhappy spring for the German Navy – turbulence among the men, tension among the officers. On 8 May the peace terms were made known to Germany. On 11 May they were published in the Press. When he read them, van Reuter decided that there were three courses open to the German government: Germany might accept the conditions outright (which seemed to him unlikely because of their severity); she might refuse the conditions; she might negotiate (which seemed to him the most likely).

If she accepted, the German Fleet would simply have to sit in Scapa Flow and await events; it would have ceased to exist as an instrument of power or policy. If she refused, there would, van Reuter believed, be a renewal of hostilities, in which case the British would surely take possession of the interned Fleet straight away – an act which it would be his duty, however hopelessly, to resist. But if there were to be negotiations, the possibility existed that the Fleet would be needed by the German government as an instrument of barter to obtain some advantage from the Allies.

Van Reuter was in a quandary. The Kaiser's instruction was incontrovertible; he must at all costs prevent the High Seas Fleet falling into enemy hands; yet he feared to destroy what might prove a valuable asset to his country if the negotiations he expected took place.

He decided it was his duty to make all the necessary plans for the destruction of his Fleet by scuttling, so that if the need arose the Kaiser's edict could be instantly and efficiently enforced. He began to draw up secret orders for his commanders outlining the conditions under which they were to take this drastic yet – to him – honourable action.

Events moved slowly towards a crisis. The spring days slipped by. Meanwhile, the German government was presenting its counter-proposals to the Peace Commission, Van Reuter was trying to read between the lines of his four-day-old newspapers, and Admiral Fremantle was maintaining his distance and his silence.

On 17 June the last batch of disaffected sailors was repatriated from Scapa Flow and van Reuter felt safe in issuing sealed orders to his officers outlining his plans for the sinking of the Fleet. On 20 June van Reuter saw *The Times* of 16 June, which printed the news that when the German government received the answer to its counter-proposals it would be given a respite of five days in which to decide its course of action. By the end of this period the Peace Treaty would have to be signed or its terms refused. Van Reuter deduced that his government would have received its answer on the day *The Times's* report was published – in other words that the Armistice would automatically cease to exist without further warning *on the following day* – Saturday 21 June. Assuming that the British might swoop on his defenceless Fleet the moment the Armistice expired, he concluded that the most likely moment of expiry was noon – since such a take-over would be simpler by day than by night.

In fact, the Armistice was extended by an extra forty-eight hours, but no one informed van Reuter of this fact. Therefore, when he saw Admiral Fremantle take his battle squadron out to sea from the Flow for a much-postponed torpedo-firing practice at 10 A.M. on Saturday 21st, he jumped to the conclusion that the activity among the British ships was a sign of the imminent resumption of hostilities. He decided to act in the spirit of the Kaiser's standing-order and at 10.40 A.M. he issued the pre-arranged signal to scuttle. The signal passed from ship to ship and shortly after noon the *Friedrich der Grosse* began to list and the loud single strokes of her bell – the signal for 'abandon ship' – sounded across the water. In a few minutes she capsized and sank. The time was 12.16 p.m. It was only the beginning. The men on the guardships left in the Flow could not believe their eyes.

¶ The guard squadron had gone out for an exercise, and I was standing on the deck of the *Victorious* when I noticed a number of small boats pushing off from the German ships. In minutes the German flags were hoisted on the ships, and then as in a dream of fantasy I saw them moving. Some wobbled, some rolled over on their sides, many sank stern or bows first, the lighter craft sank squarely; many were enveloped in clouds of steam. The alarm had been given at first sight by a vigilant signalman and soon all our picket boats, pinnaces, and ships' tenders were rounding up the Germans and bringing them to our ship, the *Victorious*. As they climbed the ladders or the booms they were marshalled aft to the quarter-deck behind a row of armed Marines. Most of the Germans were cheerful, some boats came alongside cheering and singing a national song, and even top brass did not mind lugging their kit-bags or cases along the deck.[7]

* * *

¶ Ships of all sizes were rapidly sinking, some by the stern, some nose first and yet others turning on their sides as they went down. Captain Naylor immediately ordered boarding parties out to try to avert some of the sinkings but the damage was done and of all the German capital ships in the harbour, only three destroyers were saved. The sea was swarming with German sailors who had taken to their boats and others who were swimming, waiting to be picked up.

The sight of the massive battleships sinking in Scapa Flow that day was a thing that I can remember as vividly as if it was yesterday.[8]

A frantic signal went out to the squadron firing its torpedoes in the placid summer seas outside the Flow. Captain R. C. V. Ross was then a junior officer on board one of the destroyers.

¶ Guarding the Germans in Scapa Flow was a squadron of Revenge-class battleships with its accompanying destroyers, and a patrol of armed trawlers. On 21 June 1919 the big ships and destroyers had proceeded to sea for gunnery and torpedo practice. I was on board one of the destroyers and we were actually picking up our torpedoes after a run when we received the electrifying signal: 'German Fleet sinking. Return to harbour at full speed.'

With our great speed we were back inside the Flow far ahead of the battleships; and what a spectacle met our eye. In all directions the great German super-dreadnoughts and cruisers were indeed sinking: some rolling over and going down with great bubbles, others settling on an even keel, or sliding under bows first. Apart from an astonished party of schoolchildren from Stromness, who had been on an excursion trip round the Fleet, and the few scattered patrol trawlers, we were the first to witness this unique spectacle.

Friedrich der Grosse, Grosser Kurfurst, Hindenburg, Moltke, Von der Tann, Kaiser and *König*: for many an hour we had studied their silhouettes in the gunroom, and now unbelievably they were sinking before our eyes.[9]

The schoolchildren from Stromness, on board the *Flying Kestrel*, were on an excursion round the German ships and had a ringside view of the unique historic event. The younger ones thought it was a show put on specially for their benefit. The bewildered teachers hustled them below decks for safety. No one knew what would happen next: no one, indeed, really knew what was happening then.

On H.M.S. *Royal Sovereign* the Chaplain, G. L. Bourdillon, wrote down the events of the preceding twenty-four hours in a letter to his wife, which she fortunately kept.

¶ At 9.30 yesterday (Saturday) morning we left the anchorage at Scapa – the whole squadron and all the destroyers – for torpedo exercises outside. We spent the forenoon running torpedoes, and were just preparing to continue after lunch, when a signal came through to say that the Germans, taking advantage of our absence, had hoisted their ensigns and were starting to sink their ships. Everything was at once abandoned, and we made off back at high speed. Meanwhile all preparations were made to receive the Germans as prisoners on board. Another signal reported that two battleships had already gone under, and others were sinking! In order to get the best seat for the show, I went up into the fore-top.

The first sign we saw was the masts of a ship at a sharp angle over Flotta. Half the German ships had *disappeared*, and several of the remainder were *in a sinking condition*! One battleship had her quarter-deck awash, and as we watched thro' glasses, we saw her gradually lift her bows out of the water, roll over, and disappear below the surface, leaving nothing but a vast patch of bubbling foam. It was one of the most thrilling sights I have witnessed.

We steamed into the middle of the Flow and dropped anchor. Immediately scores of trawlers and other small craft surrounded us, towing boatloads of German officers and men, the boats flying the flag of truce. It was an extraordinary scene, so different from the usual quiet routine of the Flow. All around were sinking ships. Here was a light cruiser with a heavy list: there the huge side of a battle-cruiser on her beam-ends showing above the surface: there the upturned bows of a destroyer cocked high in the air: farther off several destroyers aground with their decks awash – and all about were numbers of our destroyers, trawlers, and other vessels picking up German prisoners. In one or two places large white patches of foam showed where a ship had sunk.

It was 2.30 P.M. when we anchored. By 10 P.M. all that remained of the whole German Fleet were (as far as we could see) one battleship, one battle-cruiser (sinking), three light cruisers (beached) and some destroyers. I made some pencil sketches, and then came down to see the prisoners coming aboard. Boatload after boatload, in they poured, officers and men, till we had over 400 of them on board! They were quartered mostly in the batteries both sides. All the arrangements worked smoothly, but there wasn't much sleep for anyone last night.

We left (except *Resolution*) at 6 A.M, for Cromarty – I scrambled my way (by a roundabout route) down to the Church at seven o'clock – not that I expected anyone to come to a Celebration, but just to show that in spite of all the upheaval, it was Sunday and I was ready for service.

Well, we didn't stop long at Cromarty! Arrived at noon, and left again at 5 P.M. well on our way back to Scapa, in spite of all hopes to the contrary. They say we are going to do some salvage work on the sunken ships, which ought to be interesting. It didn't take long to get the prisoners out of the ship – and we are now tidying up. The mess everywhere was awful, and the odour!!![10]

Not altogether surprisingly, on that incredible midsummer Saturday some of the custodians gave up trying to cope with the situation as the fantastic ballet of warships continued out in the Flow.

¶ I was one of an R.A.F. shore party issued with rifles and side arms, but no ammunition, with orders to fire on anyone who came ashore and offered resistance. Absence of ammunition rather restricted us from doing this, so our spread-out line along Houton Bay gradually became a group clustered together in ring-side-seat fashion, excitedly watching the ships turn turtle and disappear under the water. Subsequently an officer appeared and placed us all under arrest for disobeying orders and leaving our posts. The result was fourteen days' punishment.[11]

In the general confusion there was some random firing from boarding parties and in a corner of the Royal Naval cemetery at Lyness there are eight headstones bearing German names and dated 21 or 22 June 1919.

Earlier in this chapter we quoted two German Fleet communications which were picked up by F. W. Tuckwell of the *Royal Oak* while helping to rescue some of the German ratings from the sinking ships. Here is another – a *cri-de-coeur* from Naval officers in Germany to their Fleet, shut away in shameful confinement across the North Sea. Their world at home was crumbling away: the old naval discipline in the interned Fleet was being undermined by mutinous revolutionaries: they clung to a fading ideal of dedicated patriotism and stern duty.

To Our Comrades at Scapa Flow

The proud edifice of our Fatherland suddenly collapsed. The deafening noise of the cracking beams, the rubble of the crashing walls confused our ears and eyes; there was nothing to hold on to; around us and beneath us everything seemed to sway and to collapse. There was no guiding spirit, no leadership left inside Germany. There was only the implacable demand from outside – the surrender of our ships into enemy hands! The surrender of our ships which had come into being by unremitting labour in peace-time, never defeated in war. Our victorious Navy in enemy hands! – Ignominious demand! For you, comrades, the execution of a most bitter duty!

The service which you rendered to your Fatherland in her greatest need, must not be forgotten by Germany. Self-denying obedience, and now self-sacrifice in the situation over there, in the saddest place in the world, on ships without flags, among fellow-countrymen who are confused in their feelings. The love for your Fatherland that you showed then will shine forth in the future as an example of simple German devotion to duty.

We greet our comrades at Scapa Flow!

The Baltic Union of Naval Officers

Von Hornhardt

1. & **2.** The Beauty of the Flow, at sunrise and sunset. *Above*: a winter dawn looking out from Stromness, 1960s; *below*: an evening view over Scapa Bay taken shortly before the Second World War. *(Malcolm Brown and W. S. Thomson)*

3. Part of Orkney's Atlantic coast at Yesnaby. *(Ernest W. Marwick)*

4. The Old Man of Hoy. *(W. S. Thomson)*

5. The old town, Stromness. *(Ernest W. Marwick)*

6. *Left*: A street in Kirkwall. *(W. S. Thomson)*

7. *Below*: St Magnus' Cathedral, Kirkwall. *(Ernest W. Marwick)*

8. The Churchill Barrier in Water Sound, when completed. *(W. S. Thomson)*

9. Water Sound and part of one of the blockships, 2001. *(Jenny Suddaby)*

10. The Ness Battery, Stromness, during the Second World War ... *(W. S. Thomson)*

11. ... and as it was in the 1960s. *(Malcolm Brown)*

12. & 13. *Above and below:* The exterior and interior of the Italian Chapel, Lamb Holm. *(Malcolm Brown and Douglas Shearer)*

14. The *St Ninian*, a troopship in both world wars. *(North of Scotland, Orkney and Shetland Shipping Company)*

15. Marines drilling on the quarter-deck of a battleship in Scapa Flow during the First World War. *(Imperial War Museum)*

16. The 'Green Room' of a battleship. Officers making up for a show. *(Imperial War Museum)*

17. A concert-party progamme from HMS *Benbow*. *(A. F. B. Bridges)*

18 & 19. Ship-board routine. Coaling ship, and 'holystoning' the decks. *(Imperial War Museum)*

20. Lord Kitchener leaving the destroyer *Oak* to lunch with Admiral Jellicoe on the *Iron Duke*. Within hours Kitchener was lost at sea with most of the crew of the *Hampshire*. *(Mansell Collection)*

21. Marwick Head, with the Kitchener Memorial at the cliff-top. It was off this rocky coast that the *Hampshire* went down in June 1916. *(Malcolm Brown)*

22. The surrender of the German Fleet off the coast of Scotland, 21 November 1918. British sailors watched the *Hindenburg* steaming towards its enforced harbour. *(Hulton-Getty Collection)*

23. Aerial shot showing the flagship SMS *Friedrich der Grosse*, *König Albert* and *Kaiserin*. (*Imperial War Museum Q29615*)

24. *SMS Grosser Kurfürst, Kroprinz Wilhelm* and *Markgraf* as seen from a British warship. *(Imperial War Museum Q19299)*

25. A König class battleship taking up her moorings in Scapa Flow. *(Imperial War Museum SP2901)*

26. & 27. *Above and below:* Two views of SMS *Seydlitz* taking up her moorings. *(Imperial War Museum SP2697 & SP2902)*

28. German High Seas Fleet in Scapa Flow, November 1918.

29. A scene on deck of an interned German destroyer in Scapa Flow, with her captain (later Vice-Admiral Ruge) playing the guitar, early 1919. *(Vice-Admiral Friedrich Ruge)*

30. German sailors abandon ship after the order to scuttle. *(C.W. Burrows)*

31. SMS *Bayern*, 21 June 1919. *(Imperial War Museum SP1626)*

32. The scuttling of the German destroyer *G.102*, 21 June 1919. *(Imperial War Museum SP1625)*

33. The scuttling of SMS *Hindenburg*, 21 June 1919. *(Imperial War Museum SP1635)*

34. Scapa Flow after the Great Scuttle of 1919. The battleship with only her funnels showing is the *Hindenburg*. *(Thomas Kent)*

35. Cheerful British soldiers guard a beached German ship. Their war was over and the German Fleet had finally succumbed. *(Thomas Kent)*

36. & 37. Between the wars private salvage operators laboriously and ingeniously raised some of the German ships from the bed of the Flow. *(William Hourston)*

38. Libertymen leaving the *Royal Oak* on the drifter *Daisy II* the day before the attack by *U-47*. *(Herbert Johnson)*

39. 'Libertymen at Lyness', a painting by Charles Cundall Air Ministry artist, 1941. *(National Maritime Museum)*

40. The triumphant return to Germany of the *U-47*, following the sinking of HMS *Royal Oak*, 1939. *(Courtesy Korvetten-Kapitan Hans Wessels)*

41. Kapitan Leutnant Gunther Prien, commander of *U-47* (left), being congratulated by Admiral Saalwachter (centre) and Grand-Admiral Raeder after returning to Wilhelmshaven from the sinking of HMS *Royal Oak*. *(Imperial War Museum)*

42. Prien and his engineer officer Hans Wessels on the triumphant return to Germany after the sinking of HMS *Royal Oak*. (Courtesy Korvetten-Kapitan Hans Wessels)

43. The *Royal Oak* memorial bell in St Magnus' Cathedral, Kirkwall. *(Jenny Suddaby)*

44. Churchill ordered barriers to be made for the sounds penetrated by *U-47*. Above is the concrete block-casting yard at St Mary's Holm, on the north shore of Kirk Sound. *(G. Gordon Nicol)*

45. 'Boom Defence Vessels', a painting by Charles Cundall. *(National Maritime Musuem)*

46. A typical page from the
Orkney Blast, with a signed
photograph of Evelyn Laye,
a great favourite at the Flow.

47. A cartoon by Strube
envisaging the worst exile
for Hitler.

48. *Above:* Dame Vera Laughton Mathews, Director WRNS, inspects a contingent of Wrens at Lyness. *(Ministry of Defence)*

52. *Below:* A film show below decks on a destroyer, with men watching on both sides of the screen, in a drawing by Gordon Rowland.

49. Convoy PQ18 under attack *(Imperial War Museum)*

50. The effects of ice in northern waters *(Imperial War Museum)*

51. A common sight in both world wars: capital ships steaming in line ahead through heavy weather. *(Imperial War Museum* SP1681)

53. A view of the Flow at the end of the Second World War. *(G. Gordon Nicol)*

54. Peaceful Scapa Flow. The view from Houton, 2001. *(Jenny Suddaby)*

THE SECOND
WORLD WAR

BLOODY ORKNEY

This bloody town's a bloody cuss
No bloody trains, no bloody bus
And no-one cares for bloody us
In bloody Orkney.

Everything's so bloody dear
A bloody bob for bloody beer
And is it good? – no bloody fear!
In bloody Orkney.

The bloody flicks are bloody old
The bloody seats are bloody cold
You can't get in for bloody gold
In bloody Orkney.

No bloody sport, no bloody games,
Ho bloody fun, the bloody dames
Won't even give their bloody names
In bloody Orkney.

Best bloody place is bloody bed
With bloody ice on bloody head
You might as well be bloody dead
in bloody Orkney.

from *The Orkney Blast*

15

Loss of the Royal Oak

For several years after 1919 the Flow lay littered with derelict German warships – some out of sight under water, others with keel or superstructure riding clear like some artificial island, others beached like wrecks washed ashore by a storm. Their novelty soon wore off, and they were seen for what they were – an ugly detraction from the sombre beauty of the Flow, and a menace to the ships that used it. In 1924 the firm of Cox and Danks moved in on Admiralty contract and started the formidable task of clearance. Ten years later Metal Industries Ltd took over, not ceasing their operations until the Royal Navy came back into occupation in 1939. They stopped before they could finish their work on the battle-cruiser *Derfflinger*, which had been lucky to escape at the Dogger Bank action and was severely mauled at Jutland. With her incredible gift for survival, she lay bottom upwards off Hoy throughout the six years of the Second World War, finally to be towed away for break-up in 1946.

Scapa did not exist as a base between the wars. By the end of 1919 the booms had been removed and the minefields exploded. In February 1920 the Admiral Commanding Orkney and Shetland hauled down his flag. A month later the base-ship *Imperieuse* and the dockyard-ship *Victorious* sailed away. The dismantling of the batteries began, the air-stations were closed, the seaplane base became a tuberculosis hospital. Scapa was left to the Orcadians and the hardy salvagers out in the Flow.

Occasionally the Home Fleet – the title of Grand Fleet had been discarded in 1919 – would sweep in through Hoxa Sound, and a new generation of sailors would take a look at the famous anchorage where so many of their predecessors had spent the days of the Great War. As the 1930s wore on they did so with greater curiosity, since it was becoming increasingly likely that Scapa might be called upon to resume its central role in British naval strategy.

¶ I first saw Scapa Flow in the early summer months of 1937 when, as a young Able-Seaman, I was aboard the cruiser *Newcastle* and, in company with other ships of the Home Fleet, we dropped anchor there after completion of Fleet exercises.

To me it was by no means a forbidding place – everything seemed so natural, the vast expanse of clean water, the dust-free air on which one could feed one's lungs – no clatter of continuous noise as one hears in the Naval dockyards.

Our Captain, John Vivian, spoke to us of the days when as a young naval officer in the First World War he came into Scapa Flow and saw ships of all kinds anchored in line ahead and across the whole width of the Flow. He said that in his opinion the time was not far off when we would see the same pattern return again. 'At least,' he said, 'you have all seen Scapa Flow in peacetime. The next time you come here we shall be at war and things will be very different.'[1]

In 1938 – year of the Munich crisis – a new Commander-in-Chief, Admiral Sir Charles Forbes, took his Fleet to Scapa Flow. When he reached it he found the Navy busy with two strangely contradictory activities. A party of Royal Marines had just finished dismantling the last of the gun emplacements of the First World War, while boom-defence vessels were preparing to lay the anti-submarine nets that were eventually to be used in the Second. He examined Scapa's defences and found them disturbingly inadequate. In particular, his eye was caught by the tiny entrances through Holm Sound on the eastern side. He found that some of the blockships sunk there in the First War had been so savagely handled by the storms that they were askew their channels rather than astride them. Indeed, he was confronted not so much by a line of blockships as a litter of wrecks. There and then he bought for £100 a large concrete barge sitting on the foreshore at Stromness and had it towed across and sunk in Holm Sound. But it was little more than a gesture. The loophole remained, and a year later the Navy was to pay a high price because of it.

Despite Forbes's urgent recommendations little was done in the year between Munich and the outbreak of war to make Scapa safer for the Fleet. In April 1939 a Senior Naval Officer, Scapa, was appointed and took up residence in the Kirkwall Hotel, but owing to lack of funds he could not be provided with a boat with which to carry out his work.

What helped to confuse the issue was that the Naval Staff was in favour of Rosyth as main base in the event of war; but Forbes was for Scapa, and so too was the man who became First Lord of the Admiralty in September 1939, Winston Churchill.

'Winston is back' was the famous signal flashed to the Fleet as Chamberlain announced his War Cabinet. The Navy was back too, in Scapa Flow. And in the final weeks before hostilities, preparations had at last been put in train to receive the Fleet into its wartime home.

The same young Able Seaman who had first seen the Flow in 1937 on the cruiser *Newcastle* found himself back there in 1939 in one of the Fleet's famous battle-cruisers. It was a verification of his former Captain's prophecy.

¶ On 4 September 1939, on board the *Renown*, I returned to Scapa Flow. On arrival in the Flow, having passed through the boom defences, we dropped anchor inside the anti-torpedo defence nets. Other ships were there also, including three decoy battle-ships and one decoy aircraft-carrier. Buildings, mostly of wood and corrugated sheets, were beginning to spring up at Lyness, Flotta, Rinnigill and Longhope and even the dark grey paint of the ships blended well with the scenery, the atmosphere and environment of Scapa. One could also see the odd shore A.A. guns, quickly erected on Flotta with the army tents close to hand.[2]

Lyness had succeeded Longhope as the main base and it was to Gutter Sound off Lyness that the *Iron Duke*, Jellicoe's flagship at Jutland, came at the end of August. She had a humbler role now. Stripped of two of her five turrets, too old for sea-warfare, she was to be a depot and transit ship; but she still had the dignity of a flagship, for she flew the flag of the newly appointed Admiral Commanding Orkney and Shetland, Admiral Sir Wilfrid French.

There was a memorable scene on her quarter-deck in mid-September when the new First Lord came north to re-acquaint himself with the Fleet.

¶ A number of officers and ratings from various ships were taken across to the *Iron Duke* and we were all assembled on the quarter deck to await 'Winnie's' arrival. It was, as so often in the Flow, a windy day, and I well remember watching the fast motor pinnace making its way through the waves towards us from the distance. W.S.C. was piped aboard and was immediately conducted aft, where he mounted the capstan and addressed us. He spoke of the First World War and of the policy then adopted, which often involved for the Fleet many months of waiting. He said we might have to be prepared for such an experience in this war.[3]

An officer of *Iron Duke* remembers the same occasion.

¶ Wearing yachting cap and cigar, Mr Churchill hoisted himself on to the after-capstan grating, and informed us that almost exactly a quarter of a century before, in the same capacity of First Lord, he had come to the same ship, in the same harbour, to stand in the same position in which he was standing on that day to address the ship's company.[4]

So Scapa Flow went to war for the second time. And for the second time she was to lose one of her mighty capital ships within her protective shores. The horrifying tragedy of the *Vanguard* was, in essence, to be repeated. The circumstances and the cause would differ, there would be a higher proportion of survivors, but this second disaster would kill even more men than the first.

When on 26 August the *Iron Duke* steamed in towards her moorings, she was observed from the decks of another battleship of the First World War which had already dropped anchor in the familiar waters of the Flow. This was the *Royal Oak*, the ship which had been entertaining that fortunate handful of officers from *Vanguard* on the night of 9 July 1917. Ironically, she was to be Scapa's second great victim.

The *Royal Oak* was not as old as the *Iron Duke*, but she could not match the speed of the Navy's front-rank battleships and battle-cruisers. So she tended to be omitted from the strenuous patrols which began even before the actual declaration of war. When on 3 October news came from Coastal Command that the German battle-cruiser *Gneisenau* and the cruiser *Köln* were prowling off the Norwegian coast, the Home Fleet sailed from Scapa in force, but left *Royal Oak* to the more humdrum duty of sweeping the Fair Isle channel with an escort of two destroyers. The Fleet that Forbes took out towards Norway was a galaxy of famous names – *Hood, Repulse, Nelson, Rodney, Furious* – but it was the older *Royal Oak* that was soon to find a place in the world's headlines.

Forbes returned to Scapa on learning – the news had a familiar ring – that the Germans had slipped back to base. The *Royal Oak* returned too, having received a severe buffeting from a North Atlantic gale. She moored in the north-eastern corner of the Flow in Scapa Bay, within sight of the tower of Kirkwall's St Magnus' Cathedral and only about a mile from the shore. After dark on 12 October, thanks to that same sense of insecurity that had plagued Jellicoe in the early months of the First War, Admiral Forbes took the Home Fleet away to Loch Ewe in the west of Scotland. The *Royal Oak* stayed behind in the Flow, where she could fulfil the role of anti-aircraft battery for Kirkwall. Such an assignment was no sinecure, since the general belief was that this was to be above all a war in the air. Massed air-attacks on Britain had been expected from the moment that war was declared.

German planes did fly over Scapa, but with cameras not bombs. The photographs they brought back to Germany exposed to the eyes of Commodore Doenitz, Commander-in-Chief of the U-boat force, that fatal flaw in the eastern defences of Scapa Flow which had so worried Admiral Forbes. Inevitably, it had worried

Churchill too. On taking office he had been appalled at the insecurity of the Fleet's main base. He wrote in his memoirs: 'As a result of the conference on my second evening at the Admiralty many orders were given for additional nets and blockings.'

One blockship intended for Holm Sound had been sunk *en route* to the Flow. Even as the German reconnaissance planes were flying over Scapa another was steaming northwards. But the gap was still unplugged, the gate still open.

Two tiny islands sit athwart Holm Sound as it curves in from the North Sea to join Scapa Flow. The northernmost of the three channels made by these islands, Kirk Sound, was the one that particularly attracted Doenitz's attention. He became convinced that courage and seamanship of a high order might effect an entry through Kirk Sound and achieve a killing in the Fleet base itself. In the First War it had been a German dream to break into the Flow and create havoc among the ships of the Grand Fleet. One U-boat had attempted it in 1918 in a brave but suicidal run. Now Doenitz saw his chance to make this twenty-five-year-old ambition a reality.

He chose his man, Kapitan-Leutnant Gunther Prien of the *U-47*, and sent him on his bold mission. The *U-47* crept in through Kirk Sound on the evening of Friday 13 October. Prien had been led by the last photographic reconnaissance before he sailed to expect the Fleet in full occupation of its base. Instead he found the normal Fleet anchorage empty, turned north-eastwards towards Kirkwall, and there discovered the *Royal Oak*.

It was just after one on the morning of Saturday 14 October that the *U-47*, sailing on the surface of the Flow, approached the *Royal Oak* and fired a salvo of torpedoes. Only one struck her – a glancing blow forward. There was an explosion which to some survivors was 'terrific', to others 'muffled'. It caused some confusion and a good deal of puzzlement, since its origin was by no means evident to those on board. About a quarter of an hour later, the *U-47* having re-loaded, fired again. This time the torpedoes struck home. Within minutes the *Royal Oak* had sunk.

There were terrible scenes below decks. As the ship lurched to starboard and slowly heeled over, the electricity failed, and hundreds of men were left floundering for the hatches in the dark – a darkness that was savagely illuminated in places by cordite flash racing in fireballs about the ship from the magazines, killing and maiming as it went. Those who were not incinerated were trapped and drowned as the ship capsized. Nearly 400 survived. Over 800 died.

Captain R. F. Nichols was the Commander of the *Royal Oak* at the time. His is one of the most remarkable stories ever to come out of Scapa Flow for he, in July 1917, was the young Midshipman of H.M.S. *Vanguard* who decided at the last minute to attend the concert that was being presented in *Gourko* by the sailors of the *Royal Oak*, and thus escaped the first great disaster that took place in Scapa Flow. Similarly, in 1939, he survived the second.

¶ That night, as usual, we darkened ship and were alert to air attack. I turned in at about 10.30 P.M. only to be awakened by a heavy shaking of the ship. The time was four minutes past one. Throwing on a coat I went on deck but no one could tell me what had happened so I continued forward to the forecastle where there was an acrid smell. I could see by the light of a faint aurora that the stopper on the starboard cable had parted and the cable run out to a 'clinch'. Evidently the trouble was below in the cable locker flat where I found the Captain and the Engineer Commander. It seemed an explosion had occurred in the inflammable store and a man was going down in a smoke helmet to investigate.

Then, just thirteen minutes after the first explosion, came three more sickening, shattering thuds abaft us on the starboard side. Each explosion rocked the ship alarmingly, all lights went out and she at once took a list of about twenty-five degrees. There was no doubt in my mind what had happened this time, nor what was going to happen. How on earth had a submarine got through the defences?

In addition to the heavy damage done by the torpedoes there were a large number of portholes open, fitted with 'light-excluding ventilators'.* I knew every one of these on the starboard side must be submerged and it would be impossible to close them against the incoming rush of water.

---

* These ventilators, which allowed fresh air into the crowded mess-decks but were not waterproof, were only intended for use in the safety of harbour.

There was no electric power to work the derrick to hoist out any of the large boats and, because of the ever-increasing list, many of the smaller boats could not be lowered.

Just eight minutes after the second salvo of three torpedoes had struck her, the *Royal Oak* sank. In the short struggle that followed, I recall only a frantic rush and scramble up the ship's side as she spun round in the act of sinking, and, when she sank under me, how cold the water was on my feet as my short seaboots fell off. Then, in the darkness, an intense feeling of loneliness seized me and I remember little else until I found myself sharing a raft with several others – all of us soaked in a foul-smelling, slippery, chilly mixture of sea water and oil fuel.[5]

Herbert Johnston was a Stoker on *Royal Oak*. An Orcadian, his home was the little village of St Mary's, on the northern shore of Kirk Sound.

¶ At midnight I went down below to the refrigerating room on watch and just before one A.M. I put the readings in the engine-room register (they had to go in every hour). A moment or two afterwards there was a terrific explosion. I thought we'd blown up, I thought we'd hit a mine, and then I decided that there had been an air-raid, so I closed down the machinery, shut the doors and the hatches and went up on the main deck.

When I got up on deck the people there seemed to think that there was probably an explosion in the CO_2 compartment. However, my appearance cleared that up and then they assumed it was probably an explosion in the inflammable store.

In the meantime, all very gas-conscious, I decided to go and get my gas-mask. I went down to the stokers' mess-deck and down there there were a few people stirring and one fellow said, 'Why don't you people be quiet and let us have some sleep?'

However, I picked up my gas-mask and set off back with the intention of restarting my refrigerating machinery, but there was a huddle of people about so I decided to hang back a little until they'd thinned out. But I couldn't settle and after a few minutes, I suppose ten minutes after the first explosion, there was another, slightly farther aft. The ship immediately began to list to star board and there was a foul smell as of cordite. I decided that I had better go up on the upper deck in case there was something serious wrong.

When I came to the ladder there was a big crowd around it. I went up and as I put my hand on the hatch-combing to go on deck the lights in that area went out and I saw the sky.

When I got on deck I didn't know what to do. After a few minutes I saw Lieutenant Sclater go over the 4-inch gun shield and slide down into the picket boat, so I went over the guard rail and followed him down. The ship was well heeled-over then, the lower boom was up at a very high angle, and that had pulled the picket boat in close to the ship's side.

I slithered down into the boat and the boat gradually filled up. After a few moments there was another series of explosions, at an even speed, that appeared to go from forward to right aft. Meantime the ship was heeling over very rapidly and the picket boat was getting fuller and fuller of people. After only two or three minutes, the *Royal Oak* rolled over and submerged. As she was rolling over, a few people came down her side towards the sea.

In the picket boat somebody started up a song, but it fizzled out before the end of the first verse. About that time the picket boat became so overcrowded and top-heavy, that it capsized. I was thrown into the water; I swam a couple of strokes away and turned to see what had happened. I thought I would go back to the picket boat because she had righted herself; but as the men clambered back in she went over again so I decided that that was no longer any use. By this time our attendant drifter, *Daisy II*, which had been tied for the night near the quarter-deck on the port side, was moving about picking up survivors. I decided to swim to her.

As I swam along I decided to get rid of my boiler suit. I took my waistbelt off which was outside my boiler suit, then decided that because my money (about three pounds) was in the purse in the belt I would try and save this. I put the belt in my teeth to take my boiler suit off, but after a few strokes, changed my mind and decided that if I didn't get away, the money wouldn't be any good to me, so I let it go.

As I got near to the *Daisy II* I got hold of a lifebuoy on a rope and they helped me into the boat.

After they had picked up numerous survivors, I don't know how many, they took us over to the old seaplane carrier *Pegasus*, which was lying in Sandoyne Bay. We were taken down to the engine room to keep warm. There was a long queue for the bathroom. We had to be cleaned up because we were all plastered in oily fuel. After a while they took us over from the *Pegasus* to a merchant cruiser near Flotta, the *Voltaire*. They gave us a tot of rum and put us all in cabins for a sleep. By this time I was very nervous and I carefully made sure the porthole was open. I had a sudden impulse to put a lifejacket on but it was the hard cork variety so I decided to leave it on top of my pillow instead.[6]

The tiny *Daisy II*, which was moored under the towering flank of the *Royal Oak* when she was hit, deserves a most honourable mention. The battleship was fitted below the waterline with huge anti-torpedo 'blisters', which, as she listed to starboard, almost lifted the *Daisy* clean out of the water, tilting her over to port and threatening to capsize her. Her crew frantically cut her moorings and the ship rode clear. She then began her task of picking up survivors. When she finally headed towards *Pegasus* there were 386 men on board a vessel seventeen feet wide and a little over a hundred feet long. They were squeezed into the boiler room, the engine room, the holds and the cabins; they were standing on engine-room casings and clinging to the rigging; and those too injured or exhausted to move were lying on deck.

The skipper of the *Daisy II*, John Gatt – although a civilian, like his crew – was awarded the Distinguished Service Cross for his work of rescue.

A member of the crew of the *Pegasus* recalls his ship's part in the story.

¶ On the morning of 14 October at about 1.20 A.M. two terrific bangs on the side of *Pegasus* woke the ship's company. I, with other messmates, jumped out of our hammocks. I put a raincoat over my pyjamas and went on deck. Everything seemed quite normal. We could see the silhouette of the *Royal Oak* against the skyline.

Suddenly huge sheets of sparks shot into the air from forward and aft of the *Royal Oak*, followed by the sound of three explosions.

Then, almost immediately, the quartermaster on *Pegasus* started blowing his pipe and shouting 'Away all boats' crews'. Men were colliding with each other as it was very dark. Then I heard our engineer officer shouting: 'Mechanician Rowley'. I found my way to him and said: 'Yes, sir.' He said: 'Up in the speedboat, quick.' The speedboat was on the davits. I was still wearing my pyjamas and raincoat. I climbed up into the speed boat and several other dark figures followed me. We were dropped into the water, I started the engine and we shot away into the darkness. I do not know how many survivors were picked up but when we got back at about 3.30 in the morning I went along to my mess. Outside were men badly burnt and in my mess were several survivors in very bad shape. Down in our engine room were dozens of naked survivors. The ship's company of *Pegasus* gave all their spare clothes and among all this horror one could not help being amused to see officers from the *Royal Oak* dressed in all kinds of sailors' clothes.[7]

One of the macabre elements in the tragedy of the *Royal Oak* is that it took place while Kirkwall slept peacefully only two miles away, and while the other ships in Scapa Flow scarcely knew that anything was amiss. But when the news spread the comparison with the *Vanguard* suggested itself immediately; and, like *Vanguard*, the *Royal Oak* was to become a name that no one in Scapa could ever forget.

¶ I was woken at a very early hour to be told of the disaster, and all the officers dressed and gathered to discuss the news. The general consensus of opinion was that this was another *Vanguard* disaster due to an internal explosion reaching a magazine. It never occurred to anyone that a submarine could have entered the Flow.

Next day we in *Iron Duke* received several of the survivors. They did not include our Admiral's Cook, who had gone into Kirkwall the night before, and mistaking the drifter in the dark at Scapa Pier, had gone back to the *Royal Oak* by mistake.

The last message we had from the *Royal Oak* was that he had fetched up there . . . and there, alas, he remained.[8]

* * *

¶ I arrived in Scapa just a day or two before the *Royal Oak* was sunk. After the disaster we dropped wreaths over the spot.

One of the divers we talked to gave a graphic word-picture of the state of the *Royal Oak* on the bottom – men still in hammocks as the fish swam about them.[9]

* * *

¶ I was a gunner in the Orkneys and spent some time on a gun-site on the edge of Scapa Flow. That site has poignant memories for me. I was there some months after the torpedoing of the *Royal Oak*, and we were told that a steel net had been placed over the sunken warship to prevent things from floating to the surface. I do not know whether this was true or not, but every morning we used to go beachcombing and would often find articles of Naval clothing washed up during the night, a boot, or a jersey, or a cap with someone's name in it, pathetic evidence of a great tragedy.[10]

Today a buoy marked WRECK sways above the spot where the *Royal Oak* lies in Scapa Bay. The buoy is easily visible from the shore, and at times from the aircraft that fly across the Pentland Firth to Kirkwall one can see the discoloration in the surface of the Flow made by the oil that is still slowly escaping from the sunken battleship. If she is ever to be salvaged it will not be for a long time to come, for she is the only grave of over 800 men, and neither the relatives of those killed nor the people of Orkney wish to see her disturbed.

In St Magnus' Cathedral, Kirkwall, there is a simple brass plaque in the north aisle in memory of the 833 officers and men of the *Royal Oak* lost in the disaster. But in Orkney they say that the real memorial is the cathedral itself, for from its tower the place where she last rode at anchor can be clearly seen; and it is not forgotten that she was there in Kirkwall's defence.

Bolting the Stable Door

On Saturday 21 October 1939 a new blockship – the S.S. *Lake Neuchatel* – was sunk in Kirk Sound. But the damage had already been done. The *U-47* had returned in honour to her base with the sailors of the warships in harbour lining their decks to cheer her in. The German newsreels ran these exultant scenes at considerable length in their cinemas, to the accompaniment of that aggressive and blood-stirring song '*Wir fahren gegen England*' – 'We are marching against England'. They also showed the U-boat's crew riding in open cars through a wildly cheering Berlin and receiving the congratulations of Hitler himself. It was like a triumph in ancient Rome.

In Scapa the loss of the *Royal Oak* was a heavy blow to morale. Incredibly, after only a few weeks of war, one of those melancholy trains crammed with survivors was on its way south from Thurso. There was a sense of angry injustice. How could it happen that over 800 men could die far inside the Fleet's main base and scarcely a mile from shore? It was a disaster that shocked not only those there at the time, but also, when the full story became known, those who had guarded the Flow twenty-five years earlier, when the threat of such a raid by a U-boat was never very far from the minds of its defenders.

¶ I was stationed on the shores of Scapa Flow from September to December 1914. I was one of a company of territorial artillerymen manning a battery of four 12-pounder guns guarding the eastern entrance to the Flow.

We guarded the entrance through which Prien navigated the *U-47* while fully surfaced, on his way to torpedo the *Royal Oak* twenty-five years later. I can swear that had he tried that caper in 1914 by night or by day, he would never have made it. We were on strict watch day and night and not a moving object would have escaped our attention. We old artillerymen regret to think there must have been great negligence on the part of the three branches of our armed forces when a submarine could go unde-tected while cruising on the surface on an autumn night in the unpolluted clear air of those northern climes.[1]

Three days after the loss of the *Royal Oak*, even before the *Lake Neuchatel* was sunk in her position in Kirk Sound, Scapa was attacked again – from the air. Four German bombers flew over at high altitude, then swooped down towards the Fleet base at Lyness and the cluster of ships lying just off shore. For a soldier of the Royal Artillery just arrived in Orkney this was his first glimpse of war.

¶ I came to Scapa Flow one moonlit night in October 1939 and saw for the first time at close quarters the silent bulk of the old battleship *Iron Duke*, flagship at Jutland, then still proudly floating. I was a gunner, Royal Artillery, with three months expe-rience of square-bashing; one of a band of reinforcements to join the islands' own Territorial Battery charged with the anti-aircraft defence of the naval base at Lyness on the Island of Hoy.

Within a day or two of my arrival in Scapa the air-raid sirens sounded and the throbbing of German bombers quickly followed. This was to be the first active service action for the battery, whose eight guns formed the whole of the land-based defence at that time. My vantage point in an old cowshed – as a new recruit I was not then entrusted with a job – gave a grandstand view of the Fleet anchor-age with the *Iron Duke* lying peacefully at anchor. It soon became obvious, as the bombs hurtled down from what appeared to be a great height, that the old ship was to be the main object of attack.

In what could only have been a matter of minutes it was obvi-ous that one at least of the many bombs spouting up from the water had scored a mortal hit and the great ship began to heel over at an alarming rate. The water was thick with swimming men and scurrying small craft but, when it looked as if she would turn turtle at any moment, the list was arrested miraculously and the ship towed or pushed on to a sandbank.

The German planes did not get away scot free. One came down in flames and exploded amidst the heather not far from one of the battery sites. It was, I remember, stoutly claimed by both the battery and the Naval gunners.[2]

* * *

¶ We felt a little bare in *Iron Duke*. There was no life-saving equipment; personal life-jackets became standard equipment much later in the war. The water looked very cold, and the beach a long way off. A fellow-officer – former solicitor – and I decided that we would help ourselves to the wooden name-boards outside the quarter-deck lobby if the worst came to the worst.

Three days after the sinking of the *Royal Oak* we caught our own little packet. I was in the Admiral's office right down aft when the first bomb landed in the water alongside the port engine-room, and opened a large hole in the ship's side. The next one came over the quarter-deck and exploded in the water almost underneath us, shaking the stern like a dog's tail. By that time I was in the after lobby where we had on display Admiral Jellicoe's frock-coat in a glass case. When I picked myself up off the glass-strewn deck, I found the said frock-coat hanging over my shoulders! Some have greatness thrust upon them! The ship took an alarming list, and I emerged on to the quarter-deck to see the last of the action, and a Heinkel coming down in flames . . . later claimed by every gun in Gutter Sound but awarded to the Lewis-gun section ashore around the oil tanks in Lyness, commanded by an ancient Captain of Royal Marines.

A permissive order was given to abandon ship, and the Sound was soon well filled with bobbing heads. I saw my solicitor friend balancing on the tilting deck with a large *Iron Duke* name-board under his arm, but the water looked very cold and we remained on the quarter-deck awaiting events. Those up for'ard had been busy, and though it seemed inevitable that we must turn over at any minute, we eventually got under way, towed by a Metal Industries tug, which beached the ship in Ore Bay where, by night-fall, the quarter-deck subsided gently into the water. We had meanwhile endured a long air-raid throughout the afternoon, but without further casualty to the now sitting duck. A cheerless night . . . and next day the ship was evacuated. Never had the land seemed more inviting, even if only Lyness-on-Mud.[3]

* * *

¶ Out in the Flow the destroyers were hammering away with their anti-aircraft guns and for a few minutes all hell was let loose. We in our little drifter *Mist* had no answer to the German planes but foolishly we stayed on deck and watched the fight. One of the destroyers found a target and down came an enemy plane, well away from us. I shall never forget the cheer that went up from the leading destroyer and the remark from the skipper as he steamed past us: 'My bird, I think!' He could have been on the grouse moors. I think the plane fell at Lyness. One did, I know, and within a few days it had been torn to pieces by sailors wanting keepsakes.[4]

The German bomber thus transformed into myriad souvenirs gave some satisfaction to the twice-bitten garrison of Scapa Flow. It was its first blood. There would be more to come.

But the Home Fleet – the reason for Scapa's existence as a base – was far off in Loch Ewe or Rosyth. In Beatty's phrase from the First War, it had been pushed off its perch. Scapa had to be made secure for it to return.

This was the urgent task for the next six months. On the last day of October, Churchill again went to Scapa to hold a conference with Admiral Forbes. They agreed on a comprehensive programme of reinforcement to the defences of the Flow – more booms, more blockships, more patrol craft, more batteries covering the approaches. There were also to be more anti-aircraft guns, numerous searchlights and a formidable balloon barrage. Substantial fighter protection was to be provided from Orkney itself and from Wick in Caithness. The Flow was to be ready for reoccupation by March 1940. Meanwhile Scapa could continue as a destroyer-refuelling base, but the big ships would be elsewhere.

The Senior Naval Officer who came to the Kirkwall Hotel in the spring of 1939 had become King's Harbour Master on the outbreak of war. Now, with *Iron Duke* beached and humiliated, his launch – he had a boat now – was commissioned as H.M.S. *Proserpine*, so that the H.Q. organization of the Admiral Commanding Orkney and Shetland (A.C.O.S. as it was generally known) could be moved officially ashore to Lyness.

Lyness was scarcely worthy of the dignity of her new name. *Proserpine* – 'Proper Swine' to her ship's company – was a primitive place in these early days of war. She did not endear herself to the sailors who found themselves there.

¶ Scapa! I was there in 1939 when the 'amenities' were mostly claptrap huts floating on a sea of mud. Shocking conditions. The wet canteen was a large hut, a trestle table, and two or three large beer-barrels. Imagine the Klondike in the earliest days, and you have it.[5]

The staff of A.C.O.S. plunged into their immense task in scarcely encouraging conditions. The only accommodation for the new H.Q. was a small accounts office, into which the Admiral, Chief of Staff, Flag Lieutenant and Secretary had to cram themselves. Secret and personal interviews had to take place in the W.C. The Captain's Secretary slept on a small table. The men slept in the canteen and the poky rooms adjoining.

Proserpine she might be in the ship's books, but she was Lyness-on-Mud in those early months, for, as one officer recalls, the mud lay thick that winter and sea boots were worn on all occasions throughout the base. There was much snow too, which is unusual for Orkney. One Naval Writer remembers his Arctic introduction to Lyness in January 1940.

¶ Our arrival at Lyness was unforgettable. We staggered along the old wooden jetty in a gale of wind and swirling snow, unable to see the landward end of it. A sailor materialized out of the snow and directed us to the 'canteen', which sounded exciting but turned out to be a wooden building of 1914–18 vintage nestling amongst the oil tanks and used as a general mess and barracks. It had a rough bar at one end and a tiny stage flanked by two tiny wing rooms at the other. One of these rooms, about six foot square, was to become my mess, shared with about twenty other Writers, Cooks and Jack Dusties.

There were hammock rails in the canteen and most times beer was available in the evenings. Liberty parties came ashore from the Fleet and other islands – thirsty men from hard convoys and isolated gunsites. The beer was strictly rationed but the fun was fast and furious and sometimes there were fights. The only place to get out of the way to write a letter was in one's hammock so we slung up and got in as soon as the bar opened. In the morning one awoke with a first-class hangover from the noise and beer fumes without having touched a drop and swung out of the hammock onto the beer-sodden floor.

We moved out from the canteen after a bit and joined some mates who slept on top of the boilers in an oil-pumping house. It was warm there with oil instead of beer fumes. Eventually we were discovered and slung out because it was alleged to be unhealthy. We then moved into the billiard room. This was in a large corrugated iron shed (1914 war) which housed our stores, transport and office and which later became the cinema. The roof was riddled with bullet and rust holes and the snow seeped gently through. The two ancient billiard-tables were moth-eaten but kept the snow off when we slept under them.

In the office was a bogey stove and we sat in a line away from it in order of rank. I was at the remote end. We often wore our overcoats at work but always had roll-neck sweaters and mittens and wrapped mail bags around our feet. When it became too cold to hold a pen we fell in and ran around the building to restore our circulation.[6]

The Army, arriving in increasing numbers to share in the strenuous task of making the base secure, were living, if anything, in even more primitive conditions than their Naval colleagues in the Lyness canteen.

¶ The battery had two sites on bluffs a mile or two on each side of Lyness. The men there in the summer had been under canvas. Preparations for permanent hutted accommodation were under way but had been overtaken by events so that many of the less fortunate spent the winter of howling gales and lashing rain in soggy tents, which maintained only the slenderest hold in the squelchy peat of the island.

We new arrivals were put into the huts which were nearest completion and even those, lacking doors and glass to the windows, could scarcely be classed as the acme of comfort, particularly as there were no beds. Every inch of floor space at night was covered with a tightly packed mass of sleeping men. Gradually conditions eased as more huts were made habitable and soon a motley collection of iron bedsteads began to appear, acquired by devious means, all strictly unofficial. I paid 1s. 6d. for a magnificent specimen which had been spirited out of the naval base and carried across the intervening bog with a confederate who 'knew the ropes'.

There was no water in the camp, no sanitation and only the most rudimentary type of field kitchen, consisting of a couple of large boilers sheltering under a sheet of corrugated iron. In consequence there was a certain lack of variety in diet since everything had to be tailored to fit one or other of the boilers.

It was strange that in such a wet place water should be a problem but this had to be carried from the Naval base at Lyness, perhaps three miles or so by a very rough road. Transport was by means of an open galvanized tank on the back of an open lorry, which made 'water fatigue' a very cold wet job in the middle of winter. Water was collected from a well in the Naval base which disgorged a muddy brown fluid faintly resembling flat beer. It had no noticeable taste but had the peculiar property of making tea look like cocoa whilst cocoa took on a slatey-blue colour.

Not much water could be spared for washing purposes but some tin bowls set on planks in the open air did duty for the whole camp. Unfortunately the water supply for this establishment, another galvanized tank, frequently froze in the winter and it was then that I learned that a satisfactory shave could be obtained from the remains of the breakfast tea.

Washing of clothes was out of the question and posed a problem, until I found a crofter's wife who was willing to do a week's wash for 1s. 3d. and who also, out of the kindness of her heart, prepared for my weekly visit an enormous meal and a seat for an hour or two beside her peat fire. That was my first introduction to the hospitality and kindness of the islanders, which came to mean so much in the ensuing eighteen months or so.

Sanitary needs of the camp were provided for by a pole across a trench dug many feet into the peat, some privacy and shelter being provided by a canvas screen. Primitive perhaps, but not without its lighter moments, such as when one of my friends was missing one dark night and was discovered some hours later at the bottom of one of these trenches which, fortunately, was still awaiting its Opening ceremony.[7]

The work of mounting the guns that were to defend Scapa against air and sea attack was perhaps the toughest of all.

¶ The job was given to a Marine Naval Base Defence Organization and to see those bearded men battling in the icy winds of February and March 1940, putting in gun emplacements and guns weighing many tons, with rough tackle and brute strength, with numbed fingers and ice in their beards and Balaclavas, was a reminder to many of us lesser mortals of the grim purpose behind their work. They were a race of real men and their good humour and devotion to duty in wickedly biting snow blizzards and gales will remain for ever with those of us who were privileged to witness it.[8]

* * *

¶ It was a hard winter, but the weather really helped us, for it discouraged the G.A.F. (German Air Force), and gradually the work went forward to provide the base with the guns and barrage balloons and air cover and boom defences which it needed, and by the spring of 1940 it was safe for the Fleet to return.[9]

It had indeed been a remarkably thorough and successful piece of work, all the more creditable because it had been carried out in that doldrum period known as the 'phoney war'. The First Lord was satisfied.

Churchill indeed had intended to return with the Fleet to Scapa on the bridge of Admiral Forbes's flagship, *Nelson*, and duly sailed on her from Rosyth. But when a report was received that mines had been dropped by German aircraft near Hoxa, Forbes decided that he must stand off for twenty-four hours while the channel was swept. Since H.M.S. *Hood* was already in the Flow, Forbes suggested that Churchill might tranship to her in a destroyer. Churchill agreed, and so entered the Flow through Switha Sound – 'the tradesmen's entrance', as it was called in the Fleet – and spent the night on board the *Hood*. It was an emotional moment for him, and a proud one, for it was evident that, though there were still things to be done, the peacetime neglect at Scapa had been repaired. 'At last the Home Fleet had a home. It was the famous home from which in the previous war the Royal Navy had ruled the seas.'*

There was, however, one major task still to be accomplished. The eastern narrows which had given access to the *U-47* were to be sealed completely, and not just with blockships. In spite of the daunting difficulties presented by the fierceness of the tide race through these small but surprisingly deep channels, specially constructed barriers were to be thrust across them. In Churchill's view, concrete was the only sure guarantee that a disaster like that of the *Royal Oak* would never happen again.

The work took four years and cost £2 million. It changed the life as well as the landscape of Orkney, for once the great concrete blocks were in position a road was built over them from the northern shore of Kirk Sound to South Ronaldsay across the little islands of Lambs Holm and Glimps Holm and the larger island of Burray. This little archipelago thus became in all but name a long south limb of the Orkney Mainland.

The building of these great causeways was carried out by over 500 British and Irish workmen and 1,200 Italian prisoners of war. It was a formidable task and one not without its risks; ten lives were lost in completing it.

---

* Winston S. Churchill, *The Second World War*, Vol. I, Chapter 23.

It was a sombre war for the Italians, living on a bare island and suffering the very un-Mediterranean climate of Orkney. But they left behind them a remarkable memorial of their captivity. A member of the W.R.N.S. described an outing later in the war.

¶ I remember going on a visit to a small island where the Italian prisoners of war lived who were building the causeways. We were shown how these men – far away from home – had built their own Italy in the north of Scotland. They had taken a Nissen hut and turned it into a cathedral. An artist had painted paper so like stone that it looked immovable. The blacksmith had done all the ironwork for the altar screen, and the altar had embroidered cloths, paintings, and candles in brass holders. Every object had been made out of scrap and the result was a sight to behold.[10]

The chapel still stands, the only building on a small green island, and is one of the sights of Orkney. The prisoner who carried out the painting – now a successful artist in Italy – returned in recent years to touch up his work. A committee of Orkney people watches over it and, once a year, on the Sunday nearest to the anniversary of the sinking of the *Royal Oak*, Mass is celebrated there. The Italian Chapel too, in its way, like St Magnus' Cathedral, is a memorial to the great battleship sunk in 1939 in Scapa Bay.

To some extent the building of the Churchill Barriers – as they came to be known – was a psychological rather than a strategic necessity. The fortress gates, in fact, were already closed; the barriers added a reassuring if costly portcullis. The Germans would not attempt Scapa again.

Indeed, the defence that above all guaranteed the security of the Fleet in Scapa Flow for the rest of the war was not so much the barriers at sea-level as the impregnable barrier overhead. For this war did in fact become to a substantial degree the war in the air that everyone expected. Coventry and London were forerunners of Dresden and Hiroshima. The fact that the Home Fleet in Scapa never suffered the kind of attack that savaged the American Fleet in Pearl Harbor was due to that remarkable phenomenon known to everyone who served in these northern islands as the 'Orkney Barrage'.

17

The Orkney Barrage

Looking back at the history of the two world wars, it seems as if the only people who never forgot the vital importance of making Scapa Flow a secure rendezvous for the Fleet were the men of Orkney. While Whitehall was neglecting its obligations and ignoring dangers ahead, the islanders were drilling and training in a military tradition that went back to the eighteenth century.

In 1914 it was the spare-time soldiers of the Orkney and Shetland Volunteers who shouldered the burden of guarding the unprotected shores of the Flow until the Royal Marines could take over. Fortunately for the Navy and the nation, the Orcadians kept the tradition going between the wars, as part of the Territorial Army. Within their encircling islands lay a priceless national asset. They quietly made it their business to be ready, whenever the call should come, to man the defences of the Flow again. When the war came at last, Orkney could muster the 266 Heavy Anti-Aircraft Battery R.A. (T.A.), the Orkney Heavy Regiment R.A. (T.A.), and the Orkney Fortress Engineers (commanded by Major Eric Linklater).

In September 1939, 226 Battery took on the anti-aircraft defence of the Naval base and anchorage. The Orkney Heavy Regiment manned the coastal guns at Stanger Head, Ness and Stromness, assisted by the Orkney Fortress Engineers on the searchlights. With the arrival of reinforcements of men and material, the Orkney troops were eventually regrouped into three regiments mustering nineteen batteries between them.

These loyal Territorials were the nucleus around which the Orkney and Shetland Defence Force (O.S.D.E.F.) was built. Massive artillery support arrived from the south. All over the islands there sprang up anti-aircraft sites with supporting searchlight batteries; balloon barrages against dive bombers and aerial torpedoes; more coastal defence guns overlooking the entrances to the Flow. There were intermittent air-raids but they were promptly beaten off.

When in March, 1940, the anchorage was considered safe for its return, the Fleet added its own guns to the strength of the defences. Now Orkney could put up a barrage that was deadlier even than that of Malta, through which enemy aircraft dare not pass.

The last big bombing attack on Scapa came on 10 April 1941. Between fifty and sixty enemy planes took part. They were met with such concentrated fire that for the remainder of the war only an occasional reconnaissance plane, flying very high, dared to approach the main anchorage of the British Fleet.

Inevitably, however, it was precisely their success in frightening the enemy away which recoiled upon the defenders themselves. From the sailors in the First World War waiting for the Germans to come out, to the gunners in the Second waiting for them to come over, Scapa Flow must have housed more highly-trained and under-employed men than any other theatre of war. To be ceaselessly on watch, without hope of a crack at the enemy, and yet always to be alert and at the peak of efficiency called for the stiffest kind of morale.

Most of the time was spent waiting by the guns. One night in three was spent entirely on duty. On other nights a man was at two minutes' call. The guns were manned throughout the day – one-third of the battery ready for immediate action and another third on reserve.

They took up rug-making, ship-modelling, lamp-shade making, to help to pass the weary hours of the night watch, while the war went on, rather more noisily, in other places.

¶ Our main and strongest emotion, I'm sure, was frustration at our enforced inactivity in that remote backwater at a time when most of our comrades of the A.-A. Command were firing themselves shell-happy in the blitz. Believe me, we envied them.

Mud, cold, darkness and wind formed the general background. We found our way about the site on a precarious network of duckboards. The cold was such that there were times when I couldn't understand how water could feel so cold and yet remain unfrozen. It never really got light at all and the gloom of midday was more depressing than the night itself.

* * *

¶ The order of the day was practice, practice, and more practice. Irrespective of weather or times of day or night, we moved out to practice firing – dragging guns through mud and peat, sleeping and living rough, more than often soaked to the skin, from one end of the island to the other and back. There were innumerable 'stand-tos' in the middle of the night in temperatures below freezing, with everyone asking if Jerry was on his way – came dawn and the 'stand down', with the inevitable crack that Jerry had taken one look at the place and b—d off![2]

* * *

¶ The Army Kinema Corps provided a mobile cinema which visited the site weekly, generally on a Saturday or Sunday afternoon. It was inevitable that in the middle of a show the alarm whistles would sound and we would turn out for the weekly visit of a German recce plane. The frequency of this occurrence was such that many felt certain that the German Air Force were in possession of the film roster and paid his visit just to keep us on our toes.

During our service there the provision for ground defence was shocking, considering the Flow was the most important Naval base in the country. There were never enough rifles to go round – most of our unit were equipped with 'pikes' – long broomsticks with a bayonet fixed to the end – and one old Lewis machine-gun. If the rest of the islands were as ill-equipped, a landing force could have captured Scapa intact in a few hours.[3]

* * *

¶ My unit, 302/99th (London Welsh) H.A.A. Regiment, R.A., left Felixstowe in spring, 1941. Our final destination was a camp some three miles out from the little village of St Margaret's Hope on South Ronaldsay.

We were there until mid-1942 and saw very little action the whole time, with not half-a-dozen shoots at high-flying Germans, and a dawn-till-dusk stand-to at the time the 1st U.S. Task Force arrived – *Wasp*, *Wichita* and *Washington* were the names we heard. There were practice shoots and the usual camp fatigues; daily maintenance of equipment and lining up of guns and predictors – and such jobs as painting the sloping sides of our Nissen huts with water paint, even though at the time it had started to pour with rain. But they had to give us something to do.[4]

* * *

¶ One cannot think of Orkney during wartime without mentioning *schemes*.

These were thought up by the powers that be to keep us on the alert and try out tactics, etc. Unfortunately for the poor old soldiers they always occurred at week-ends – from after duty Saturday till late on Sunday night, with everyone, needless to say, confined to camp.

It was usually the infantry or the commandos etc. attacking one particular camp, and one couldn't be sure whose, as there were such a lot of camps all around. You would hear bangs and shouts going on and wonder if you would be next.

On one such occasion we had been confined to camp, and had been alerted on and off all Saturday afternoon and two or three times during the evening. Each time it meant grabbing your rifle and dashing to man the defences, and everybody was fed up.

About 1.30 A.M. on Sunday morning, we were all dozing on our beds, ready for any emergency, when in dashed the officer in charge. 'Man the defences,' he shouted, 'the enemy is about', and off he went. We were so fed up, someone said, 'So-and-so the defences, it's another false alarm', so no one stirred. The next moment the Nissen hut door was flung open, in poured black-faced troops, they let off fireworks, bangs, smoke, yells, and out they went through the other door.

Needless to say we had a good ticking off when it was all over. Bad show, chaps! etc.[5]

* * *

¶ While I was up in the Orkneys there was very little aerial attention from the Germans. In fact most of the time we forgot about the war altogether: we were far too busy trying to keep warm and dry amid the endless gales which swept the merciless rain in grey horizontal streaks across the darkling waters of Scapa Flow. But when there was an air-raid warning, or a practice, all the fire and thunder of Dante's *Inferno* was let loose. Punctuating the slow *stam . . . ! stam . . . ! stam . . . !* of the steel-hooded 5·2-inch Army anti-aircraft guns would be the *pom! pom! pom!* of the cluster of pom-pom guns mounted on the *Iron Duke*. And over all a cloud-puffed screen of bursting shells.[6]

When the Army and Navy joined forces every now and again to unloose the famous Orkney barrage, the experience was positively therapeutic for the men of the batteries.

¶ There were periodic trials of the Scapa Barrage, an anti-aircraft box barrage said to be deadlier than Malta's, and, although this was never tried out under battle conditions, to participate in its operation was a great experience. All vessels in the Flow would combine with the land forces to put this up. The noise was frightening, and the Orcadian population of sea-birds would take the air in their thousands, only to suffer many casualties.[7]

* * *

¶ Just to ensure that every man woke up at least once a month, the Orkney barrage was fired. Every anti-aircraft gun on the Islands would put out intense fire and all the ships would join in, and for one minute there would be a deafening roar as thousands of shells screamed skywards.

The islands would seem to vibrate. The roar would echo and re-echo amongst the cliffs and hills and as it grew fainter the great slumber would again descend. And the billowing clouds would play around the island hills waiting for the next gale.[8]

Perhaps, as they looked out upon the Fleet confidently going about its business in the peaceful waters of the Flow under that great, invisible umbrella which was held over it, the Army felt some small glow of pride. Perhaps – but as one N.C.O. said at the time, just one Messerschmitt a week would have kept them perfectly happy.

18

'In from Out'

There was one vital difference between the role of the Grand Fleet in the First World War and that of the Home Fleet twenty-five years later. There was no possibility of a battle of the giants this time. Neither Admiral Forbes nor the C.-in-C.s who succeeded him expected to fight another Jutland because Hitler's Navy was radically different from the Kaiser's. It had as its principal elements a high-mettled and rapidly growing U-boat force, and a handful of ultra-modern and immensely powerful capital ships and cruisers, whose intended function was to move rapidly about the oceans in pairs or alone and to concentrate on the killing of merchant ships and convoys. They were to be raiders; the last thing that they were expected to do was to challenge the British Home Fleet to a stand-up battle of the big guns.

In these circumstances the duty of the Home Fleet was to confront these highly armed warships whenever they put to sea, and in the meantime to concentrate on the steady routine of patrolling the seas and getting the convoys through. The result was a war of ceaseless vigilance, of constant and wearisome activity for some, of a good deal of waiting for others. It was a war in which the occasional dramatic encounter got the headlines, but the long arduous grind of the battle for the sea-lanes ensured the victory.

But before the Home Fleet could settle to this new pattern of war, there was the brief, dispiriting Norwegian campaign of April to May 1940. The beginning of April found Scapa full of ships ready to forestall any German move against Norway, but when the German invasion fleet sailed on the 7th the Admiralty mistook the unaccustomed activity in the North Sea for an attempt to smuggle the battle-cruisers *Scharnhorst* and *Gneisenau* into the Atlantic and failed to take appropriate action. Thus the Germans struck at Norway without meeting the swift intervention that had been prepared for them; and when to their seizure of Norwegian ports was added the capture of airfields in both Norway and Denmark, they established themselves in an almost impregnable position. The British made a number of landings on Norwegian soil, of which the most important was their assault on Narvik, but under constant and effective air-attack their withdrawal was only a matter of time. Hitler's successful drive into France in early May – which turned Norway into a sideshow – was the final argument. By the end of that month all operations in Norway had been abandoned.

The Norwegian episode was a failure, but it had its moments of outstanding heroism, as when Captain Warburton-Lee in H.M.S. *Hardy* led his flotilla of five destroyers up the fjord towards Narvik and challenged the ten German destroyers lying there. He sank two and damaged three others, but on withdrawing ran into five more. Thus trapped between two fires, the British lost two of their ships – the *Hunter*, which was sunk, and Warburton-Lee's own *Hardy*, which was so badly damaged that she had to be beached.

A member of the crew of one of Scapa's boom-defence vessels remembered the departure of this force on its dangerous mission.

¶ Being on a 'gate' boat, I saw many ships leave never to get back, and the most outstanding memory of all was to see Captain Warburton-Lee lead his flotilla of five destroyers out one day. He was standing alone on the top bridge, legs astride, and waving his cap to all as they left the boom. On the ship's hailer was played an old gramophone record of 'A-hunting we will go!' Truly a wonderful sight of a great man, marred a few days later on hearing he had died on the beach in Norway and had been awarded the V.C.[1]

Equally remarkable was the heroism of the destroyer *Glowworm* in ramming the German cruiser *Hipper* (though the full story of this incident was not known until after the war, when the *Glowworm's* few survivors were released from their German prison camp), and that of the destroyers *Acasta* and *Ardent*, who were discovered by the *Scharnhorst* and *Gneisenau* while escorting the carrier *Glorious* home from Norway. They steamed straight towards their powerful opponents at full speed and, though they failed to save the *Glorious* and were themselves swiftly despatched by the German battle-cruisers, they did not go down without inflicting a crucial blow, since the *Acasta* was able to strike the *Scharnhorst* with a torpedo which put her out of effective action for six months.

A new and important lesson of the Norwegian campaign was that air-power was to be as much a factor of the war at sea as it was of the war on land. Almost all the German Navy was involved in Norway but it was the German Air Force which made the British attempts to seize coastal key-points so difficult. The cruiser *Suffolk* brought this discovery home to the garrison of the Flow in vivid form when she returned from her bombardment of Stavanger airfield, having suffered nearly seven hours of continuous air-attack during her withdrawal. A Marine of H.M.S. *Rodney* was amongst those who watched her arrival.

¶ I remember H.M.S. *Suffolk* limping into the Flow early one morning, her stern low in the water from bombing. Volunteers were called for from the more senior men to go over to her to sort out the casualties and dead sustained during her action off Norway.[2]

'The pitiful *Suffolk* with her back broken' was an ex-R.A.F. man's evocative description of her as she came in with her quarterdeck awash through Hoxa Sound. But the *Suffolk* was shortly to be back in service and to play a significant role in one of the most famous naval episodes of the Second World War.

After the German seizure of Norway and the defeat of France, the Royal Navy resumed as its paramount duty in Atlantic and northern waters the task of ensuring that the sea-lanes to Britain were kept open. Grand Admiral Raeder, Hitler's Naval Commander-in-Chief, saw the role of the German Navy in precisely opposite terms:

It is imperative to concentrate all the forces of the Navy and the Air Force for the purpose of interrupting all supply shipments to Britain. This must be our chief operational objective in the war against Britain.

The battle was now fully joined. Already the U-boats were taking a high toll in the Atlantic, and by late 1940 Raeder was preparing to launch his fast and superbly armed capital ships on to the ocean highways. The *Scheer*, *Hipper*, *Scharnhorst* and *Gneisenau* were fully ready for action, and two more ships were not far from completion – the cruiser *Prinz Eugen* and the huge battleship *Bismarck*.

Through the winter of 1940–1 the Home Fleet carried out a series of sorties from Scapa following reports that one or more of Germany's raiders had put to sea. But their speed, their policy of avoiding contact with superior or even inferior forces and the vastness of the Atlantic made the task of tracking them extremely difficult. The British steamed thousands of miles but failed to bring any of them to book.

In May 1941, however, news reached the Admiralty that the *Bismarck* and the *Prinz Eugen* had slipped north to Bergen in Norway and were obviously poised for a major incursion into the sea-lanes. The *Bismarck* in particular was a remarkable and formidable opponent. She was 42,500 tons, and, in Churchill's words, 'a masterpiece of naval construction'. Before they sailed from Germany, Hitler had inspected his new ships and addressed their crews. He had especially warm words for the men of the *Bismarck*. 'You are the pride of the Navy,' he told them.

If one ship more than any other was considered the pride of the British Navy it was H.M.S. *Hood*. She was not new, having been launched in 1918, but she was at 42,100 tons the biggest ship in the Fleet, powerful in her armament and handsome in her design. She was, however, not a battleship but a battle-cruiser, similar in concept to the beautiful but vulnerable 'Cats' of Admiral Beatty. These two giants were soon to meet in memorable and, for the British, tragic circumstances.

Orkney played an important part in the opening stages of the *Bismarck* action. It was an experienced observer from the Royal Naval Air Station at Hatston, Commander G. R. Rotherham,

R.N., with Lieutenant (A) N. N. Goddard, R.N.V.R. as his pilot, who made the vital discovery that the Bergen fjords, where the *Bismarck* and the *Prinz Eugen* had temporarily dropped anchor, were empty. The Germans were out and the hunt was on.

By the time Commander Rotherham had signalled his message to Admiral Tovey (the Home Fleet's new Commander-in-Chief), the *Hood* and the new battleship *Prince of Wales* were already well north of Scapa. Their destination was Denmark Strait, the channel between Greenland and Iceland which, it was considered, the Germans were most likely to use as their point of entry into the Atlantic. On patrol in the Strait were the two cruisers *Norfolk* and *Suffolk*. Vice-Admiral Holland, in command of the British heavy ships and flying his flag in the *Hood*, was to give support to the cruisers and attempt to bring the enemy to battle.

In the early evening of 23 May the *Suffolk* sighted the *Bismarck* and the *Prinz Eugen* off the north-western corner of Iceland. Thereafter she and the *Norfolk* shadowed the German force from just beyond extreme gun range while the *Hood* and the *Prince of Wales* closed in at high speed.

Unfortunately, when the British finally engaged their opponents the next day they did so from a position of some disadvantage. The shadowing cruisers had lost contact with the Germans for a short period during the night and in that brief time-gap the British capital ships had 'lost bearing' on the enemy – in other words, instead of being head on to him they had fallen astern. Because of this, when they sighted the two raiders at dawn on the 24th the British were considerably less well placed than the Germans to use their fire-power. Moreover the range was such that shells directed at the *Hood* were more likely to plunge on to her relatively unprotected decks than hit her more adequately armoured sides.

Bernard Campion saw the ensuing action from the *Prince of Wales*.

¶ We had all been at our 'action stations' since midnight, which meant that the first watchmen of the previous night had been on duty for nearly ten hours. However, there were few thoughts of sleep as, festooned with anti-flash clothing of white asbestos, inflatable life-belts, intercommunication telephones and so forth, we prepared for the coming Armageddon.

At 5.53 A.M. the guns of all four ships roared into action simultaneously, from a rapidly closing range of 25,000 yards. The *Bismarck* concentrated her fire on the *Hood*, while the *Prinz Eugen* took on the *Prince of Wales*. Almost immediately shells from the *Bismarck* penetrated the *Hood* from a high angle about her after-turret, engulfing her quarter-deck in flames. Seconds later the pride of our pre-war Navy disintegrated in a deafening explosion with fragments flying in all directions as a column of orange cordite flame and thick black smoke shot upwards into the grey sky.

A minute or so afterwards an 8-inch shell from the *Prinz Eugen* crashed into our bridge, killing most of the personnel working there. I was in the remote control radio office, situated well up the fore-superstructure just below this carnage, and through the vertical voicepipes connecting the two positions the blood of the casualties came down, splashing over our signal pads and operating keys. In the midst of the confusion the navigating officer burst in with the flesh hanging down from his shrapnelled cheek and a blood-soaked signal in his hand for us to code and transmit. It began with the chilling words, '*Hood* sunk'.

Ask me for the most terrifying memory I could conjure up from my twenty-seven years in the Royal Navy in peace or war and without hesitation I would recall that bleak early morning of Saturday 21 May 1941, when we – in Britain's newest battleship – saw the proudest and most powerful of our battle-cruisers disintegrate before our eyes, leaving us not only stunned by this unbelievable loss but also alone, badly damaged, taking in water, afire in several places, one quadruple 14-inch turret jammed and other big guns unable to bear – within virtually point-blank range of two highly efficient German warships, both unscathed as far as we then knew.[3]

The *Prince of Wales's* signal was flashed instantly back to the Fleet base.

¶ I have a vivid recollection of the news arriving at Scapa that the *Hood* had been sunk. A signal had just been received from her saying that she was engaging the enemy at extreme range and her position and that of the *Bismark* had been plotted on the huge wall map. The *Prince of Wales* then signalled the bald message 'Hood sunk', and I remember the messenger – I believe it was one of the Paymaster staff – bringing the signal to Captain Weld, R.N. who was in charge of the operations room where I was on duty, and he could not believe it. He ordered the messenger to take the signal to the signals officer personally to check the decoding, whereupon the signals officer appeared to confirm the message. The silence was unbearable.[4]

There were only three survivors from the *Hood's* complement of ninety-five officers and 1,324 men.

Four days later the *Hood* was avenged. The hunting of the *Bismarck* was a drawn-out and complex operation that involved naval units from Scapa to Gibraltar. At one time it seemed as if she would escape, but Swordfish aircraft from the Gibraltar-based *Ark Royal* attacked her as she raced towards Brest and succeeded in immobilizing her steering engine. Many ships had a hand in her despatch, the *coup de grâce* being delivered by the torpedoes of the cruiser *Dorsetshire*, which was sailing northwards with a convoy from West Africa when the chase began.

Such moments of high drama – and tragedy – were rare. For the ships of the Home Fleet it was more often a war of drudgery without exhilaration; of patrols so routine and wearisome that they were simply not worth talking about during one's few days of respite in the Flow.

'In from out' had been the catch-phrase of the First War; now it was revived in the Second. For the men whose ships were mostly on the move, who were more often battling with the North Atlantic than resting in harbour, that was precisely what Scapa was. There, thanks to those innumerable guns ringed round the Flow, they were safe from the enemy. They could lie in, get some sleep, look around them, have a run ashore, forget a little, before going back to war.

¶ Scapa was the haven to which we would come after weeks at sea. Here we would long for the homeliness of familiar streets

– blacked-out and blitzed though they were. When the first excitement of war had worn off we would come to long for the sound of a woman's voice – of footsteps on pavements, or the aroma of food being cooked in a civilized kitchen.[5]

* * *

¶ Scapa seemed bleak. Yet a month later when we returned from convoy duty, we were ready to see it in a more favourable light. At least it was calm and you had 'all night in'.[6]

For the men caught up in this interminable routine of long spells at sea interwoven with periods of quiet inactivity in the Flow, it often seemed as if they would remain in their strange limbo world indefinitely, as if nothing would ever change.

¶ There was the temptation to become settled in one's cooped-up ways of living on board ship. Though there were cinema shows most evenings, men tended to foregather in small groups or 'cabooses'. These were generally small compartments – sometimes offices – not used for any official purpose during off-duty hours. Here the bright lights and piping days of peace would be discussed. Here the place and time of the long-expected Second Front might be 'divulged', together with the part our own ship was to play in the operation. Doubt would then be expressed that we would ever be released from the monotonous runs we were continually being ordered to carry out off the coast of northern Norway.

'Of course,' some rumour-monger would point out, 'that's where the Second Front will be!'

These trips were of little more than nuisance-value to the enemy, but they often ended in death for someone. Sometimes we might lose a pilot or an observer – sometimes it might be a rating of the flight-deck crew. No one could tell who would be the next to go; yet these niggling losses went on. A stray bullet – not necessarily an enemy one – or a mishap occurring during landing-on, and another Union Jack-draped coffin would disappear over the ship's side.[7]

One consequence of such actions as that against the *Bismarck* was an increasing reluctance on Hitler's part to put his surface raiders at risk. Inevitably, this meant less work for the big ships of the Royal Navy, whose sailors found themselves caught in the kind of doldrum that had so exasperated the men of the Grand Fleet twenty-five years earlier. The Fleet flagship *King George V* even earned herself at one period the nickname of 'H.M.S. Neverbudge'. As in the First War, it was a case of 'waiting for them to come out' and 'swinging round the buoy'.

¶ One got very bored. The B.B.C. news was always grim in those grim days and when the German blitz started, particularly on the naval ports of Portsmouth and Plymouth, an occasional officer, sailor or Royal Marine would be sent hurriedly on a few days' leave, usually to bury his dead wife or mother, killed by the bombs.[8]

* * *

¶ Harbour routine at Scapa was the same day after day: clean guns; clean ship; watch-keeping; divisions; evening quarters; store parties and sometimes a day on the Island of Flotta doing military training and fraternizing with the local crofters and A.-A. gunsite crews based on the island. Their lot was more monotonous than ours. I remember tombola, the odd film show. Someone leaves the ship under observation – suspected mental-case. I wonder there were not more.

Another recollection was a submarine scare in Scapa Flow itself. The Fleet raced to sea at action stations while the Flow was given a depth charge pounding by our destroyers. Forty thousand tons of our ship shaking like a leaf. God help the submarine!

Back in the Flow again and settle down to harbour routine. A storeship manoeuvring alongside. What sort of Yankee or Canadian food or stores are we getting this time? The chap who had the dogs – middle and forenoon watch – was not interested. He had his 'make and mend' and 'all night in' to look forward to. Eat, sleep and work was our life in the big ships at Scapa Flow during the Second World War.[9]

As in the First War, the United States Navy came to the Flow. With the men of the Royal Navy in Scapa, the Americans left two abiding impressions – their totally different way of doing things, and their generosity.

¶ I recall the arrival of the Yanks, especially the U.S.S. *Washington*, and their impressive slow entrance into the Flow. Lieutenant, or Lieutenant-Commander Douglas Fairbanks Jr soon came ashore in his capacity of liaison officer.

A number of British officers were invited to dine aboard U.S.S. *Washington* and I was one of the fortunate ones. An American officer was detailed to look after each guest and after a sumptuous meal which seemed incredible after the rations on which we had become accustomed to subsist, we were more or less given the freedom of the ship and our escorts guided us round every deck.

I was amazed that no rating attempted to come to attention on the approach of officers but continued with their noisy game of 'Crap' and betting money was in full evidence all the time. The space between the mess-decks seemed massive.

Naturally the Yanks wanted to play baseball and a football pitch was allocated to them. They came ashore laden with gear and also cardboard cartons containing canned beer. Unfortunately, no one had warned them that foxholes had been dug alongside the road and, as was inevitable at Scapa, had filled with water upon which a scum had formed, making them appear to be part of the field. The Yank with the canned beer walked right into a foxhole and the beer sank to the bottom. Spectators and players were soon diving head first in to salvage it.[10]

* * *

¶ One thing I can't forget: when the American ships were in the Flow, many times when the wind and tide were in the right direction, they chucked boxes overboard – supposed to be empty. In those boxes were tinned peaches and cream, fresh fruit and all sorts of good things that we had almost forgotten. Bless those Yanks![11]

As well as the Fleet's warships resting in Scapa between convoys and patrols, there were also those other ships that were permanently 'in', whose duties never shifted them from their moorings – the base ships.

¶ I was posted to H.M.S. *Iron Duke*, Jellicoe's old flagship doing duty as a base ship for armed trawlers and M.L.s, which left her dingy, grey sides to patrol the island seas.

To those in her the *Iron Duke* was a cold, lonely, inconvenient, ship. Her unnecessary, motionless guns mocked her former glory; she rested ignominiously on the sea-bottom in Longhope Sound. It came as a surprise to learn that her magazines still contained 13·5 inch shells. Might she still fire in anger? Or were her shells just relics, as ghostly as Admiral Jellicoe's uniform in a glass cabinet down aft?'[12]

* * *

¶ I served on H.M.S. *Tyne*, the depot ship for the destroyers, from 1940–4. She was a large ship (11,000 tons) and had a large complement of below-deck ratings. The Commander of the ship during one period was a keep-fit enthusiast, and every morning at 7 A.M. most of the ship's company were called on to the upper deck and instructed to run round the complete perimeter of the ship's deck, jog-trotting along as in 'follow-my-leader'. This was invariably carried out to the tune of 'The Old Brown Cow – She Ain't What She Used To Be', played over the ship's loud-speaker system.

Looking back, I can't help wondering what any U-boat commander might have thought if, after surfacing his periscope, he espied a British warship with the whole of its crew belting round the ship's deck and up and down ladders, singing their heads off about some Old Brown Cow That Wasn't What It Once Had Been![13]

Perhaps the best known among the base ships was the *Dunluce Castle*, since hers was usually the first deck that the arriving sailor set foot on when he came to Scapa Flow. She was accommodation ship, general store house, General Post Office. She was said by Scapa sailors to be not so much floating as sitting on years of 'gash' thrown over the side. She was also remarkable as being the only vessel in the Flow to perpetuate that ancient ritual which had aroused such antipathy among the sailors of the First War – coaling ship.

¶ Although never going to sea she had steam continuously in her boilers as a great deal of work was always being done by winches and dynamos had to be kept running. To do this she burned coal.

She must have been one of the very last ships to 'coal ship', which she did every fortnight. Everyone was roped in for this – some shovelled in the collier alongside, some worked derricks or shovelled in the holds. I was one of those roped in to run backwards and forwards with sacks on a sort of porter's barrow. We began at 6 A.M. At 6.30 a large wireless loud speaker wished us good morning and received a sarcastic answer from the men. From then on the B.B.C. programmes continued to entertain us. There was a break for breakfast and stand-easy, then with music while we worked we went on till noon, when followed the no less arduous task of getting clean.

On all other days the men's work was unbelievably monotonous – tying up ships alongside, loading mail and stores – and coaling ship was really a welcome break in the monotony.[14]

Another familiar sight off Lyness was the Royal Fleet Auxiliary *Demeter*.

¶ In 1943 I, an Admiralty civil servant, was appointed to the *Demeter*, a storeship moored in Gutter Sound. We carried three holds of naval stores, two of victuals and one of N.A.A.F.I. and our task was to supply these items as required to warships and auxiliaries based on Scapa.

She was a Swedish cargo liner, formerly the *Buenos Aires*, but a mine had cracked her bedplates and she was therefore a hulk, but a very active one with full auxiliary machinery. Her winches were constantly on the go taking in bulk supplies from small coasters up from Aberdeen and issuing stores to vessels alongside – anything from a motor boat to a destroyer. The ship was manned by Merchant Navy personnel and Admiralty civil servants. The ship's officers were mainly Royal Fleet Auxiliary personnel recalled from retirement, and some who had had an arduous time at sea and were in need of a respite.

We were allowed leave three times a year. Once I did not bother to go ashore between leaves. After the novelty had worn off there was little to go to Lyness for – a film show or a drink of the bloating wash that wartime beer had become.

During our leisure hours we played table tennis; walked interminably up and down the boat deck; read, wrote letters and played chess. Sometimes we would fry eggs on the bottom of an electric iron in someone's cabin. Sometimes we rowed in the bosun's skiff or sailed in one of the ship's lifeboats. Always there were ships to watch, the sunsets and the subtly changing colours of the heathers, lichens and scrub on the treeless islands surrounding us.[15]

The Home Fleet, in fact, was more than the sum of the ships in – or out of – the Flow. It was kept fully operational by a massive team of administrators and craftsmen who got little of the glory for their hard labour. Among these few had a more important role than the men of the Navy's Construction Department – the 'repair-men' of the Fleet.

¶ We base workers had the job of keeping the Fleet in good shape and fighting trim. We went out to the Fleet and sailed with the ships when time did not allow repairs to be completed in the Flow.

I well remember a little Scots iron caulker being sent out to a certain battle-cruiser to carry out repairs in one of the oil tanks. He went off on the Monday and didn't turn up at the base camp until five days later.

'Where the hell have you been?' we asked him when he got back to the mess.

'Ah came up for my snap,' he said, 'and we was half way up the bleeding North Sea chasing the – *Bismarck*.

I myself was carrying out repairs on the cruiser *Sheffield* afloat in the Flow when she suddenly put to sea. My mate and I were down in the bowels of the ship working by feeble lights in an empty oil tank. Suddenly my driller went into the ship's bottom a little too far, and a great gout of water shot up over both of us. 'What's that?' he said, nearly falling over his own air hose.

'Scapa Flow, you bloody idiot. Did you expect the Medway?'[16]

It is almost impossible to recapture the infinite varieties of mood of the men who found themselves 'in from out' in Scapa in the days of war. There was relief at escaping from the dangers outside, fear of returning to them; boredom, war-weariness, frustration; determination, a mature acceptance of whatever was to come; and – at the sight of this still great armada riding at anchor in the security of the Flow – a sense of pride, even of awe.

¶ To a very Ordinary Seaman aboard a light cruiser swinging round the buoy in the winter of 1940, Scapa Flow was a desolate place. Lonely too when the weather clamped down, and the snow, driven by frenzied winds made it impossible to see even the ship moored nearest to your own.

But when the gale had blown itself out overnight, and the dawn arrived brilliantly, chasing away the last clouds of that wild storm, then the sense of loneliness disappeared, and a mood of utter peace and majesty took over.

The large expanse of water would be as smooth as glass. Only the sound of gulls would break the stillness. There would be no wind, and the smoke from the drifters would rise into the cold air and then smudge horizontally over the Flow in opposite directions. Shielding one's eyes against the bright rays of the morning sun one could make out the enormous shapes of the battleships and battle-cruisers of the Home Fleet – the *Nelson*, the *Rodney*, the *Hood*, the *Renown*, the *Prince of Wales* – all still and awe-inspiring, as the sky overhead changed colour as would the sky-cloth of a theatre.

I remember thinking of a line from a hymn: 'As Earth's proud Empires pass away . . .' and reflecting that this Empire would surely never pass away as long as it could muster such a force.[17]

19

The Small Ships

'There always seemed to be a certain amount of resentment between the men on the small ships and those who served on the big capital ships,' wrote a Wren. 'If a drifter passed within hailing distance of, say, H.M.S. *Rodney*, any sailor visible would be asked: "Wot's it like living in barracks, mate?"'

'When people speak of the Royal Navy and its part during the war,' wrote a veteran of the minesweepers, 'the general imagination is of great battleships, aircraft-carriers, cruisers, etc.; of well-dressed commanding officers pacing their well-kept bridges, the epitome of Noel Coward in the film 'In Which We Serve'. But the facts were entirely different. The very nature of operations called for small units of every size, shape and purpose, to be crewed by men different from the peacetime regulars.'

'A marine menagerie,' somebody called it. There were the boom-defence vessels, minesweepers, steam drifters, motorized fishing vessels, and even a number of yachts. For the men in the small ships, service in the Second War differed hardly at all from the First in its undeviating monotony and discomfort.

The distances to be covered in Scapa Flow were such that it was considered essential for efficiency and morale in harbour for each battleship and cruiser to have a drifter attached. Aircraft-carriers had two.

A network of ferries served most of the islands around the Flow and a regular two-hourly routine was maintained for five years. The Orcadians were allowed to take advantage of the service and to travel free.

¶ Shortly after the start of the Second World War when the Fleet had assembled in Scapa Flow, I was on board H.M.S. *Royal Oak*. I was a very young Leading Seaman at the time, twenty years of age. The *Royal Oak* was allocated three fishing drifters. I was made 2nd Coxswain of the drifter *Mist*, while the famous drifter *Daisy* was manned entirely by a crew of civilian fishermen. It was while I was on board *Mist* that I came face to face with all the varying moods of Scapa.

The *Mist* was an all steel drifter, armed with a three-pounder gun, a machine-gun and depth charges. I soon found that our duty was to guard one entrance to Scapa Flow, and the routine was to sail along the length of the boom defence, awaiting flare signals from the buoys on the nets, indicating that a submarine was caught in the nets.

After the sinking of the *Royal Oak* our duties were intensified and our off-duty spells became less frequent. At one period we steamed up and down the boom defences for seventeen days without stopping engines. We were almost all the time without fresh vegetables and meals were very monotonous. The weather at times was really foul and life was very grim. Tempers were often frayed, and having lost the bulk of our kit on the *Royal Oak*, our appearance became somewhat less Naval-like.

You can imagine how much we looked forward to being relieved of our monotonous patrol in order to go back to H.M.S. *Greenwich* in Lyness Bay to re-store. After a bath and a general tidy-up, we would be sent alongside the pier at Lyness to commence a short spell of shore leave.[1]

* * *

¶ Crewing the duty boats in the Flow was a real nightmare in bad weather, far worse than normal harbour work. One night we tied up alongside with our wheelhouse gone. Our coxswain took the pinnace under the yawning stern of a big Fleet Auxiliary in the pitch blackness and the straining stern-cable

of the merchant-man went straight through our superstructure
like a band-saw.[2]

The boom-defence vessels opened the gates for all who left
Scapa Flow and counted the losses as they returned, knowing that their vigilance made it certain that there would be no
losses *inside* the Flow. They served the Fleet with quiet and
steadfast devotion.

¶ Everyone remembers the boom-defence ships, those patient
drudges on whose monotonous work the safety of the anchorage greatly depended. A small flotilla of landing craft, coming
up from the south, was driven on to the boom in a gale. There
was a lot of damage and loss of life. Scapa could be dangerous as
well as dreary.[3]

*   *   *

¶ In one boom ship every man on hearing that volunteers were
wanted for two-man submarines offered his services . . . I remember taking prayers on the mess-deck of one ship which had just
lost five of its men. Returning from shore in the only little boat
allotted to them they had been swamped . . .To all intents and
purposes these ships were completely cut off.[4]

*   *   *

¶ Our duties were laying new nets, repairing old ones, and various other jobs to make the Fleet anchorage comparatively safe.
On one occasion a trawler on 'close-net work' around one of our
'big uns' – *KG.5.*, *Howe* or *Anson* – lifted a net only to see a torpedo hanging from it. She immediately returned to base with the
damned thing hanging over her bows. Imagine the panic when
she came alongside. This shows the nets were necessary – in this
case there could have been another *Royal Oak* disaster.[5]

The crews of the armed trawlers which patrolled the waters
outside the Flow through which the convoys passed had a

rough, tough life of it and for a lad not yet broken to the nautical life it could be a rude introduction.

¶ I went to Scapa Flow as a last-minute stop-gap because the signalman of an armed Naval trawler fell under a bus on his last night ashore following the ship's re-fit. The remark of a regular sailor in barracks as I left on draft laid sombre guide lines for the future. 'Going to sea for the first time in December, on the Northern run, in a trawler – you poor bastard!' I joined the ship in West Hartlepool and was sick before we cleared the river. The 1st Lieutenant, hearty rather than kind, hit me between the shoulders as I retched miserably over the rail and cracked the hoary quip about 'If there's any good in a boy the sea will bring it out'. He also cautioned me that should a small circle appear on my tongue I was to swallow it – 'for Christ's sake' – for that would be my anus. I sat on the steps of the gun platform where the cook obligingly passed me platefuls of rice pudding which I ate and immediately spewed over the convenient rail. But one day I wasn't sick any more. I could stand with the watch going on duty and urinate in the scuppers before climbing to the bridge and guns.

When Christmas came we were ordered to lie alongside H.M.S. *Nelson*. No one seemed to know why. To give us a better Christmas, we heard, and were doubtful, since it meant scouring the ship as for an Admiral's inspection and wearing our No. 1 uniforms instead of comfortable dungarees and sea boots. 'So they can look over the side and see a ship that really goes to sea,' said Jock. There was an unkind legend that ships like *Nelson* only moved from their moorings when the 'gash' (rubbish) thrown over board accumulated to the extent that they went aground on it.

We cleaned ship and ourselves and went alongside *Nelson*, feeling like a rowing boat as we looked up at her. We were certainly made welcome. We went to the ship's cinema, lying on palliasses in the 'flats' (open spaces between decks), munching 'nutty' (chocolate) and watching 'A Yank at Oxford'. Some of us went to church, through a carved Gothic door so deep in the ship one seemed to leave Scapa and the Navy entirely and be back at home on a Sunday.

We ate Christmas Dinner aboard our own ship, but the food ('big eats' we said) came from the *Nelson*. We fetched the gravy in our big tea kettle (we were always short of utensils in a trawler) and the *Nelson's* 'chef' raised his eyebrows 'so high his flickin' cap was nigh pushed off' said the gravy carrier.[6]

In the vast and complex defence system which protected Scapa Flow, the role of the minesweeper was 'monotonous, hard and miserable' and yet the veteran of that service who wrote the following graphic account of life aboard one of the trawlers could speak of it with affection.

¶ I was sent from the *Dunluce Castle* to the base at Lyness, to see the Commanding Officer Minesweeping, Commander Bull, in company with a few more rookies. We must have looked a miserable sight to him, young, tired, uniform askew, not knowing or caring much about anything.

I eventually was drafted to the magnetic and acoustic trawler, H.M.T. *Michael Griffith*; an uninspiring name, but I was to be part of her crew for over two years, and I grew to love her, as only men can love their ships, which, after all, become their homes.

The trawler had in fact been built for the 1914 war by the Navy, who had built a couple of hundred of her class to be used for minesweeping and other duties. Between the wars she, like the others, had been sold to fishing companies. The Second World War found the majority of these ships under the White Ensign again.

The earlier part of the war found these trawlers manned by a curious crew. The Skippers (that was their official title) were either British fishing skippers or quite often Norwegian ones, with a rookie 1st Lieutenant of the Volunteer Reserve – wartime Navy officers. The rest of the crew was as follows – hard-bitten seamen and stokers, nearly all fishermen, who had been on the reserve in peace-time, getting reserve pay and hoping that a war would never come; and young fellows like myself average age about twenty, who were new to the sea, but who had been trained as signalmen, telegraphists, electricians, motor-mechanics, radar and asdic operators – tech in other words. So there was quite a strain in these crews; the young ones were more fright-ened of these rock-hard fishermen than of the enemy. They in turn resented the fact that they had been caught up with the war, and were on a very low rate of pay, compared with their mates who were still fishing and making fortunes.

They disliked us because our duties excused us doing the more menial jobs of work aboard; they thought they had to be the lackies of young, ignorant boys. We were certainly ignorant of the sea, but at least we did master our own jobs, which were new to everyone, and in the event the lives of the crew quite often depended on us doing our job well.

The massive expanse of the minesweeping service, including more and more ships, as the war progressed, lessened the dif-ference in the make-up of crews – later most of the crews were young men, 'hostilities only' ratings.

Our 'group' of minesweepers were based in Longhope Sound. We tied up to buoys on a level with the old battleship *Iron Duke*. We used to watch the ceremonial aboard the *Iron Duke*, especially on Sundays, when they had 'divisions' with all the necessary 'bull' – Marine band, marching, padre, etc. That sort of thing was of course absent on our ships.

Our job was to go out into the Flow every day, and sweep the 'channel' – the main area along which the Fleet sailed when enter-ing or leaving Scapa. We swept with an 'LL' sweep for magnetic mines, trailing two long cables which floated on the water, one cable three times the length of the other. A massive current was pumped through the cables twice a minute, which caused a magnetic field in the water, which in turn would activate a mine lying there.

For the acoustic mines, we had an 'A Frame' hinged on the bows, which carried a device in an enclosed box, which was low-ered in front of the bows, pointing in front of the ship, thereby activating an acoustic mine ahead. So we swept ahead for acous-tic, and behind for magnetic.

This was our role for days, weeks, months, and even a couple of years; the only exceptions being trips to Aberdeen for the annual refit, and other periods of duty as relief to certain places off the Scottish coast, such as Loch Ewe, where we went for a few weeks in 1941 as relief for a trawler that had gone for refit.

There was a canteen and cinema at the base at Lyness, but it took such a long time on the ferry to get to Longhope, and so long to return, that most of us never bothered going ashore. There was one period when I did not leave the ship for three months. We were more content to await our leaves, and write our hundreds of letters home.

We used to get quite a lot of things from our 'Comforts Fund' at the base. Each ship would get a sack of woollies, records, books etc. about once a month. These came from the good-hearted people at home. It was customary for everyone to draw lots when these woollies arrived. Jumpers were most popular, gloves and socks the least, and as there were only a few jumpers each time, this was considered a fair way to share them out. More often than not this resulted in a small fellow getting a long jumper, and a big chap getting socks that wouldn't go over his big toe, and all sorts of perms in between. But a lot of these woollies were very well made, and all were appreciated.

We also acquired a good selection of records – everything from symphony to the pop of the day, Bing, Geraldo, etc. One was a march called the 'Phantom Brigade', played I think by the Black Dyke Mills Band. It was adopted by us as a signature tune.

On certain nights, after the day's sweeping, we had to do a 'Scapa patrol'. That meant we had to leave our base at Longhope, and go to the Flow and watch all night; in the event of aircraft dropping mines we were to mark them.

So when we left Longhope in the evening, an old gramophone was taken to the bridge, the 'Phantom Brigade' put on through the loud hailer, and off we would go. We used to sing, 'We are off to the Scapa Patrol, Scapa Patrol', and other invented words. We usually got signs of derision from the other ships.

Commander Bull sometimes made a midnight inspection of the sweepers, whilst tied to their buoy in Longhope. There was no forewarning; it was his way of testing the watch on each ship, because, of course, one man was supposed to keep an eye on Flotta signal station for any message being flashed.

He would come alongside in a small motor boat, very silently, and if possible would creep aboard, unless he was challenged. If he managed to get aboard undetected, he would rouse the officers and the rest of the crew out and give us a thunderbolt.

When he came to inspect the ships normally in the daytime, he would line the crew up, and even though we were dressed properly in the 'rig of the day', he always said that we looked like a lot of bloody pirates.

On occasion we would go to Mill Bay near Lyness, for a boiler clean. This would take about a week. We were without heat or light, but I used to couple the ship's electrical system to the massive banks of batteries used for the sweep, so that we had light in the evening for a few hours. This was absolutely forbidden by order, but my own officers did not complain, for they got the benefit too, and the lads were very pleased to be able to write their letters and read in peace. So much for regulations.[7]

The men of the small ships had their consolations. They escaped the discipline and spit-and-polish of the big ships and many of them could boast of the fact that they were serving on 'a ship that really goes to sea'.

For them the war never let up: there was no relaxation in their duties. It was all day and every day. Small ships they may have been, but they were a vital part of the Navy and sailed under the same flag as the great ships whose names have passed into history.

¶ I saw the carriers old and new, including the *Victorious* straight from the builders. Four of the *K.G.5* class battleships – *K.G.5*, *Duke of York*, *Anson* and *Howe*. I remember the American carrier *Wasp* coming in for a period – she was later lost in the Pacific.

We watched them come and go – the great and the small – the 'big Navy', and us the 'scruff', both under the same ensign.[8]

20

'You Lucky People!'

The Navy had Orkney almost to themselves in the First World War. The Royal Marines were on shore manning the gun batteries, the Royal Naval Air Service were launching their Walruses, and Scapa Flow itself belonged exclusively to the sailors. In the Second War they had to share it.

The islands were alive with the Army and Air Force. They had started to arrive in the feverish months after the *Royal Oak* disaster and soon built up into formidable numbers. The countryside was studded with camps. There were sappers building; infantry and Pioneer Corps unloading cargoes of ammunition, vehicles, building materials; the Ordnance Corps doling out stores; aircraftmen gouging out runways for the fighter squadrons. The Fleet Air Arm stations – H.M.S. *Robin*, H.M.S. *Tern* and H.M.S. *Sparrowhawk* – and the R.A.F. stations at Skeabrae and Grimsetter flew legions of sorties covering convoys and patrolling the North Sea passage.

It was months before there was anything like adequate accommodation for such an influx of men. The primitive living conditions which prevailed in O.S.D.E.F. in the early part of the war must have been unique within the British Isles. The units on the Mainland were the best placed as conditions gradually improved, but at first there wasn't much to choose between any of them. Every unit thought they were the ones who were having the worst of it. 'You lucky people!' was a popular catch-phrase of the time. In Orkney it had a somewhat bitter ring.

¶ Our life in the Pioneer Corps was hard, dull, and monotonous. We were roused at 6.00 A.M., usually by the Orderly Sergeant running a stick along the outside of the corrugated iron sides of the Nissen huts, which had the effect of an earthquake on the sleepers inside. Rising in the total darkness – for there were only about six hours of daylight in the Orkneys at that time of year – we would huddle on our trousers and rubber boots (for we slept in the rest of our garments) and staggering and sliding in the mud, would lurch down to the ablutions ('absolutions' one Irish sergeant called them), and either in darkness or by candlelight attempted to wash and shave in icy water. I remember slipping as I emerged from the shed one morning, shooting spread-eagled into the mud. Razor flew one way, soap the other. I never recovered them, or tried to. Nor did I trouble to go back for another wash. There was no need anyway, for the first parade was held in the strange grey light of the Orkney dawn, the steely glitter of Hoy Sound catching the first light, the black mass of Hoy rising behind.

The Sergeant-Major read the detail by torch-light. We were formed in our sections, and an odd company we must have looked. No two were dressed alike, some wore oilskin jackets, many wore leather jerkins like medieval bowmen. Headgear was as diverse – Balaclavas, forage caps, usually with the flaps down, sou'westers, steel helmets, battered old cheese-cutters – there was even one individualist who wore an old trilby. Against the almost continuous rain we wore gas capes or groundsheets buttoned like cloaks. Others wore their greatcoats, but the majority preferred to keep this garment as an adjunct to their bedding. For some reason rifle-slings were scarce, so lengths of rope were used instead.

As each detail was called, they would slouch off, mess-tins clanking, to their jobs.

For the first few weeks my section was employed in building a camp at Caldale at the other end of the island. This was considered the best job of all as it entailed nearly two hours' travelling. We would assist each other into the lorry – I always liked to get near the tail-board so that I could admire the scenery – and away up the hill out of Stromness. It was just getting to full light as we passed the Top Dump, where some of our people would already be working. Then over the Bridge of Waith, where the first bomb of the Second World War fell; past the steely gleaming waters of Loch Stenness, fringed by the mysterious Standing Stones. Then on over the rounded bare hills to the cross-roads at Finstown, There was a little shop there, and the lorry always used to pull up so that one of us could slip over the tail-board to buy cigarettes, since there was always a shortage. Then on again, over the grey-green hills, until the sea appeared on the left and we were going over the long causeway into Kirkwall, often, when the wind was high, with the waves breaking right over our truck. We skirted the town, and arrived at our work site, just outside. Here we did whatever we were required – erecting Nissen huts, two or three days digging a septic tank.

Friday night was pay night, and after a pay parade by the hissing light of Tilly lamps in the mess-room, the majority of our comrades rushed off to the N.A.A.F.I. canteen to return their few poor shillings to their employers. The majority of the Company were southern Irish, and with the exception of our small band of conscripts, the remainder were men whose volunteering had been inspired by economics rather than patriotism. To them, nothing was more enjoyable than an evening's drinking, and this they were only able to enjoy one evening a week. After the first hour, the N.A.A.F.I. resembled nothing more than the saloon of a 'B' Western film.

After one experience of alcoholic affection alternating with drunken belligerence, my friend and I decided to retire to our hut. We would tuck ourselves in our blankets, and quietly write our letters home, or play a meek game of chess on his minia-ture board, until the dreaded hour when the door was flung open and they lurched in. Always some of them would fall over our recumbent bodies and roll over us, but at last they would gather themselves up and, arms round each other's shoulders, would sing in a swaying semi-circle around the stove. I never knew before that so many Irish songs had been written. As they went on they got sadder and sadder, until some of the songsters themselves were in tears. At last it would end, visitors would stagger out into the night into their own huts – you could hear the splashes as they slipped over in the mud outside – and peace would settle at last, to be broken as those of our own hut who had been visiting crept in, mud-covered in their turn, falling over us, beery, lachrymose, musical, and anecdotal. At length even they would fall asleep, and the hut would be still, the red glow of the stove on recumbent bodies, and silent but for the shattering snores and the pattering of the mice with which we abounded. They would race over the shelf over our heads, eating any food that lay there, eating our letters, engaging in vigorous races. On one occasion a mouse fell right over the edge of the shelf clean into the open mouth of the snoring Corporal below.[1]

* * *

¶ I was a nineteen-year-old aircraftman, stationed at an airfield a few miles out of Kirkwall opposite the island of Shapinsay. This place was appropriately named Grimsetter.

Compared with airfields in the rest of Britain, life at Grimsetter appeared primitive because, until the main generators arrived, there was no electricity available for lighting so that until January 1943 billets were lit by candles, each man keeping a private stock of these which he bought from the N.A.A.F.I. He also, like the Navy, had to do his own weekly laundering for which he received a half-day off; one extra soap coupon and 1s. per week extra pay. In practice, most of us did our washing in stages nightly, using the time off allowed either to go collecting unrationed eggs from the farms or to visit Kirkwall, provided one was prepared to walk miles as transport was scarce and at that time no bus services existed on the island.

With these conditions discipline had to be slightly relaxed and I can well remember the fortnightly pay parade being attended in (besides the inevitable gum boots and seamen's wool stockings) a mixture of oilskins, leather jackets and balaclava helmets. The resulting scene would have given the pay office a heart attack anywhere else.[2]

* * *

¶ As the months slipped by, we improved our lot at Orphir. We were fortunate in taking over the local church hall adjoining the camp, and there we held sing-songs, travelling cinema shows (everybody, including the locals, invited) and an occasional 'hop'. At first the dances were dead as there were few local females, but someone hit on the idea of sending trucks into Kirkwall and Stromness to collect partners and return them home after the dance. We used to refer to the trucks as 'passion wagons' but I could never understand why, as once inside the hall no one was allowed out until the dance was over, when the girls were ushered back into their respective trucks and driven home.[3]

That was the Mainland. Across the Sound, on the island of Hoy, they lived in a world of their own but there seem to have been some intrepid spirits who refused to be quenched.

¶ I was stationed on Hoy about 1941, manning a newly built twin-six battery on the shore. The only access was by walking from the road up the side of a hill and then down to the Nissen huts which were wired down by means of ropes slung over the roof and pegged into the ground because of winds of up to 100 m.p.h. All rations and stores were brought by road to the pick-up point on the hill side. Then a single file of off-watch soldiers carried stores down to the site in sacks or tea chests, whichever were available. This was a daily task which caused much slipping and sliding if the weather made the heather wet.

Another fatigue duty was picking up rocks and stones from the beach and throwing them into the paths between the huts and the beach. They seemed to disappear into the mud as fast as they were thrown in. Coal was delivered by drifter to the beach and then carried from the beach to the cookhouse.

Beer and diesel oil were brought to the camp by being rolled down the side of the hill, two soldiers to each barrel or drum. Many a drum of diesel oil ended up in the heather after striking a rock on the way down, or else fell in a hole and had to be sweated over to get out again.[4]

*   *   *

¶ The rigours of rough living in an isolated camp on Hoy imposed a severe strain even on resilient youth and I remember a feeling of horror when an outbreak of meningitis started to remove men suddenly and stealthily, some never to return.

Although the second largest of the·Orkney islands, Hoy did not boast a town or even a village of any size; indeed few inhabitants and those widely scattered in isolated crofts. There was a pub some ten miles by rough road from the camp to which as many men as could be spared from duty for an hour or two were taken by lorry once a week. Some relief from the monotony of the first dark winter was provided by fleeting visits by stars of the entertainment world. I remember vividly Evelyn Laye and Frank Lawton; Douglas Byng; Tommy Trinder and Beatrice Lillie, all of whom gave freely of their best on an improvised platform in the camp dining hut. Seldom, I think, could they have received more spontaneous and heartfelt applause.[5]

*   *   *

¶ The winter mornings were pitch black and remained so until about 11 A.M. It was terribly cold and one had to take off up the road about two hundreds yard from our battery site to the ablutions. No lights existed, so one groped around until one found a steel dish to hold the water which came from a tarn and contained brown sediment. The water was always freezing cold and one's face ached from the sting of it. Some of the chaps carried stumps of candle, about half an inch in size, which they blew out and carefully put away for the next morning.

Bathing became quite an art. The bathing hut was a room with a shallow trough about four or five inches deep and three roses, similar to those on a watering can, attached to another pipe, running along the ceiling. These were our showers. Unfortunately, only one of the roses was ever in working order, and even that didn't work properly, the sediment in the water having clogged it up. This water was heated from an oil water drip which did not give off much hot water. About twenty of us would strip and endeavour to bath, having managed to lather our bodies with soap, we then tried to rinse the stuff off. This was a joke because you had to be something of a magician to get under the one working shower. Trying to dry oneself and then dress without your clothes dangling in the water on the floor was another work of art. Never in all my life did I feel so filthy dirty, for after the so-called bath I felt even worse than before I started.[6]

Small units were like small ships in escaping the 'bull' and discipline of the big battalions and the 'pusser' battleships – but they could not always do so. Occasionally pomp and circumstance could reach even the remote hinterland of Hoy.

¶ My wind-swept Arcadian existence as searchlight detachment commander on Hoy came to a sudden end. We were to be inspected by a Very Great General, so aweful a presence seemingly that he had to be escorted everywhere by a posse of red-tabbed staff officers. So there we were one sunny day awaiting the majesty of his arrival, all smartly 'brittled up' in full battle-order standing to our First World War searchlight and sound-locator. George, my star Lewis-gunner, stood by his 1916 Lewis Gun and I awaited the arrival of God and his star-studded satellites with frozen confidence.

We waited . . . and waited . . . for over two hours. Punctuality may be the politeness of mere princes, but great generals, apparently, were not subject to the rules of mortals. And George was desperately feeling the call of nature. 'I'll have to go, Sarge, I can't hang on to it any longer . . .' he pleaded. When you have to go, you have to go, and George went. And he stayed, too. He must have been very constipated.

In his place I posted the spare man, a recently-joined surly unwilling conscript. And that was when the General and his entourage arrived. Trotting along in the rear with his eyes goggling in terror was our Battery Commander. The General, with commendable understanding of military priorities, inspected the cookhouse and asked me about our rations. I told him we were quite well fed, but that we were sometimes short of bread. The Battery Commander's frightened eyes signalled a black mark behind his shining black-rimmed spectacles. I would now never be made up to full Sergeant. And George was still communing with nature in his tiny wooden cubicle.

Ominously the great man approached the machine-gun. The spare man was ordered to fire at a rashly hovering sea-gull. Twenty rounds missed the lucky bird, of course. I don't think the new man had fired a machine-gun before. But the bird fluttered off with a frightened squawk of annoyance at the interruption of its fishing-trip and honour seemed satisfied. The cortege was about to move off.

But the stupid little Battery Commander ruined our near-success. 'Clear the gun, man!' he hissed sideways. 'You haven't cleared the gun!' The gun-barrel was now horizontal again. Nervously obedient the spare man touched the trigger. 'Whizz-spat!!!' and a tracer bullet embedded itself in a sandbag between me and the General. And just then George approached from his secret cabinet. But everyone was too shaken to remark on the appearance of an unexplained extra man.[7]

There were smaller islands than Hoy, each a strategic site for a battery, and the smaller the island the tougher the life for those installed upon them.

¶ There were several isolated outposts for observation and such like – usually manned by two men only. They led primitive and rather Bohemian lives, contriving their own electricity supply from rudimentary windmills. One such post used to declare that with a good breeze they got three pips before the News and in a Force 8 gale six pips before the News, but never – ever – the News.[8]

* * *

¶ My unit was soon to be scattered in detachments of ten over various islands in the Orkney group. We all agreed, I think, on one point – we had never seen such isolation. Certainly we weren't adequately clothed for the cold months that were to follow, and more often than not were very hungry. Man's first thought is for survival, and as on one occasion we only had one loaf and a little marg per day between the ten of us, we decided we had to do something about it. Someone remembered that Orkney cockles are reputed to be the best in the world, so picture us all complete with our tin bowls scraping in the sand. Our search was very soon rewarded, but the pleasure of having our bellies filled was soon to be replaced with acute discomfort and regret, for cockles and dry bread make a diet which no gourmet could recommend.

In one of the bays lay a ship which we were told was a torpedoed Danish tanker. One night three of us landlubbers decided to venture out to her and see if there were any biscuits or anything which could make life more endurable for us left aboard. We knew where to get a small rowing boat (all Orcadians seemed to possess one) and the two of us who could row a little laboriously made our way to the side of the stricken craft.

Now we were near she seemed to take on huge and fearful proportions and the uncanny noises made by the sea as it swished through the crippled vessel made us wonder if we should turn back. I think it was only hunger that made us complete our mad mission. We made fast our borrowed boat, and clambered up the sloping deck. How we made our way around I shall never know. We even ventured down below, managing to find mattings of various sorts, and biscuits, etc. Groping around like we did – three men with one small torch – was quite some feat, and we were all quite agreeable to get back to the boat when we had as much as we could each carry.

Upon doing so we found to our dismay that the tide had receded leaving the boat hanging almost clear of the water by the rope to which we had tied it. We cut it free, threw in our booty, and jumped in desperately. Then the gravity of our situation dawned on us! Which way were we to row? It had been fairly easy on the way out for we could see the ship silhouetted against the sky line, but now it was quite dark, and we couldn't see the shore. Worse still our craft was letting in water. Frantically we rowed for our lives. I shall always remember the chap who was baling with his hat, he couldn't swim a stroke. His name was Jimmy Drake, I think the other chap's name was Bill Parkinson. I wonder if they are still alive. Truly all our guardian angels were with us that night though, for just when we thought Jimmy's efforts were to be of no avail we spotted a blurred outline of land. More remarkable still, the spot where we landed was less than fifty yards from where we had started.[9]

But wherever the defenders were located, there was no escaping the weather. 'You luck b—s!' said a sergeant-major, taking his leave of a detachment embarking for Scapa. 'Not for you the road to Mandalay: you're going to the frozen north, where even the sheep wear jerkins and gumboots!' And there was nowhere so remote that the Orkney wind could not find them out. One Naval officer even claimed that he saw an aeroplane actually drifting *backwards* over Kirkwall.

¶ The real master there was the wind. A quiet day up there would rate as a gale in England. I think it's no exaggeration to say that a sixty m.p.h. wind was normal. All camp buildings, both our overcrowded Nissens and the wooden administration huts, were anchored down by steel hawsers slung over the roof and attached to deeply-buried steel stakes. I recall evenings in the canteen when we felt the floor rocking and bucketing under our feet as the whole hut strained against its wires. What was more important, the barrels were rocking too, so there was no draught beer for us.[10]

* * *

¶ The wind was the fiercest I have ever experienced. If you faced it you could bear forward at an alarming angle and be supported by it. I found that many times I had to turn my back on it and walk backwards, because I felt my lungs would burst. I recall having to walk to our other gun position, about two miles away, under such conditions, to pay the men there. The road lay parallel with the coast, and we received the full force of the wind. On arrival at the other camp, we were unable to carry out the pay duties until we had recovered from the dizziness. The effort of walking through the wind had made us appear intoxicated.

I also recall the wind causing the steel ropes holding the barrage balloons to break away, carrying away the cables supplying the electricity from the generator to the huts and plunging us all into darkness. As the winter days started going dark after 3.00 P.M. this caused great discomfort, because repairs of this kind always took months. The more inventive-minded chaps made their own lamps by obtaining some paraffin and making a hole in the lid of an empty cigarette tin and inserting a length of string, but the chances of reading after one's duties were nil. All in all, the winter months were treacherous – rain, hail, snow, wind, gales; everything that was possible to be had we had. How we cursed those islands.

The island was ringed by barrage balloons and when these were up it appeared to be suspended on the water. How I wished we could cut the ropes and let the whole lot sink![11]

The very real problem of personal cleanliness was met by the military authorities with typical briskness, and with a solution which conjures up visions of paupers in a Victorian workhouse:

¶ Each section was given one day off in seven (no account being taken of Sundays, which were ordinary working days), but the free day was hardly a holiday. One was excused the first parade, but later had to parade for baths. For this we paraded in best battle dress, clean underclothes wrapped in a towel, and were then marched through the narrow street of Stromness to a disused whisky distillery. Here we disrobed, leaving our clothes on benches round the wall, and picking our way delicately over a thin film of slimy mud covering the stone floor, climbed into the mash tub, some twenty feet across, and scrubbed ourselves as clean as we might under a spray falling from water-can roses fitted overhead. As more and more warriors arrived, so the mash tub got fuller and fuller, so that it was packed tight with hairy naked bodies.

'Noo I'll shift thae boogers,' said the N.C.O. in charge as he adroitly switched from hot to icy cold, and with howls the tub emptied, and there was a frantic search for one's own garments, which would be lost under piles three or four bundles deep.

To add to the simple pleasure of this exercise, gas respirators were worn on the march to and from the baths, so that I for one saw little of Stromness by daylight through a film of steamed-up glasses.[12]

There was one good thing about those pioneering days: they couldn't get worse, they could only get better. And so they did. Major Eric Linklater, who as an Orcadian Territorial had seen the early struggles of the defence forces, revisited the islands later in the war and noted the change: 'The vital confusion had settled down and become vital order. The guns were in position, ceaselessly manned. The cargoes of corrugated iron had become villages and between the huts were tidy paths; in front of them gardens had been planted. The occupation was becoming a military civilization.'*

¶ The food was good and plentiful and there were plenty of eggs to be had. Two eggs and bacon for breakfast were quite usual. Orderly Officer: 'Any complaints?' Lance-Corporal: 'Yes, sir.' Orderly Officer: 'Well?' Lance-Corporal: 'One of my yolks is broken, Sir.'[13]

---

* *The Northern Garrisons,* by Eric Linklater (Central Office of Information).

21

'Orkneyitis'

There was a 'disease' widespread in wartime Orkney that was unknown to any medical text-book – 'Orkneyitis'.

'Orkneyitis' seems to have been, in particular, a disease of the Second World War. No doubt it existed in the First World War, for the conditions of life were basically the same, but the service men of 1939–45 brought out into the open, and named, discussed and dissected, an attitude of mind that seems largely to have been taken for granted by the servicemen of 1914–18.

'Orkneyitis' was compounded of many elements. Monotony, isolation, loneliness, living too closely with the same few men for too long, the lack of all normal healthy outlets, the inhospitable and bleak surroundings, the bad weather (especially that maddening Orkney wind), the Arctic nights of Scapa's winter and the endless daylight of her summer – all these plus the inevitable anxieties of wartime and the usual irritations of service life worked together to produce a kind of *cafard*. Those most in action had it least. Those who saw little of the 'real thing' but merely went through a series of tedious dress-rehearsals for a great day that never came, and watched a war drag interminably on which they themselves were powerless to shorten, suffered from this strange northern malaise most of all.

It took as many forms as there were causes. It was sometimes comic and sometimes deadly serious. It could be the subject for a concert-party joke; it could also lead men to suicide. One sailor

defined it as a 'sense of impending nervous breakdown'; for others
it meant the creation of a day-dream world that gave them consolation – even a kind of serenity – in a situation which they
would normally find intolerable.

An airman recorded how he came across the symptoms of
this strange sickness of the Orkneys in his first crossing of the
Pentland Firth.

¶ I sat on deck somewhere near the prow of the ship and a sailor
returning from leave sat next to me. He hated the Orkneys; he
hated that bloody Scapa Flow which was the reason for his being
there; he'd rather be anywhere than in the bloody Orkneys; he
was going to see his C.O. and ask for a Middle East posting; he'd
rather go without leave than be up here. Life up here was too
bloody lonely, too bloody meagre, too bloody cold! He broke
down and cried. Nonplussed, amazed and innocent, I offered
him my only bar of chocolate as consolation.[1]

But for the most part 'Orkneyitis' showed itself less in outright diatribes against Scapa and the tyranny of the prevailing
conditions there, than in deviations from normal behaviour
which began as mere quirkishness but which eventually grew
into something not far short of insanity. It was usually, of course,
insanity of a fairly mild kind, and was all the more innocuous
because it was so widely shared. For it was not a case of a few
isolated individuals showing major aberrations, but of almost
everybody being very slightly round the bend.

¶ The main problem among us Army men on the island (Flotta)
was boredom. A few of the town-dwellers found the solitude too
much for them, and were invalided out of the Service after spells
of rehabilitation farther south in England.

The rest made up for this by catching the dread disease
called 'Orkneyitis' – a convenient term to cover any deviation
from the norm. Flotta's contribution to this was the acquisi-
tion of imaginary pets. Invisible budgies, dogs, cats, lions,
tigers and ducks followed their masters everywhere, and were
fed, groomed and quartered by their owners amid ceremony

and serious respect. It was occasionally a trick to obtain extra helpings from the cook-house but, surprising though it was, it became generally accepted amongst the rank and file that these creatures actually existed.[2]

* * *

¶ In one ship there was an imaginary garden located somewhere about the bridge. The watch coming off duty would solemnly be asked: 'Any spuds through yet?' or 'Didn't you bring some greens down with you?' The watch going on duty would be as seriously enjoined to 'Run a hoe through that starboard bed if you've half an hour to spare' or 'I noticed Geordie left his flickin' rake lying around when he knocked off. Watch out you don't tread on it and knock your flickin' teeth out.'

One character (who never got any mail) received imaginary letters from an imaginary grandmother. Holding any odd piece of paper in his hands he would add his comments to those scraps of news and interest we all exclaimed at as we first skimmed our letters. 'Cor, that's rough. Well, the rotten old bleeder!' Of course, we always 'fed' him: 'What's up, Bob? Grand-dad making trouble again?' 'Not 'arf. Listen to this.' Holding the scrap of paper up to the light with exaggerated deliberation, Bob would intone: 'I am sorry to write that your grandfather has deserted me. He has run away and joined a circus.' Mumble, mumble from Bob. Then, 'Hey, listen to this then, that's not the worst of it. "I am sorry to tell you too that he has left me in the family way."' Loud cries of outrage and sympathy from all hands. '*How* old's your grand-dad, Bob?' 'Ninety-two.' 'And how old's grandma?' 'Eighty-six.'[3]

The people for whom one feels the most sympathy are, inevitably, those who were most alone. Cities are supposed to be the loneliest places of the twentieth century; but nowhere could one be lonelier than in the tiny communities that kept and polished and exercised some of the remoter batteries that guarded Scapa Flow. There one might indeed feel that one had been totally forgotten, that one was being made to endure inhuman miseries for a purpose that had ceased to have any significance. It was in circumstances like these that 'Orkneyitis' could go beyond a joke and even become tragic.

¶ The main thing I remember is the intense isolation of life on the A.-A. sites, for they were placed several miles apart and in most cases many miles from the capital, Kirkwall. The only regular visitors we had, the twelve or so of us, were the despatch rider who came with mail and orders about every two days and the ration lorry which came once a week. Apart from these visitors, and the irregular inspection visits by an officer, we were alone for long stretches, surrounded by mile upon mile of featureless, treeless and barren hills. If you were very fortunate you had a farm within reachable distance, and if so you could at least see people working in the fields and have someone to visit.

For entertainment on site we had a radio, and off site there was Kirkwall, where we could either spend the time in a Forces canteen, or, if you were lucky enough to get a seat, in the one cinema. There was nothing else, and often it was a case of going for a long walk in the hills just to get away from the all-too-familiar faces of the other men on the site. The isolation, lack of entertainment, the unending and unfillable hours of daylight, and the boredom, inevitably led to friction and personality clashes. We were constantly oppressed with the feeling that we had been forgotten and that we would still be there when the war ended.

I remember having a demonstration of the effect of loneliness on men when I was acting as Troop Clerk for a short spell. Two men had been detailed to guard huts and equipment on an abandoned and particularly isolated site and it was part of my duty to deliver rations and mail to them once a week. All was normal for the first two weeks, for the men were enjoying the unaccustomed freedom from discipline and authority, but I noticed a difference on subsequent visits. There was a growing warmth in the welcome they gave the driver and myself and a growing reluctance to see us leave, and out of kindness we used to spend far longer with them than we should have done.

As time went on they used to think up all sorts of transparent schemes designed to keep us there, such as having ready a full meal we had not the heart to refuse, heating the water in the bath house and persuading us to have a hot shower, having a chess or draughts board laid out, and even putting the clock back an hour or so and swearing that their clock was right and that my watch was wrong. Each was so sick at seeing only the other man week after week that they would do anything to prolong our visit as long as possible. I shall never forget seeing them waiting for us at the beginning of the track that led from the road to their hidden site, and then running beside the truck, grinning with pleasure and shouting greetings, nor seeing them, from more than a mile away, two small figures with upraised arms, as we departed and left them to another week of loneliness.[4]

* * *

¶ We used to man a disused site near Longhope. There were two men together to keep each other company. When leave came round one was left on his own. The store truck failed to renew his supply of paraffin, so he was unable to start his generator which provided electric light. We were notified by the coast-guard that a man was running around waving a chopper. Without light etc. the life of loneliness had got him down. He had cut his leather equipment to pieces, and said that the rats took his sausages out of the pan before he could eat them. His mind was temporarily deranged. The site was not manned again.

Another man from Welling, Kent, took his own life. He was missing for forty-eight hours. After a search, he was found hanging by his braces under a small bridge over a stream that came down from the hills. He was a very quiet fellow; evidently army life in the Orkneys got him down.[5]

As a postscript to this chapter, we include a letter written in Scapa Flow on one of the ships in 1941. The secretary of the distinguished person to whom it was addressed sent it back north to be dealt with by Rear-Admiral, Scapa. One of the Admiral's officers eventually 'collected' it, and preserved it as an illustration of the kind of effect that Scapa could have on some men, even in three days.

H.M.S. *St Sunniva* was one of the small craft charged with the defence of Scapa Flow.

> *H.M.S. St Sunniva*
> 24 July, 1941

Mr Winston Churchill
Sir,

Knowing you take an interest in the R.N. and always anxious to help individually or collectively. Well Sir I have just completed a commission abroad and I had my leave, came back and was in Barracks (Dev.) exactly 26 hrs before I got a draft chit up to this ship, and there are men who have been walking around Barracks for years. I am not exaggerating Sir it is true and there are several murmurs going round about it. I would not have minded if I had gone back abroad, preferably the Med. Can you help to get me there I have a brother with M. East Forces and I long to take my whack of it. I don't mind dyeing although I am still young (21) it would be an honour to die for a just cause. Although I have spent considerable years in approved Schools, Borstal, and prison, it was only for devilment I did these things.

My brother was fortunate to get away from Dunkirk and Crete. I do envy him.

This present ship is a yacht and R.N.V.R. and R.F.R. Officers are trying to run it like a Battleship pre-war, you just can't do it. We don't go to sea which is no good to me and I am smothered in a cold. I told the Doc I had a cold but he said Oh open your mouth, he said 'alright' and went out to have dinner with a whren. Gracie Fields gave a show tonight and at the gate a fellow said all civilians at the front can you beat that. Well Sir they are only a few things as to what goes on up here which as come to my notice since I joined on Monday 21st. So please Sir, help me to get out in the Med. and fight with the boys. This climate is killing me.

> Your loyal and
> Obedient Servant,
> A/B W—A—
> P.S. I hope you are well and carry on the good work.
> Your last speech was a knock out.

There is a tragic footnote to this letter. *St Sunniva*, a handsome lively ship with a clipper bow, had not been built as a unit of the Navy. In peacetime she had run regularly between Leith on the Scottish coast and Lerwick in the Shetlands. She was in fact a sister-ship to those other 'Saints' of the northern waters – the *Ola* and the *Ninian*. She was commandeered at the outbreak of war, and it was then that she took the prefix H.M.S. Later in the war she was sent on northern convoys as a rescue ship. On January 1943 she suffered the fate which was a constant threat to ships on the run to north Russia. Her masts and rigging were so encrusted with ice that she became top-heavy and turned turtle. There were no survivors.

22

The Suicide Run

By the time the *St Sunniva* sailed from Scapa on her last voyage, the Russian convoys in whose cause she was lost had been running for almost a year and a half. The convoys were a product of the new political situation that arose following Russia's enforced entry into the war in mid-1941. As Hitler's divisions moved eastwards into the Ukraine, the Soviet Union ceased to be a mistrusted neutral and became overnight a welcome and heroic ally. There was to be no question of allowing suspicion of the Red Flag to take precedence over fear of the Swastika. Hitler was the real enemy, and any country locked in battle with him was at once to be claimed as a friend. 'Any man or state who fights against Nazidom will have our aid,' Churchill told the British nation in a broadcast speech delivered on the very day that Hitler launched his invasion; and he gave an urgent assurance to Stalin that Britain would do everything that 'time, geography and our growing resources allow' to help Russia in her struggle.

The convoys to Russia were a major ingredient in the fulfilment of this promise. Indeed, until the launching of the Second Front in Normandy in 1944 they represented by far the most important counter in the hands of the western powers in the delicate relationship that soon developed between London and Washington on the one hand and Moscow on the other. When the convoys were in operation Stalin was approachable and quiescent. When their running was interrupted, however legitimate the reason, Stalin taunted Churchill and Roosevelt with bitter and scornful accusations.

There were three possible routes by which war-supplies could be sent to Russia: across the Pacific and through Siberia; through the Persian Gulf; and round the northern coast of Norway to Murmansk or Archangel. In the end, the greater part of the arms and equipment sent to Russia between 1941 and 1945 arrived by the Persian Gulf, but this easiest and most suitable of routes only came into prominence late in the war. Stalin, reluctant to see the British and Americans establish themselves in Iran, insisted at the outset that the route round Norway should be the one on which all efforts were to be concentrated. It was indeed the most direct route, but it was also by far the most exposed. With the Germans strongly entrenched in Norway, convoys sailing to Russia round the North Cape and through the Barents Sea had to run the triple gauntlet of Goering's Luftwaffe, Doenitz's U-boats and Raeder's battleships and cruisers. As the First Sea Lord, Admiral Sir Dudley Pound, wrote in May 1942 to his American counterpart, Admiral King: 'The whole thing is a most unsound operation with the dice loaded against us in every direction.' The Navy had an even pithier way of putting it. They called it 'the Suicide Run'.

As if the hazards prepared by the enemy were not enough, they were compounded by those provided by nature. The convoys had to sail through one of the most forbidding stretches of water in the world, a region of violent storms and fogs and Arctic cold. The polar ice-cap shifted to and fro, at times acting in unconscious alliance with the Germans by forcing the convoys even more dangerously near to the Norwegian airfields. In winter there was almost perpetual darkness, with a murky twilight for two or three hours at mid-day providing the only relief. Winter did at least keep the bombers away and made U-boat attacks more difficult, but this was the time when ships would suddenly change in colour to a ghostly and menacing white and when many anxious hours had to be spent chopping ice away from decks and rigging and guns. In summer, by contrast, there was almost perpetual daylight, which meant that the convoys could be easily spotted by German reconnaissance planes and were open to attack all round the clock.

To the Home Fleet based on Scapa fell the responsibility for superintending these convoys and protecting them, as far as was possible, from enemy attack. It was a task which continued for well over three and a half years, from the first convoy which sailed from Iceland in August 1941, to the last which finally returned to the Clyde on 31 May 1945. A succession of highly professional Commanders-in-Chief applied their best energies to this work: Admiral Sir John Tovey from its commencement till May 1943, Admiral Sir Bruce Fraser (later Lord Fraser of the North Cape) until June 1944, and Admiral Sir Henry Moore until the cessation of hostilities. The United States assisted from time to time with the loan of naval detachments, but it was the British Home Fleet that bore the brunt of this wearisome duty, which was later to be described by Admiral of the Fleet Lord Cunningham as 'one of the most thankless tasks of the war at sea'.

Through the autumn and winter of 1941–2 the convoys completed their missions with minimal losses. But with the spring of 1942 the task of molestation began in earnest. Convoy PQ13,* sailing in April 1942, lost five of its twenty ships to attacks by enemy destroyers, aircraft and U-boats. It set a pattern that was to become all too familiar throughout that hard and anxious year.

¶ Merchant ships full of ammunition seemed to be blowing up all over the place. How many survivors there were from those ships I shall never know. I saw several ships just disintegrate in huge balls of orange flame.[1]

The loss of merchant ships was tragic enough, but more crucial was the loss of the naval escorts, which were even less easily replaceable. The cruiser *Edinburgh* sailed with PQ14 to

---

* The convoys were given the code-name PQ on the outgoing leg to Russia and QP on the return leg. Later the designations were changed respectively to JW and RA: perhaps not before time, for the PQ–QP convoys were perpetually dogged by misfortune.

Murmansk, and was returning westwards with QP11 when she was struck by two torpedoes from the German submarine *U-456*. P. J. Spearing was an Electrician serving on *Edinburgh*.

¶ I remember returning from leave just before we sailed on that last voyage and seeing *Edinburgh* lying alongside the wall in North Shields. The whole of the outside of the ship had been painted white. Several times I heard the remark, 'Change a ship's colour and you change its luck'.

The day after we left Russia we left the convoy for some unknown reason to do a sweep in its rear. We were without destroyer escorts and were a sitting target for any submarines. About four o'clock in the afternoon of a perfectly fine day, two explosions shook the ship. There was a greenish-blue smoke coming through the mess-deck I happened to be in. One torpedo had exploded in the oil-tanks underneath the quarter-deckmen's mess-deck and the stokers' and Marines' mess-deck. The other torpedo blew the stern off and wrapped the quarter deck around X and Y 6-inch gun turrets. The *Edinburgh* listed over but did not sink. We were shortly joined by two destroyers from the convoy, *Foresight* and *Forester*, who stood by us. We managed to turn the *Edinburgh* back to a fairly even keel, and it was decided that they would try to take us back to Murmansk, with one destroyer towing us, and the other steering us from astern. After many attempts had failed due to the amount of water in the *Edinburgh* and tow wires had snapped, it was decided to use the anchor cable from the cable locker. We hauled cable all night, passing it to one of the destroyers. The weather was freezing in those Arctic waters but eventually we were making two knots.

Next morning found us limping slowly eastward. The attempt to tow us had been given up and we were only able to steer with our engines. Then suddenly over the horizon came three German destroyers in line ahead, cutting in for a torpedo attack to finish us off. They came from astern on the port side. Both *Foresight* and *Forester* opened fire on the German destroyers and positioned themselves between the *Edinburgh* and the German ships. But in spite of this the Germans fired off a salvo of torpedoes at us as they came streaking towards us through the icy

Barents Sea. We were helpless to do anything – we were a sitting duck. How many torpedoes hit us I do not know but we heeled over to starboard again. The forward 6-inch gun crews of A and B turrets were at action stations and, firing locally with electrical supplies from their turret batteries, engaged the German destroyers. By this time both the *Forester* and the *Foresight* had been damaged and had stopped, but the *Edinburgh* succeeded in disabling one of the German destroyers, which shortly sank. The other two Germans picked up the survivors, then turned tail and ran for home.

Edinburgh by this time was settling low in the water. Fortunately three minesweepers appeared over the horizon and were recognized as British ships. They came alongside and we were ordered to get the injured and sick off first. Wooden planks were pushed across between our 4-inch gun-deck and the minesweepers. The sick were wrapped in blankets and pulled across these planks, and when they had all been got on board the minesweepers the order to 'abandon ship' came and we crawled across these planks on our hands and knees. A welcoming hand pulled me aboard the minesweeper *Bramble*. When all the survivors were aboard the minesweepers *Bramble*, *Gossamer* and *Harrier* we cast off from the *Edinburgh*. She did not look as though she wanted to sink but she was slowly going down. When we were some distance away we saw her finally tilt and slip beneath the sea.[2]

The *Edinburgh* was in fact almost cut in two by the torpedo attacks of the German destroyers, but was so reluctant to sink that she was finally despatched by the last remaining torpedo of H.M.S. *Foresight*.

The most unfortunate Russian convoy of 1942 – indeed, of the whole war – was convoy PQ17, which left Iceland on 27 June. The decision to send it was a political one taken in the face of immense misgivings. It was a large convoy of thirty-four merchant ships, with a substantial close escort, and a force of two British and two United States cruisers giving immediate support. In addition, distant cover was supplied by the Commander-in-Chief, Admiral Tovey, in the battleship *Duke of York*, which, together with the United States battleship *Washington*, the carrier *Victorious*, three cruisers and a flotilla of destroyers, was to cruise to the westward of the convoy's anticipated route.

The Admiralty was aware, as the convoy sailed eastwards from Iceland, that the new and formidable German battleship *Tirpitz* was waiting at Trondheim in Norway with the cruiser *Hipper*, and that the pocket battleships *Lutzow* and *Admiral Scheer* were similarly poised at Narvik. All this, of course, was in addition to the strong force of U-boats and aircraft that was ready to give PQ17 the now traditional welcome to these northern waters.

It was the *Tirpitz* that dominated the Admiralty's subsequent course of action. She slipped out from Trondheim on 3 July, and it was assumed in London, with some reason, that she had sailed to intercept and destroy the convoy. On the evening of 4 July, Admiral Pound took a decision that was to become one of the most controversial of the whole war. Knowing that the cruiser force could not possibly withstand an attack by the *Tirpitz* and that, if the Germans acted quickly, Tovey's heavy ships would be too far off to intervene, he ordered the cruisers to withdraw westwards at high speed and the convoy itself to scatter. In the event, at the time when these signals were being received with horrified incredulity by the escorts of PQ17, the *Tirpitz* was at anchor to the north of Narvik at Altenfjord. When she finally put to sea, the merchant ships of the now scattered convoy – of whom a high proportion were American – were being despatched with such pathetic ease by German aircraft and U-boats that she was soon ordered back to port. The *Tirpitz* had never been near the convoy but the threat of her presence had accomplished its virtual destruction. Of the thirty-four merchantmen that sailed, twenty-three were sunk. Admiral Pound's motives were beyond question, but the abandonment of a large and important convoy before the enemy's movements were incontrovertibly established left a bitter taste in the mouth. It produced, in particular, an angry reaction from the United States, which lost fourteen valuable merchant ships in the disaster. It did considerable harm to the high reputation of the Royal Navy. In Churchill's words, 'This was one of the most melancholy naval episodes of the whole war'.

Richard Aldridge sailed with PQ17 as an Air Artificer on H.M.S. *London*, flagship of the escorting cruiser force under Rear-Admiral Hamilton.

¶ The small Icelandic port of Seydisfjord looked peaceful that morning, with the towering walls of the fjord reflecting the rays of the sun on to its cluster of houses and tiny white church. Here was assembled the largest escort force yet to take the hazardous northern route to Russia, while farther south in another fjord was gathering a large concourse of merchantmen. Leaning over the rail with the sounds of activity beginning to echo over the ships, I thought to myself that this time we really must have a good chance of getting through.

One by one, led by the London, the escort force slipped out to sea. We made rendezvous with the merchantmen and PQ17 formed into convoy order. The escort was quickly about its familiar duties; we for our part began the routine which had almost become second nature of preparing to launch one of our faithful old Walrus aircraft for its anti-submarine patrol, while around us the defence crews closed up at their guns. Below decks the galley staff began the job of baking hundreds of the Navy's specials, Tiddy Oggies;* these and soup would ensure that in spite of abandoning regular messing times everyone would have an adequate supply of hot food at their action stations.

Within hours we were joined by an 'old friend' – a German reconnaissance plane who would never leave us during those endless hours of daylight, his job being to relay information back to his Norwegian base. He was always circling the convoy just out of the range of our guns; no matter where one looked he was always there.

As the distance between us and the coast of Norway lessened, waiting for the initial air-attack became unbearable. Finally it came with a large force of torpedo bombers and the sky at once became dark with shell bursts as every ship joined in a terrific barrage. From then on the battle was joined. Both sides suffered casualties during the following days, while lurking U-boats

---

* Known to Civvy Street as Cornish pasties.

added to the danger, picking off more than one ship at the rear of the convoy.

And then the climax. Mid-afternoon and the alarm buzzers for enemy surface attack sounded. The cruisers and destroyers left the convoy, taking up battle formation and proceeding at full speed in the direction of the Norwegian coast. The major German units led by *Tirpitz* were out. This was what we had trained for and now at last we were to be asked to prove our worth. Darkness fell and still we headed east, closed up at our action stations all night. Fortified by the Navy's noted cocoa we waited for the dawn, but before daybreak came we had the surprising order to stand down for defence watches. I climbed into the cockpit of one of our Walrus and to my amazement discovered that, according to the aircraft compass, we were now on a course steering south-west and plainly heading back towards Scapa. With all sorts of rumours flying about we continued in this direction until finally our Admiral informed the crew that he had been instructed to leave the area and scatter the convoy.

When we reached Scapa the old familiar base looked grey, dismal and forlorn to us and our spirits were low. What had begun as a great adventure had ended in a sad failure. In spite of a security clamp-down our Admiral cleared lower deck on each cruiser in turn and explained the true position.[3]

PQ18 had a far more successful passage than its predecessor. It lost twelve ships and an oiler, but for the first time it included a carrier among its escorting forces and it exacted in return a toll of thirty-three German torpedo planes, six bombers and two reconnaissance aircraft, and also accounted for three U-boats. The honours, in fact, were becoming more even. In December 1942 a yet more significant development took place. Five British destroyers and two cruisers escorting convoy JW51B succeeded in outwitting and driving off a considerably superior German force that included the cruiser *Hipper* and the pocket battleship *Lutzow*. It was a fillip for the British, and it created havoc in Germany. Hitler turned his rage on Admiral Raeder and his prized capital ships and forced him to resign. Doenitz, whose faith was in U-boats rather than surface ships, succeeded Raeder as Commander-in-Chief.

As Churchill was to write later, with obvious relish: 'This brilliant action fought by the Royal Navy to protect an Allied convoy to Russia . . . led directly to a major crisis in the enemy's naval policy, and ended the dream of another German High Seas Fleet.'

Convoy duty was not always dramatic. In winter, when the weather and the darkness kept the enemy at a distance, this twelve-day journey across the roof of the world was notable for its dreariness rather than its danger – even though the fear of enemy action could never be entirely dismissed from the mind.

E. L. Peck sailed to Russia in a Hunt-class destroyer on several convoys in 1943 when, in Churchill's phraseology, 'salt water and geography' were the enemy rather than the German U-boats and bombers.

¶ Our Arctic clothing was good stuff. The 'long hangers' were of ribbed oiled wool from ankle to waist, where they tied with a pyjama cord. 'Auntie May's' seaboot stockings were also of oiled wool; and after jersey, jerkin (from the 'Daughters of The Empire, Saskatchewan'), trousers and dungarees, you finished off with a waterproof coat – fleecy inside and canvas out. The chafing was likely to make you sore about neck and wrists, but mitts and scarf helped here. A leather cap with ear flaps and chinstrap (also Canadian comforts) just about concealed the rest; and with only eyes visible, guns' crews at cruising stations could enjoy hilarious fisticuffs – so well padded-up that you could cheerfully keep warm by thumping the daylights out of each other only retiring for lack of breath.

As it grew stormier we were allowed after a gun drill to train the twin 4-inch of X gun into the weather. But the gunshield afforded scant shelter, so leaving layer, trainer and a messenger on the gun with headsets on, the rest of the guncrew and relieved look-outs huddled in the 'caboose'. This was a 'sweating iron tank' on gun platform level, about six feet square, with iron door, porthole and bench seat. Here the violent motion, the unwisely pulled-down earflaps and the reek of 'Sweet Caporals' were likely to ensure that the less hardy, with grunted excuse, soon made for the alternative of the great outdoors!

Here the wind ruled, and grabbed you unless you grabbed something else. When called to relieve forward look-outs you judged your moment to swing down the steps from the gun platform, grabbed a monkey's fist dangling stiffly from the fore and aft lifeline, and rushed forward like a racing straphanger to the fo'c'sle and bridge ladders. If she rolled to leeward before you passed the waist you might find yourself lifted off your feet in green water and clinging to guard-rail, davits or such scant protuberance as a destroyer's decks possess – very entertaining for those looking down to observe your progress, but for a brief spell desperately grim for you: the pull of a wave has to be felt to be known.

When our path took us near to the convoy on our modified zig-zag, it was possible to see the nearest merchantman – a Liberty Ship slogging stiffly ahead at the tail of the outer column. Not a soul was visible – we envied them keeping their watch from the wheelhouse as we ducked vainly from rattling spray to hang on to anything handy. Her decks were stacked with crated aircraft, and frozen spray gleamed on the tarpaulins lashed firmly over the trucks. An ensign whipped from her stern, a log line trailed down into her wake and spun off her slow progress as we battled into the weather and crept north past Jan Mayen Island.

From the look-out's clamped stool in the wing of the bridge the view was limited but impressive. No boundary of sea or sky was visible; the greens and greys just merged at something like a mile away, and in the squalls at much less. The picture within our limited range was of row on row of breaking waves superimposed on an awesome swell. A corvette to port leapt with us, riding the seas better and showing her Asdic dome as she took the fences! The waves were said to be fifty or sixty feet from breaking crest to foaming trough. The wind whipped off the wave tops and streaked long lines of spume and bubbles across the green water; yet I was amazed to notice in the briefly sheltered troughs, groups of small seabirds paddling steadily ahead, presumably 'hove-to' and awaiting better weather! They left little whorls on the surface in their wake, for all the world as calm as ducks on a village pond, and strangely reassuring.

It wasn't always so unlovely. St Elmo's Fire after an electrical storm at night was deeply impressive – mast, yard, signal halyards, aerials, pom-poms, guard-rails all picked out clearly in bluish light; and even my gloved hand before my face had tiny lights in every droplet of rain and spray upon it, until I moved it and they fell away.

There was also a beauty of an eerie, even deadly, kind in the calmer days when sometimes the seas 'streamed' with snaky, wraithlike trails of fog – for all the world like the surface of a pan of water being heated on a stove. But this was freezing fog. In a matter of a few hours we would be rolling ponderously and heavily, encased in ice inches thick on fo'c'sle head, anchor chains, gun-barrels, guard-rails and rigging. We chopped and chipped off what we could. Some of the decks stayed ice-free because of boiler rooms beneath, but in the comparatively gentle rolling the icy fo'c'sle had to be abandoned as unsafe. We left heaters switched on beneath the gun breech to keep the mechanism free.[4]

In the messes of these tiny vessels bouncing through the Arctic seas, life was only marginally more comfortable than on deck. At least men could get out of that bitter wind, but there was no real opportunity to relax – though there was plenty of opportunity to consider whether the whole operation was really worth the effort and the risks involved.

¶ In our forrard mess (shaped like a flat-iron with a squat cylindered pillar in the centre which bore the weight of the guns above) battened-down deadlights and escape hatch admitted a steady trickle, naked deckhead bulbs gleamed and a few small electric fires gave a warm but ineffectual glow (they had their uses though: you could press slices of bread right up against the element to make quick toast!). The motion was violent and noisy. The sea through which we made our passage made a groaning, squealing and complaining like shunted trucks in a railway siding as it rushed past outside – separated from us only by the plating of whose thinness we were very much aware.

As the bows careered vertically downwards into the abyss ahead, near weightlessness was something with which we were familiar. With a crash they would bite down into the water which then squeezed and compressed them, then they would assert themselves and spring outwards with a deafening clang.

'All for them bloody Russians!' says a member of a poker school, hanging on grimly to the mess table as he surveys his hand. 'Remember that woman sentry who followed us all round the streets with her rifle at the ready last time in Polyarnoe?' 'And the way they broke up our football match with the *Poppy*, and shoved us all in the shelters when the air-raid warning went. Surly b——s.' 'Still, that was a damn good choir came to sing to us all on board the cruiser later on.' Strains of the 'Cossack Patrol'. Pause. 'Dear Mother, sell the pig and buy me out!'[5]

'All for them bloody Russians!' One of the unhappiest aspects of the story of the Russian convoys is that the men who sailed on them came to expect a cold welcome at their journey's end. The Soviets provided little in the way of protection even when the convoys were in sight of Russian shores. They showed few signs of gratitude. Attempts at fraternization were quickly crushed by the political commissars.* There were no runs ashore except under strict surveillance and then only to the chastely exuberant concerts of the 'Red Club' at Archangel or its namesake at the Naval base of Polyarnoe near Murmansk. In the early months the injured were kept in squalid and airless hospitals, though a British-run hospital at Vaenga, on the opposite shore of Kola Inlet from Polyarnoe, improved the situation from the beginning of 1942. There was also on the Allied side no means of knowing to what ends the mountains of equipment, arms, ammunition, tanks and aircraft transhipped by the convoys were used. Indeed, there was 'a general feeling among both the British and American Chiefs of Staff that Russian demands were in excess of their requirements, and that there was much waste of the goods

---

* We are grateful to the former 1st Lieutenant of the British Naval Party 100, whose headquarters were at Polyarnoe, for the following story. On one occasion he and his fellow-officers greatly enjoyed a Russian film, based on a traditional folk-tale, called 'The Hunchbacked Horse', but were unable to appreciate it fully because of their ignorance of Russian. Their young female interpreter offered to come to their mess to read the story to them in English. She came, recounted to them this entirely innocent and unpolitical fable, and was never seen by them again.

delivered.'** One sailor based on the destroyer depot-ship *Tyne* in Scapa Flow had this bitter comment:

¶ Fellows that went right though on those long convoys used to reckon that the Russians never gave them adequate protection on the last desperate lap, and often (they said) the previous convoy's crated supplies were still deteriorating on the quayside when they tied up.[6]

For survivors awaiting repatriation, the living conditions in Russia were often more what one would expect from the hands of an enemy than an ally. P. J. Spearing spent several months at Polyarnoe, following the sinking of the cruiser *Edinburgh*.

¶ We were taken to a sort of dormitory with double-tiered beds that had wooden planks in place of springs. The springs, they said, were required for hospital beds. They issued us with a blanket and ½ inch thick mattress and a cloth hand towel. I slept that night – the first for three nights. Next day we were lined up to go for breakfast; with a guide we trudged through the snow for about 1½ miles and finally came to a group of wooden buildings. Inside we found it to be a communal feeding centre with pictures of Lenin and Stalin around the walls. There were rows upon rows of wooden tables and long benches with piles of green enamel bowls at the end of the tables and piles of wooden spoons.

The menus varied from day to day – boiled rice or boiled black barley with yak or fish stew, and huge long loaves of black bread (made from beans) straight from the oven. Tea, or as we called it 'chi', was made from pine needles and sweetened with a small fruit like a sultana. The change of food did not agree with my stomach and for the first few weeks I could not make the return journey without having to stop somewhere along the way. I was not the only one and occasionally if we strayed off the track between the two villages, the Russian soldiers who patrolled the hill-tops would take a pot shot at us.

** *The Russia Convoys*, Admiral B. B. Schofield, p. 208.

The Russian soldiers would come off patrol and eat at the same tables in the same communal feeding centre. They would never remove their hats or clothes and with their rifles propped up at the table a few inches away from their plates would eat their food in an enormous hurry and be gone again.

For about five weeks I could not get a bath. I had tried to get into the Russian Navy base where I knew there were some showers, but was ordered off the lorry I had been given a lift in at the point of a rifle. I then found out some days later that a small building over the hills was a bath-house, so I and one or two others made tracks for the building and found an open door with big wooden tubs inside the building. We stripped off and filled the tubs and I had the only bath I can remember having in Russia. No sooner had we got into the steaming tubs when in came a crowd of women with bags of washing tied in bundles. When they saw us in their wash tubs they shouted and gesticulated. I realized then that we were in the women's wash house! We finished our bath and hurriedly made tracks out of there.

When the summer came the days were long and the sun shone at midnight. The few Russian Wrens (or Women of the Red Navy) were housed in a building a little way from ours, and although they were not allowed to speak to us or we to them, they used to sit on their verandah and play their balalaikas until past midnight.[7]

There were occasions, however, when the Russians abandoned their cool indifference and gave the Royal Navy a warmer welcome. 1943 was a mixed year on the convoy run. There was a long interlude while the western allies gave all their energies to the invasion of north Africa and the Battle of the Atlantic, but the convoys were resumed in the autumn and the year ended with the spectacular success of the sinking of the battle-cruiser *Scharnhorst* on Boxing Day. The *Scharnhorst* emerged to attack convoy JW55B but Admiral Fraser was waiting for her in the battleship *Duke of York* together with the cruiser *Jamaica* and four destroyers. The resultant encounter was a great encouragement to the Navy and made a suitable impression on the usually aloof Russians in Murmansk.

The *Scharnhorst* made two attempts to reach the convoy, but was twice warded off by the cruiser covering force under Admiral Burnett. She then turned for home, only to find Admiral Fraser moving in to cut her line of retreat.

S. H. J. Hyan was on *Duke of York*.

¶ Signals were received from Vice-Admiral Burnett that the German battle-cruiser had turned away and they were losing her because of her speed. We had closed up to action stations. I was in the port after control room, and we got reports from our gunnery officer in charge of the port after secondary armament range-finder. We rested as much as we could – men dozed or played cards, only the communications rating was alert. Then we were told: 'Stand by. We expect to make contact with the enemy in an hour or so.' Then came the report from the bridge: 'We have her on radar.' This was it. We felt the recoil as our 14-inch guns went into action.

What was happening on top? Locked away in our small control room we waited for news. Then it came: 'She's on fire; she's moving like the clappers.' Our radar was put out of action; a shell had split the cable from the aerial. The range was opening; it seemed as if she was going to get away. Then we scored another hit in her boiler room. 'She's slowing down,' we heard, then 'Cease fire!'

It was the destroyers' turn now. They went in to try and put a few tin fish in her. Then our 14-inch guns started firing again. She must have taken a terrific punishment, for I remember our gunnery officer reporting that she was ablaze from end to end. Finally we heard the report: 'She's disappeared.'

After the action we sailed on to Murmansk where we were warmly greeted by units of the Russian Navy. The Russians put on a concert for us in the ship's cinema. The concert-party was dressed in the uniform of Russian naval ratings and were led by an officer (presumably) who conducted the choir. Four played accordions and others played balalaikas. As the concert came to an end one of the choir stepped forward and sang in English the song, 'Love's last word is spoken, cherie'. The applause was terrific.[8]

So it went on – six convoys in 1943, totalling 112 ships; nine in 1944, totalling 284 ships. The losses were minimal as compared with the peak year 1942. Then over sixty ships had been lost, but in 1943 and 1944 the numbers did not reach double figures.

At Scapa the sight of ships putting to sea on the Russian run was now a commonplace, but it was still a moving sight for those who witnessed it, such as one old sailor who had served on big ships in the Flow in the First War and who found himself serving on a boom-defence vessel in Switha Sound in the Second.

¶ Often have I watched a destroyer division – six or seven boats – go through the gate spotlessly clean with pennants flying, really things of beauty, on the Russian patrol; to see them twelve or fourteen days afterwards return, weather-beaten, smashed, with shipsides bared of paint, and every rib showing like starved race horses.[9]

Always when the destroyers came back to Scapa they berthed alongside the depot-ship *Tyne*, many of whose crew carried away with them grim memories of those homecomings, particularly in the early tragic days.

¶ After the return of the convoys we often had to kit out survivors. Then amongst rescuers and rescued one met shaken men, who haltingly spoke of others who had washed past the scramble nets, stark, frozen and glassy-eyed. We sometimes took in pathetic bundles of effects of casualties from ships that had been hit by an aerial torpedo or a mine; and when all that is left of a young married chap is an overflowing ditty-box with a nude photo stuck on the lid and several bundles of letters from other women, what do you send home to his next-of-kin?'[10]

23

Six Hundred Men to One Girl

¶ At the W.R.N.S. Training Dept, a member of my course was drafted to the Orkneys. I hastened to commiserate with her. 'What are you worried about?' she said. 'There are six hundred men to every girl and *I'm* going to enjoy myself.'[1]

There was one aspect of life at Scapa Flow in the Second War which was an even greater improvement than oil-burning ships. It was something the men of the First War would never even have dreamed possible. Their memories are austere ones.

¶ We were anchored over by one of the islands – I think it was Hoy – and being a Signal Boy I had access at times to a telescope; and during a quiet spell, I was looking over at the island, and behold there was a girl, leading a cow and pony, with a cart with stone wheels held on the axle by wooden wedges. All of us boys took it in turns to gaze at this apparition before she moved out of sight.[2]

In the Second War such sights were less of a novelty in the Orkney landscape when the female population was augmented by women in uniform. The W.R.N.S. arrived in Orkney in 1939, almost as soon as the Fleet itself. They were needed at the Naval Headquarters at Kirkwall and at the Hatston Naval Air Station nearby. These girls, straight from civilian life, were plunged at once into the tragic realities of war. There was no escaping them in such a posting.

¶ I was one of those who left my ordinary office job in September 1939 and joined the W.R.N.S. My first posting was to Scapa Flow. Being the first Wren to arrive, and as I was a shorthand typist, I was attached to the Captain's office. I knew then I was truly in the war as my first job was dealing with the result of the sinking of the *Royal Oak* the night before. After the initial horror I had to settle down to the routine work of it all but the first shock stayed with me for a long time.

Later, when Norway was overrun there were the harrowing scenes of people arriving 'somehow' in Orkney and finding a real welcome among people some of whose ancestors originally came from Norway. There was a squadron of Grumman fighters on the station and they went out on daily raids over the fjords. When they were due back all work was forgotten while we crowded the windows to 'count them in', some barely making it and too many not arriving.[3]

* * *

¶ We had our heartaches at times. Consider a crowd of Wrens and a crowd of young Fleet Air Arm pilots at the Royal Hotel in Kirkwall – out for dinner, then adjourning to the bar for 'noggins'. Silly games – Cardinal Puff, the Muffin Man, etc. The squadron was due to embark next day – no one knew where. Maybe a Norwegian or Russian convoy. They didn't know and didn't care either. We Wrens in the signal office were the first to get the 'gen'. How many planes had been lost. Wondering if we'd be out again with the boys of the night before and if so, how many faces would be missing. I know it happened on operation stations everywhere, but it didn't lessen the hurt. What got me was the fact that they knew what they were going into the next day, but they just didn't seem to care – and some of them were so very young.[4]

Even the desert of Lyness rejoiced and blossomed when, in January the authorities at last allowed the W.R.N.S. to be attached to H.M.S. *Proserpine*, the shore base, with its swarming male population and lack of amenities. Dame Vera Laughton Mathews, Director of the W.R.N.S., wrote that 'the Lyness Wrens had the honour of being for three years the ears of the Home Fleet. This was the main reason for their being there, and the communications staff numbered over 200, including the Visual Signalling Wrens who did all the signalling for the Home Fleet from the Control Tower.'* She described the effect of their presence at the base as transforming 'a bleak wilderness into a place of friendship and goodwill'.

This Wren had the honour of being in the vanguard.

¶ I was stationed at H.M.S. *Proserpine* at Lyness from May 1943 for a year. I was among the first W.R.N.S. to be posted there.

Very soon news of our arrival had spread to all the various forces units up there and we were invited to parties by the Navy, Army and Air Force. A night out was quite a performance if you wanted to go to one of these functions. There would be an invitation for a certain number of Wrens pinned on the notice board; you would sign your name on the list and on the evening in question you all met at the appointed time to be taken, by lorry usually, to the place where the 'do' was to be held. You were counted out and then in again on your return, by the W.R.N.S. Regulating Officer.

If you had a date the poor man had to collect you from the regulating office and sign for you and also had to see you were back in time, when you were marked off as being 'in' once more. You were only allowed late passes for organized functions. If you went out unaccompanied or just Wrens together you were only allowed to walk on a short stretch of the road. Men arriving at Lyness after months at sea and visiting the canteen were apt to be a little boisterous to say the least, so I suppose there was a need for all the careful guarding. We did once have a rating break into the Wrennery and into the dormitories – you can imagine the stir it created.[5]

---

* *Blue Tapestry*, Dame Vera Laughton Mathews, D.E.E.

The reminiscences of the women whose wartime service brought them to Scapa – the W.R.N.S., A.T.S., W.A.A.F. and Nursing Services – seem to radiate a feeling of pride at playing such a vital part in the work of the base; of the camaraderie of sharing the duties with the men; of fortitude in the face of the rigours of the climate, which forced them to swamp their femininity with heavy, awkward clothes; of sharp awareness of the beauties of nature among which they lived, and unflagging good humour. No doubt the ratio between the sexes had much to do with their enjoyment of Scapa. Probably also they chafed less at the austerities of life up there. They could build their own domesticity around them. One correspondent felt that they had a certain advantage over the men when it came to occupying their spare time because 'we could always stay in and wash each other's hair', Whatever the situation, they made the best of it.

¶ Going out in parties, never singly, until more female personnel arrived. Going to dances organized by soldiers on lonely ack-ack posts and the touching welcome – practically all 'excuse me' dances to give all the men a turn. Going by drifter to Kirkwall and seeing the main mast of the *Royal Oak* showing above the water – a very eerie feeling and a great sadness. At work, handling long lists of casualties lost on convoys to Russia. Bitter cold weather and winds – remember warming my feet and wool socks smouldering, couldn't feel a thing. Sleeping two in a narrow bunk to try and get warm. Splicing the mainbrace for King George VI – Wrens got lime juice. Standing to attention for Colours, outside mess, with cup of tea for watchkeeper friend – blown out of cup. Going on drifter to Stromness and seeing a naval Lieutenant-Commander, immaculate with silver-topped stick, etc., falling between H.M.S. *Tyne* and *Richard Grenville*. A great cheer when he retrieved his cap and stick and was hauled up, frozen stiff on the end of a rope.[6]

* * *

¶ Wrens were renowned for being 'gannets' and were always ready for 'big eats'. We were allowed to go ship-visiting sometimes and if any Wren knew a sailor on the ships in at that particular time she took along her friends for the wonderful feast of ship's bread which was delicious – pure white – quite a luxury in wartime.

We never seemed to lack things to do. There were two cinemas where we saw very good films and sometimes famous artistes came to entertain us. I remember the visit of Yehudi Menuhin and although I'm not a lover of the violin he made a great impression on me, not only as a great artist but as a person. He played a duet with one of the Marines and I often think how proud of that moment that Marine must still be.[7]

* * *

¶ It could be beautiful up there in the summer. There was heather on the hills and it was very pleasant and peaceful. It could be very different in the winter. The wind blew so strongly that you had the breath blown out of your lungs just crossing the road from W.R.N.S. quarters to the Captain's office where I worked. The long winter evenings we spent (when not at a dance) in our dormitories – long wooden huts on stilts – usually in bed to keep warm, with the chests of drawers and bunk beds pulled well away from the walls – because we used to get mice in! We would usually scramble for a bath first to warm us up. I remember going to bed in pullover and socks to keep warm. If you were lucky the bath water was quite clean but every now and again the oil (which was stored in the hills so rumour had it) used to somehow get mixed in with the water and it is rather annoying to get out of a hot bath covered in black globules of oil and have to splash cold water over yourself to get it off![8]

* * *

¶ In our bathrooms were large notices saying 'Use Less Water – every drop is pumped to you by oil bought with the blood of the men of the Merchant Navy'. Having digested this, you would turn on the water, which flowed out a rusty peaty brown – but so beautifully soft. With the callousness of youth we would say: 'Well, I'm off to have a bath in the blood of the Merchant Navy.'[9]

* * *

¶ I was a Territorial Army Nursing Sister and early in 1941 I was posted as Sister-in-Charge of a small military hospital at Kirbister Bay near Scapa Flow.

On my arrival at Kirbister I descended from the field ambulance which had brought me from Stromness only to be felled by the everlasting wind. I remember two R.A.M.C. orderlies came to my assistance and each taking an arm propelled me into a wooden hut which was to be my home for a few months. The hut was an L-shaped wooden structure. One arm divided in five small bedrooms, one each for myself and four Sister colleagues. The other arm was the C.O.'s headquarters and in between was a communal living-room with a stove. My bedroom consisted of an iron bedstead, a wooden raw-wood locker and a coconut-matting doormat beside the bed.

My first morning I was most perturbed to find that my face cream was almost frozen and hard to rub in. Woman-like, this was a terrific problem – nothing else seemed to worry me.

The C.O. escorted me over the hospital, a double Nissen hut with windows, situated about 200 yards from the quarters over heath and heather, on the top of a small hill. The hospital surprised me. It was passably equipped with an operating theatre and even a small X-ray table. When either of the latter had to be used the C.O. signalled the R.A.S.C. unit stationed near-by for extra electric power.

Eventually a few V.A.D.s came up to swell the ranks and they were splendid girls, full of entertaining ideas to pass the time.

Word soon went round when ship 'number so-and-so' was in Scapa and we hoped for two or three visitors. There was great excitement and meagre army rations did not allow a great spread, but there was plenty of 'spit and polish' in our mess room. In the summer we would pick tiny wild flowers which abound in Orkney and although we had no vases we made displays in moss with the aid of plates and tins, a female touch which was always commented on.[10]

*   *   *

¶ On 15 February 1944 I got my posting for R.N.A.S. Twatt, Orkney – H.M.S. *Tern*. I was the 'relief' for one of the half-dozen Aircraft Direction Wrens. Our job was to train crews, disembarked from ships in the Flow, in plotting aircraft picked up on the radar screen and in directing fighter aircraft to intercept such raids. We were also responsible for the R/T on the station. Our call sign all the time I was there was 'Rabbit'. In those days radar was very 'hush-hush' and the R/T job was a 'blind'.

The radar site was some miles north of camp on the coast at Nesti Geo – slightly north-east of Brough Head. One of the previous Fighter Direction officers who lived there was one of the Lanes of Penguin Books and the call-sign of the site was 'Penguin'.

The 'Met' Wrens had to work night watches and in the early days the one Wren on duty would have been the only female on 'main camp' so it was considered necessary to chaperone her! Several of us were detailed for this job and would spend a gay time in the Met Office until about 02.00 hours entertaining 'odd bods' who would drop in for a cup of tea and a chat!

I remember walking into the W/T – R/T office one morning to 'open' the 'channel' and the Leading 'Tel' said just one code word: 'Minimize!' I felt a great thrill and knew that D-Day had arrived.[11]

*   *   *

¶ One night during the summer of 1944 I was awoken by our senior Wren Officer who wanted to know in which bunk she could find the Leading Wren in charge of the Safety Equipment. I told her and presently she left, followed shortly after by the Leading Wren dressed for going out. She said she was needed in the parachute section as parachutes were required. This was extraordinary as, having no flare-path, we did no night-flying from the station. Shortly after, however, a plane (Swordfish – the sound was unmistakable) took off.

On arrival at the section next morning we found from the signal that *all* ships had left the Flow. This had never happened before – generally the dear old *Duke of York* was left swinging round a buoy, at least!

No team arrived for training and no aircraft, but the 'String-bags' doing anti-submarine patrols took off, and no one would even drop a hint as to what was up. In the evening we were told that we may not leave camp and also told to sleep dressed, with our respirators and greatcoats beside the bunks. Our spirits sank a little lower when the names of all Wrens who could use a rifle were taken – the Wren team having won the Captain's Cup for shooting many times.

This lack of news, work or mail went on for several days. Then things gradually returned to normal. We gathered after-wards that it was thought that midget submarines had got into the Flow and parachute landings were a possibility.[12]

Of course there were never enough girls to go round. One former A.C.2 wrote that he went out with a Wren once, but she told him she was rationed! Among the men at base, competition was keen; for those on remote gunsites or out at sea, the vision of delight came but rarely.

¶ Hardships and difficulties at Scapa Flow? The biggest difficulty was finding a member of the opposite sex – the biggest hardship hanging on to her.[13]

* * *

¶ Running across the island of Hoy towards Rackwick Bay was a desolate shallow gorge, known to us as 'Death Valley' on account of a fatal aircraft disaster. In the centre of this valley we had an Army detachment whose existence was as lonely as that of an outpost of the French Foreign Legion in the Atlas Mountains. One day the 'air-sentry' gave the detachment the air-raid warning, and they all turned out on a sunny afternoon to do, at long last, the gallant stuff for which they had been training on their ancient Lewis machine-gun. No planes could be heard; the skies were empty. What was all this then? the Detachment Commander asked, somewhat peeved at the interruption of his afternoon sleep.

'There's a girl coming down the valley, Sarge . . . a real one!'

The grumbling detachment immediately clamoured for a glimpse of this phenomenal sight through the spotter's field-glasses: they hadn't seen a girl for many weeks.[14]

*   *   *

¶ I recall an E.N.S.A. concert in the N.A.A.F.I. halt at Lyness at which Nancy Evans sang. She came on the stage, dark-haired, slim and lovely in a dazzling striped black and white gown. We hadn't seen anything so beautiful for what seemed like years. One of my friends, not long back from a particularly nasty trip on a cruiser on Russian convoy duty, murmured 'Don't bother to sing – just stand there'.[15]

There is one other bird to include in this chapter – a rather rare bird but by no means unknown in Orkney – the Service wife. It took a bit of organizing, as Orkney was classified as a restricted area and could not be entered freely, but the rewards were great. One Naval wife vividly remembers her days at Scapa.

¶ Many wives went to Orkney for visits but a few of us stayed on for years: life was quite unrelated to anything in the south: the problems were unique – but it was worth it. For me it meant seeing my husband two or three times a week instead of two or three times a year.

To get permission to join one's husband was complicated because permits to land in Orkney could only be issued against accommodation certificates and in the case of Lyness Naval base accommodation was only forthcoming if one had a job. As I had worked for the Admiralty at Portsmouth I was able to find a post in the Admiral-Superintendent's office, living in a civilian women's mess. When our first baby was coming I moved into one tiny room in a little croft at Longhope, Hoy. The cottage was right on top of a hill with an endless view of sea, sky and islands. The room was about eight by ten feet with a recess bed. As our landlady said, 'It's an awfy sma' room, but it always was sma'!'

Life was governed by the weather. The prevailing westerly wind is almost unceasing and frequently at gale force. It is a wet wind and hardly a day passes without rain: but hardly a day passes without sunshine either. The rain could be seen coming as a cloud on the wind, miles out over the Atlantic. My neighbour would warn me to bring the pram in with the words: 'It's comin' another wee shoor noo.' The 'wee shower' had the strength to knock you down and soak you to the skin in one minute flat. Nothing has ever terrified me so much as the time I was blown flat and could not rise again: every time I presented any resistance to the wind I was slapped down again. The feeling of helpless horror, the insane conviction that I was clinging spreadeagled to the rapidly shrinking ball of the world was a panic-inducing nightmare, until I could drag and claw my way round the corner into the shelter of the barn.

But when it was fair, the wind was invigorating and a challenge, and the washing dried as quickly as you could peg it on the line and it was as soft as silk from the constant snapping in the wind.

Because we had a home, my husband brought friends and colleagues along for supper or a cup of tea, a smoke and a chat. They would stay until the last minute, as many as eight large young men squeezed into the tiny room, sitting on the floor, while the baby slept through the talk and laughter, tucked away on the recess bed behind drawn curtains.[16]

'There has always been a great family feeling among those who served in the Orkney and Shetlands Command,' wrote Dame Vera, and she was not speaking only for the W.R.N.S. It was a very large family indeed, and they were not all boys.

24

Making the Best of It

Women may have enriched the wartime landscape of Orkney but they could not change its fundamental character. It was still sea and sky and ships for the Navy: sea and sky and lonely countryside for the Army and Air Force. One serviceman is reputed to have written his first letter home from Scapa Flow as follows:

Dear Mum,

    I cannot tell you where I am. I don't know where I am. But where I am there is miles and miles of b—gg—r all.

Love,

Ted

During those Spartan early months of the war, Scapa was as cheerless as it had been in 1914. Churchill himself was concerned about the situation and its effect on morale. 'I am told that the amenities of Scapa are so much below those of the Naval ports that the destroyers' crews are deeply disappointed when their brief spell of rest takes place there. No doubt in some cases this is inevitable, but I trust the whole question will be reviewed with the intention of comforting these crews to the utmost extent that operations will permit.'

One sailor in those early days, gazing at the grey undulation of Hoy, with its cluster of Klondike-style huts and rows of oil-tanks down by the shore at Lyness, and at the even more desolate terrain of Flotta, decided to spend his free time on board his ship. 'Even the austere and cramped discomfort of a destroyer,' he wrote, 'seemed preferable to the ordeal of sloshing ashore and taking a walk along those bleak and deserted country roads, often deep in mud.' For another sailor any land – wet or dry – was better than no land at all.

¶ The real novelty in going ashore lay in walking on dry land. After weeks of treading a moving deck these tramps along firm flint roads were a luxury. I walked to nowhere and thoroughly enjoyed the experience.[1]

When it came to amenities, the Navy had its priorities right and soon organized a very large, very wet canteen ashore.

¶ On the island of Flotta, a particularly bare and uninteresting hummock, was a huge Fleet canteen where we were allowed to go once a week or so. We were given tickets for beer – three pints' worth I believe. This was not instead of money but only to ensure that everyone stayed reasonably sober.

There was, of course, a brisk trade in these tickets. We all had plenty of money, comparatively speaking. There was nowhere to spend it. The 'wide boys' were well aware of this and had a very large Crown and Anchor school going right under the noses of the Naval patrol in the big canteen. In fact I'm sure the patrol was in on the deal because it was quite a common sight to see two or three hundred people playing any afternoon. The promoters, who had their own paid look-outs and 'helpers', made fortunes. The winnings were escorted back to the promoter's ship in kit-bags full of notes.[2]

* * *

¶ The focal point was the beer bar which must have been the largest and most primitive bar in existence. Hundreds of sailors and Marines of all nations consuming the one brew, the object of the exercise being the consumption of as much of the vile stuff as was possible in the time permitted. The result was something like a Hogarth print; but frequently that native ability of sailors to entertain emerged and before long spaces were cleared and various ships put on impromptu shows. I recall that my ship *London's* performance never failed to attract – a huge Leading Stoker from Glasgow doing his version of an Apache dance with his undersized partner literally taking his life in his hands. Things at times became very rough.[3]

Fortunately for the non-drinkers in Scapa Flow, additional diversions were gradually organized. In February 1940 the Lyness Cinema was opened in a building taken over from the salvage firm, Metal Industries. Later, a Garrison Theatre was built on the road between Lyness and Longhope – a huge Nissen hut with a frontage like the real cinemas in Civvy Street – and from the middle of 1943 even Flotta had its own theatre.

Now the sailors had something worth going ashore for, and the men from the lonely batteries on the islands a good reason for undertaking the arduous journey to the main base.

¶ One of the highspots at Lyness was the weekly film show in the N.A.A.F.I. We got off early on the evening of our 'picture run' and would go first to the canteen and have the full bill – egg, bacon, sausage, beans and chips. After this we would go to see the film – often an old one which would break down frequently, giving rise to entreaties in rich naval parlance to 'get the — thing going again before lights out' and derisive cheers when the picture returned.[4]

But outside the corrugated iron walls the war went on, and the world of make-believe could be shattered in a moment.

¶ Imagine sitting in the back row with an affectionate Wren when a notice appears on the screen: 'Will all members of the crew of H.M.S. *Freebooter* return on board at once' – knowing that you would soon be setting out to fight your way through mountainous seas – in this case north of the Faroes to tow in a stricken tanker.[5]

When it came to entertainment, celluloid stars were good but flesh-and-blood stars were better and up in Orkney they got the best: Gracie Fields, George Formby, Gertrude Lawrence, Sybil Thorndike – too many names to list here. But they remember their favourites.

¶ There were some great shows. Beatrice Lillie came and when an air-raid developed continued her show in miniature in an air-raid shelter to the few of us privileged to share it with her. She was very brave and as witty as ever. Flanagan and Allen came and gave a delightfully 'broad' performance appropriate to an all-male audience. But the greatest of all was Evelyn Laye. We sometimes felt a bit forgotten, enduring the privations but with no glory, but she adopted us, entertained us and publicized us, and we loved her for it. I remember her first show when she arrived late due to a storm, wet through, sea-sick, and without dresses or props. She went right on stage and gave a wonderful performance.

I once stopped off in Leeds on leave and Miss Laye was there in pantomime. I sent round a note with the word 'Scapa' on it and was at once invited to her dressing-room and to a New Year's party which followed. I had the opportunity then of telling her what she meant to us in the far-flung outpost of the north.[6]

* * *

¶ I remember Pouishnoff coming – he stayed on the flagship with the Admiral. He strode to the piano in immaculate evening dress with a white carnation in his buttonhole – we couldn't think where he'd got that. He played most beautifully but when 'Requests' came and he was asked for 'So deep is the night' he seemed a little shocked but unbent enough to say he would play the Chopin original.

By contrast, Yehudi Menuhin came wearing flannels and a velvet jacket. He went out on all the little ships and played to men of the drifters and destroyers. He was immensely popular and never batted an eyelid when asked to play 'In a Monastery Garden' and 'I'll walk beside you' but gave them all his rapt and loving care. I became a devoted Menuhin fan from that day.[7]

* * *

¶ Yehudi Menuhin playing unaccompanied Bach in the garrison cinema on Hoy . . . Pale and shy-looking, casually dressed in sports jacket and soft shirt, reminding us of things that were apart from the routine of war.[8]

* * *

¶ I well remember a concert in Lyness at which Frances Day, bless her, sang to a packed house (all male). The object of her attention in the front row was none other than an Admiral of the Fleet (nameless) and the song was something to do with Her Heart Belonging to Da-Da-Daddy . . . The applause had the last night of the Proms beaten into a cocked hat! How these artistes were appreciated and what a good job they did.[9]

And when the evening ended for the revellers at Lyness or on Flotta – when the last orders had been taken, or the last act cheered to the echo, or 'The End' had flickered on the screen – it was off down the pier, and the watery journey home.

¶ The M.F.V.s would be tied up at Flotta about eight or nine abreast. Each M.F.V. had the name of the ship it belonged to on the wheelhouse. Someone would shout the name of your ship when the M.F.V. arrived and you would have to fight your way through and climb over perhaps five or six before you could reach the one that belonged to your ship. Eventually everyone was sorted out. Often hats would land up in the 'drink' in the scramble. Sometimes a matelot would jump off the jetty and try to swim back to his ship but the cold water soon made him clamber out again.

Usually, before the M.F.V.s cast off to return to their ships, there was a lot of barracking with jeers and cheers and remarks from men of one M.F.V. to another of: 'Go to sea, you "baskets"!' Then invariably there would be the song, sung with gusto:

> *Roll on the* Nelson, Rodney, Renown! –
> *This two-funnel 'basket' is getting me down.*[10]

It probably never occurred to the sailors that anyone could consider their ships in the category of entertainment, but as the base at Scapa Flow expanded, they found that one of the most popular pastimes among the Army, Air Force and Women's Services was visiting the Navy. The visitors were gladly welcomed aboard.

¶ Most of the liberty watch remained aboard for the Sunday afternoon 'make and mend'. The afternoon was often set aside as a visiting day, intended, I suppose, to relieve the tedium experienced by Army and Air Force personnel on isolated shore stations. Meanwhile one or two souls would be asleep in hammocks. Someone always is asleep on a mess-deck.[11]

The destroyer depot-ship, H.M.S. *Tyne*, mounted an even more sophisticated entertainment. She ran tea-dances. It was a far cry from the all-male valetas and military two-steps of the first war. Now there were real girls, and foxtrots and tangos and, no doubt, the Palais glide.

Like that previous generation they, too, looked to the little towns of Kirkwall and Stromness on the Mainland as the outposts of civilization. After all, they had real streets, real houses and, above all, real shops.

¶ Kirkwall's one main street was like Bond Street to us. We Wrens took it in turns to go and whoever was going had a long list of things the rest of the dormitory needed, usually including bottles of Dettol which we all used lavishly in the bath water.

When the drifter arrived at Kirkwall there would be a mad rush ashore on to the one and only bus (a small one) and I have never before or since seen so many people on one bus!

We'd start at one end of the main street and be in and out of the shops till we reached the other. This done we'd either go to the Church of Scotland canteen for eats or to a particular café where we'd queue up outside for a tea of eggs and chips followed by lovely Scotch pancakes, all washed down by tea. Then off to queue for the bus and our afternoon was over.[12]

*   *   *

¶ If the ship went into Kirkwall Bay a run ashore meant pubs and a cinema: but first of all the Temperance Hotel for a meal like home. Mixed grills, sausages and eggs, tea and bread and butter. But most important, the food was served on willow pattern china and the table stayed still and nobody said 'Pass the flickin' grease' (butter) or 'Raise the flickin' lighthouse' (pass the salt). Some of the cinema seats were broken and the films were old, but it was warm, and a world away. Then back to the pier where a drifter took libertymen back to their ships. One's own ship was always the last call. As the drifter circled among the moored craft, the libertymen circled round the drifter's funnel, seeking warmth and shelter from the sleet squalls which seemed to blow especially at liberty boat time.[13]

Those libertymen must have felt that when it came to time off the chaps who were actually stationed on the Mainland had jam on it. And so, quite literally, they did. At least those within striking distance of Stromness.

¶ Remember the 'Fourpenny Bash'?

I can't recall who provided it – I think it was the local equivalent of the W.V.S.* But I do remember vividly the large, square, parish-hall style room, the trestle tables arranged around, and the piles, mounds, hills, mountains of rolls, baps, scones, buns, cakes and breads of every possible variety. You entered, were greeted smilingly by an aproned angel in the lilting South Wales accent that they use in Stromness, and you were handed a very large plate. Then you wandered around, Army boots loud upon the plank floor, and you made your selection. Anything. Any quantity. If you could eat it – you could have it. Then, if you had your Army mug with you, it was filled with hot sweet tea. If you hadn't they would fill a cup, and tell you to come back for more. More buns, more scones, more baps, more tea.

Then, when the buckle of your battledress was comfortably tight, they accepted – reluctantly! – the sum of fourpence. Fourpence!

---

* It was actually organized by ladies of the Stromness churches.

To do the Services justice, it was almost a point of honour to visit the fourpenny bash only when financial embarrassment pressed – except of course for the first visit, to see if your mate had been pulling your leg.[14]

The pattern of Garrison Theatres was repeated in Kirkwall and Stromness. Stromness had its theatre by July 1942. It would have been opened months earlier except for the fact that, far away in London, somebody thought Stromness was in Iceland and the theatre was sent there. The outlying posts were not neglected by ENSA and sooner or later most people got their share.

¶ For entertainment in R.A.F. Skeabrae we had the travelling cinema show in the cookhouse; or perhaps an ENSA party would come to entertain us. To stand at the back of the hall, and to peer through the murky, stuffy, smoke-laden air for a couple of hours wouldn't normally be called enjoyable, but to us, starved of entertainment, it was wonderful.[15]

But perhaps not quite everyone, to judge by this wry comment.

¶ I heard on good authority that there was entertainment for the troops in the Orkneys, provided by ENSA, even great names like Tommy Handley. But small searchlight units saw none; we had to be satisfied with our battered dartboards and greasy packs of cards.[16]

The stars of the entertainment world shot through the wartime skies of Orkney and disappeared over the horizon, but they did not leave a complete void behind them. Unit concert-parties sprang up everywhere – 'Off Parade' on Flotta, 'The Gunnerdiers' at Longhope, 'The Live Wires' (Signals, of course), 'The Nosey Parkers' and the 'Boforters' (Ack-ack talent) and many, many more. The Army and Air Force could recruit A.T.S. and W.A.A.F.s to give their shows a touch of glamour, but on ship board they had to fall back as usual on illusion and make- believe.

¶ Those camp concerts were far and away the funniest yet saddest entertainments I have ever seen.

Imagine up to two hundred duffle-coated, rubber booted, woollen-capped men, many with beards, roaring their heads off at a troupe of 'ladies' all of whom were capable of packing any rugby team front row!

The humour was of the roughest, and the old joke about *Nelson* being the ship the Orkney shepherds feared most was heard every time the *Rodney* (her sister and identical twin) came into the Flow. On the other hand ratings off the *Nelson* insisted that it was the *Rodney's* men whose amorous appetites and poor eyesight (they thought the sheep were Wrens in duffle coats!) caused the shepherds to decamp at the sight of them.[17]

*   *   *

¶ I think the funniest act in any ship's concert was the performance by one stoker called Ben. His body was a fantastic panorama of tattooed figures: ladies that wriggled their bosoms on flexion of the arm muscles; snakes that entwined; St George on his chest and, they said, a fine hunting scene in full cry on his buttocks with the fox's tail disappearing in between!

However, back to Ben's illusionist act. After the usual stage patter, Ben got into a black box and an assistant, unskilled apparently, dramatically thrust a sword into the box which resulted in the most violent eruption of poor Ben, clutching a wounded leg, and he hopped about the stage cursing one and all with the most lurid of language while the whole audience rolled in the aisles.[18]

*   *   *

¶ Our unit had a concert-party. I remember careering along cliff roads in the dark, returning from shows with the piano in the back of the lorry, and a full rehearsal of the next show roaring out into the night.[19]

There were less uproarious recreations, too. An energetic young Sub-Lieutenant of the Fleet Air Arm launched an Arts Club in Kirkwall where service men and women of all ranks, and civilians interested in the Arts, could meet in comparative comfort and exchange ideas. He launched his scheme with a letter in the local paper.

¶ I little realized the response that would greet my rather pomp-ous letter. In no time there were several hundred members. Premises were discovered: a disused basement in a Temperance Hall. Eric Linklater and his wife who lived locally were extremely enthusiastic and persuaded John Gielgud to become President. The Council for the Encouragement of Music and the Arts assisted. Money was forthcoming from the Pilgrim Trust, and a quick flight to Edinburgh to meet the colourful Lord Provost, Sir Will Y. Darling, yielded further support, and some furniture, and a piano. A Wren artist designed the decor of the club premises, and the Marines built a beautiful fireplace out of local stone. In a very few weeks the club was complete, shows were presented and toured round the islands, exhibitions of paintings held and musical recitals given . . .[20]

This was a gift to Orkney which the Orcadians have treasured. The Kirkwall Arts Club still exists today.

Cinemas and theatre parties could, in any case, only take up a very small part of off-duty time. For the rest, the Fleet and the men of the Defence Forces were thrown on their own resources. They became cheerful experts at making the best of things.

All over the islands an infinity of activities sprang into being. There were dancing classes, quizzes, French lessons. There were debates, mock trials and mock radio programmes – on one occa-sion the 'mighty roar of Hoy's one bicycle' was halted by the H.4. Battery to introduce personalities who were 'In Hoy Tonight!' There was a football season (which began in May). There were even orchestras, such as the Flotta Island Orchestra and the South Rona Island Orchestra. And there was practically every known form of handicraft.

But football teams need a league table to climb up, and amateur public speakers need audiences, and gifted leather-workers need to exhibit their handiwork. With so many scattered and isolated units, there had to be a central clearing house for all this effort. Fortunately they had one in *The Orkney Blast* – the Forces' own newspaper.

It owed its inception to Major Eric Linklater and the first number appeared in January 1941. The sub-editor walked eleven miles through snowdrifts to deliver his copy to the printers in Kirkwall. It was this professional spirit which ensured that during its nearly four years of existence it went out without fail every Friday, with the rations, to every unit.

The Orkney Blast was produced by a handful of N.C.O.s whose first editorial office was a hotel corridor at Garrison Headquarters in Stromness. It was the prototype of all other Service newspapers which appeared during the war. It was racy, witty, comic, entertaining; never at a loss for a comment on anything from the latest inter-unit soccer news to the highest strategy of the war. Admirals, Generals and Air Marshals used its front page to send messages to the troops.

As a safety valve for discontent, it aired such grievances as the censorship of mail from Orkney.* One of its broadsides – against the practice of expecting the ordinary soldier to sleep in his underclothes – led to a successful Fleet Street campaign for the issue of pyjamas to *all* ranks of the British Army!

Correspondents from the units sent in sports results, social gossip, poems and short stories. The Football League flourished ('Scapa Lions 2, Twatt United 1'). The competitive spirit which was the great enemy of 'Orkneyitis' was fostered through its columns. One breezy gunner correspondent announced: 'We are prepared to take on the "Nore Parkers" (and anyone else who cares to have a bash) at table-tennis, darts, cross-country running, draughts, dominoes, snooker, swinging the lead, dodging the column, carrying the can, jankers, leatherwork, ironwork, fretwork, housework, network, Bagshot, Oxshott and a fig for the silly old railway!'

The Orkney Blast was a remarkable and entirely successful venture and was a crucial element in maintaining morale. It is a pleasing continuity that its sergeant editor is today the editor of Orkney's local newspaper, the *Orcadian*.

---

* Although a home posting, Scapa was treated as a foreign one in the matter of the censorship of Forces' mail. Men particularly resented their letters being read by their own officers. Green envelopes for uncensored mail were issued at the rate of one per week per man, but the majority found this a good deal less than adequate.

The Navy, which 'had no world outside the ship', and whose ships were constantly on the move, would not seem the likeliest source of constant readers for a newspaper. However, the men of H.M.S. *Tyne* discovered otherwise. The ship's company, endowed with more than its fair share of talent, had organized its own radio station – 'Radio Tyne' – which broadcast musical requests, brains trusts and play readings over the amplifying system. Then, in October 1942, a group of Ship's Writers launched the first edition of a ship's magazine. It was called *Outlook*, ran to twenty-eight pages and was written entirely by those on board. It included entertainment reviews, record releases, cartoons, sport, short stories and a 'What's On in H.M.S. *Tyne*' page. It was printed on a spirit duplicator by permission of the Royal Marines sergeant of the Rear-Admiral's staff; during any quiet period of the dog watches. It became so much in demand that commercial companies bought advertizing space and it was eventually printed by a London firm as a pocket-sized glossy magazine – being posted back to the *Tyne*, according to standard wartime practice, c/o G.P.O., London.

The popularity of *Outlook* spread from the depot ship to the destroyers and in the summer of 1944 it became 'the magazine of the Home Fleet Destroyer Command' and was sold throughout the destroyer fleet.

These spontaneously produced and truly parochial newspapers created a sense of community and camaraderie among so many who, on land or sea, felt cut off from their fellows – and almost from the course of the war – in their remote Orkney station.

The summer months brought to some a form of recreation which to others was alarming and unthinkable – taking long walks about the Orkney countryside. For those with eyes to see and ears to hear a whole new fascinating world opened before them. They became passionate birdwatchers, botanizers, geologists, antiquaries. For such as these the islands were a treasure house. They could even enjoy the supreme luxury of being alone, or the quiet companionship of a kindred spirit.

¶ There was magic in the air when my friend and I went on walking expeditions and looked down on the archipelago in the glinting sea, and the sea birds and the flora of these northern islands were a permanent fascination.

My main relaxation ashore was walking and bird-watching and I used to send in reports to the British Ornithological Trust, particularly about the fulmar investigations conducted by James Fisher. The west coast of Hoy was fascinating, with the towering cliffs of more than a thousand feet sheer at St John's Head and the coast indented by geos, or vast gullies, at the bottom of which the waves thundered and seals floundered. Standing off the rocks were stacks like the Old Man of Hoy, all teeming with vast colonies of sea birds. Cormorants below, and cliff shelves packed with kittiwakes, guillemot, razor bills above. And at the cliff tops raven and puffin and not far inland the great and arctic skuas. The skuas would dive-bomb a walker with fierce croaks, and it was always of interest to see their habit of aerial piracy – chasing a small gull and, as the terrified bird regurgitated the contents of its stomach, the pursuing skua swooped on the vomit and caught it in mid-air.

On the barren, boulder-strewn plateau in the centre of Hoy there were lonely tarns, home of the northern diver or loon with its eerie call, and in the winter one often disturbed a hare in Arctic white coat.[21]

* * *

¶ For those who did not care for crowds, a walk over the moorlands down to the loch, perhaps a row on its waters, and the crisp clean fresh air to breathe, was the best entertainment of all.

The landscape was barren, treeless and windswept, with hardly any habitation to be seen. It looked very isolated and unfriendly, but it was pleasing to me because of its isolation and remoteness. To walk across those desolate moors, with a gale blowing in one's face, was to get away from it all, to have time to think deeply of the goings on in the world.[22]

But though home was indeed far away, there were homes near at hand which were thrown open to the exiles from the south.

In the early days of the war, the relationship between the Orkney people and the thousands of strangers who invaded their islands was not always a happy one. There was a sense of offended pride when townbred servicemen were heard abusing the place they had been sent to because of its climate or because it lacked the manufactured pleasures of city life. However, as living conditions improved and welfare services spread, tension relaxed and a strong bond of friendship was forged between invaders and invaded. It is a bond which has stood the test of time.

¶ The town of Stromness was a loveable little town, stone-built throughout but the inhabitants were far from stony-hearted, as many servicemen can verify. Every home open to the man in uniform, always a meal and a welcome.

But above all this the warmth of the farms in the scattered surrounding country was something that had to be experienced to be believed. It was always the same. 'Don't knock, just walk in!' Wonderful hospitality that has never been matched. The chickens, cheeses and lobsters that we brought home on leave left our ration-bound folk not only speechless but suspicious.[23]

* * *

¶ Whereas on the mainland servicemen took home little gifts for the family, in Orkney – thanks to the generosity of the Orcadians – the leave queue seemed to be a sort of farmers' outing. Men had all sorts of things like ducks, chickens etc. slung over the shoulder, some plucked, others not, and even, occasionally, one still flapping.[24]

* * *

¶ One of the few pleasures of life in our army gunsites was to enjoy the simple and never-failing hospitality of the kind-hearted Orkney people. One remote farm I visited fairly often was owned by an elderly couple with two daughters, none of whom had been off the islands in their lives, not even to Scotland. I would sit in their spotlessly clean whitewashed kitchen and breathe the indescribably wonderful aroma of burning peat, home-cured bacon, home-baked bread, and home-made cheeses, while they listened with great interest to my descriptions of England, and particularly London. They had never seen an actual train, only pictures of one, and it was some time before they really believed that in London there were trains that actually ran under the ground. It was from them that I took home a large, round, white, goat's milk cheese that in those days of rationing caused a furore of joy.[25]

*   *   *

¶ A short distance away was a typical Orkney croft – just a stone cottage with a stone slab roof. One day I was roaming around and noticed a little girl about my own daughter's age – about 2½ years old. I said hello but she was off just like a frightened rabbit. I tried several times to make friends but she always ran away, until one day her father was there and said, say hello to the soldier, and he invited me down to the cottage. I had tea and bannocks and I became a great friend of the family.

The little girl's only toys were a pack of picture postcards which she would look at over and over again. But I may add that in spite of not having the opportunity to see trams and buses, big stores and cinemas, she did get an M.A. at Aberdeen University. After all these years we still write family to family – I wonder how many ex-soldiers can say that?[26]

All these were the things that in years to come sweetened the memories of Orkney service, but when all was said and done the best they could make of it was only second best to actually going home on leave. And because the distance was just that bit greater than most units on the British mainland had to travel, the intervals between leaves were most precisely calculated.

¶ I remember how the boys used to make their mark on the calendar when their leave was due. How happy and excited we were as we boarded the old troopship for a spot of leave. The *St Ninian* seemed like the *Queen Mary* to us then. What a cheer as she tied up at Scrabster. But, as the boys on shore at Lyness used to say, 'You'll be back!'[27]

267

SUNSET

Do you recall, my dear, how once you walked with me
Across the warm brown hills towards the shining sea
And how we lingered long upon the shore to see
Beloved ships come sailing up the Flow?

   But that was yesterday, for now they come no more
   Among the small green isles where oft they lay of yore,
   And so we linger sadly by an empty shore
   And shed a tear for lonely Scapa Flow.

We saw them anchor proudly as the sun went down
And heard a far-off bugle from the old Renown.
And o'er the gleaming water like a brave new town
A thousand port lights winked in Scapa Flow.

   But that was yesterday, for now they come no more
   Among the small green isles where oft they lay of yore,
   And so we linger sadly by an empty shore
   And shed a tear for lonely Scapa Flow.

Then for a while we walked not on that darkened shore,
No winking port lights then to glint the wavetops o'er,
And there were those who came and will return no more
And are asleep in lonely Scapa Flow.

   But that was yesterday, for now they come no more
   Among the small green isles where oft they lay of yore,
   And so we linger sadly by an empty shore
   And shed a tear for lonely Scapa Flow.

Song, *Lonely Scapa Flow*
by Allie Windwick

25

Paying Off

For the men of the Orkney defences the end came quietly. Many months before victory the tide of battle had ebbed away. There was less khaki and Air Force blue in the streets of Stromness and Kirkwall. The camps began to close down. *The Orkney Blast* ceased publication. In 1944 the new airborne threat to London – the VI and V2 rockets – claimed the balloon barrage which had been such a spectacular feature of the Orkney landscape. The secret build-up to D-Day absorbed all available men and material, and much of both were drained away from the northern garrisons.

For the Navy it was a different story. They were deeply engaged with the enemy to the last days of the war.

In spring 1944 a force of carriers sailed from Scapa, made rendezvous at sea with the Home Fleet under Vice-Admiral Moore in the battleship *Anson* and steamed to flying-off positions near the coast of Norway. At dawn on 3 April a strike of Barracuda bombers and fighters flew eastwards over the Norwegian coast and headed for the remote fjord where the battleship *Tirpitz* was lying, and where six months before she had been immobilized by a midget submarine attack of the utmost daring from which she had barely recovered. In a bombing attack lasting only sixty seconds considerable damage was done to her at the cost of one Barracuda bomber. Almost immediately a second wave of bombers and fighters flew an equally successful sortie, though again

271

one Barracuda was lost. Altogether fifteen hits were scored in this swift but brilliantly executed assault, and the *Tirpitz* was again out of the war. She was to remain so. In October she was able to sail at a humble eight knots to an anchorage near Tromso, but in November she was finally despatched by Lancaster bombers of the 'dam-busters' squadron, turning turtle under the ferocity of their attack and taking with her a thousand German lives.

Meanwhile the convoys to Russia continued their dreary round. Surface raiders were no longer a problem, but after much delay Goering had finally decided to build up his air forces in northern Norway. More crucially, the U-boats, which had virtually conceded defeat in the Battle of the Atlantic in 1944, were now in 1945 enjoying a new if reckless lease of life. The escorting forces for convoys were stronger than they had ever been, but given favourable circumstances the U-boat packs could still achieve their killings. Convoy JW65 which sailed from the Clyde on 11 March, lost three ships by U-boat action when virtually at its destination. RA66, sailing from Murmansk on 29 April, was met by some ten U-boats immediately on leaving port, but here the honours were more on the British side, two U-boats being sunk by the convoy escorts as against one success – the frigate *Goodall* – by the Germans.

The last fling of the Home Fleet came in the very last week of hostilities. On 1 May Rear-Admiral McGrigor, with a force of cruisers and escort carriers, sailed from the Flow towards Norway, to attack the U-boat flotilla base ships at Kilbotn to the north west of Narvik. On 5 May – three days before VE Day – the carriers flew off their Avengers and Wildcats on a boldly successful raid, sinking a depot-ship, a tanker and a U-boat. McGrigor's ships were on their way back home when they received the signal announcing the unconditional surrender of Germany. 'As they came in sight of the coast of Britain on the night of the 8th the lights in the houses were shining out to sea'*

Again, as in 1918, Scapa Flow was to have its tangible token of victory; not so splendid, perhaps, as the former occasion, but very gratifying for those who had spent hard and dangerous

---

* *Victory at Sea*, Lieut-Commander P. K. Kemp, (London: Muller, p. 340).

years patrolling the northern seas and ensuring the safety of the Russian convoys, and who were still at Scapa to witness it.

¶ For the most part anti-U-boat warfare is a fight against an invisible enemy whose presence is only noted by the ping of Asdic contact. For every U-boat sunk there were hundreds of weary, frustrating searches and depth-charge attacks in the tormenting Atlantic seas, which yielded nothing and resulted in sleepless, fatigued crews. Now here at last was a full sight of the enemy to give some kind of added reality to the convoy work. Here for the second time were German U-boats surrendering!

It was a sunny day with a light breeze. U-boats of all sizes – large ocean-going vessels and much smaller craft – slid slowly into Longhope Sound. Several, we noted significantly, were red with rust. They picked their way to an anchorage and then rode the water with us, German flag flying. This was the end for them and from the upper deck of the *Iron Duke* it was a heartening sight.

Two U-boats were made available for showing to the public and during this time the crews were accommodated in the *Iron Duke*. They swashbuckled aboard, these well-built young men, wearing the traditional white polo-necked sweaters and sea-boots. They laughed and joked, and sang the *Horst Wessel* song noisily to the accompaniment of a piano-accordion. A small British seaman guarded them with fixed bayonet. He looked bored stiff and clearly felt that he was supervising some kind of circus.[1]

Now Lyness began the slow task of undoing the building-up of the past five years. The Naval Headquarters at Kirkwall had already closed down in October 1944. In addition to the men of the Fleet, there had been a vast army ashore at Lyness of Naval Reserve, Naval Volunteer Reserve, Royal Marines; civilians digging out the vast oil storage tanks inside the hill above the base; boom-defence gangs who overhauled and maintained the huge wire anti-submarine nets; storekeepers and dockyard men working on the floating dock; building workers constantly erecting accommodation for all these people.

In June 1945 the floating dock, which had in its time at Scapa docked 343 ships, left Gutter Sound for the Far East. The dockyard camp and the messes gradually closed down. In spite of the fact that this ultimate result was precisely what they had all been fighting for, it must have been a melancholy business. It was presided over in its death, as in its life, by the redoubtable Admiral Superintendent, Rear-Admiral Sir Patrick Macnamara, K.B.E. He was remembered with honour by all who served under him.

¶ I was a Lieutenant-Commander in the Navy and was based at Scapa Flow for two years – 1943 until it closed down – as a pilot berthing overseas tankers and docking destroyers in the floating dock. Scapa Flow came under the command of Admiral Macnamara, who was Admiral Superintendent of Orkney and Shetland Islands.

The Admiral lived in a big house called Mill House, in Mill Bay, and a notice said on the gate: 'Please come in for a cup of tea if ashore for a walk.' He often gave a get-together party with rum punch. He had two spaniels – Scapa and Flow – which he had to show off. He would say: Scapa, bring in some logs, and if the Admiral forgot to tell him to stop, the fireside would be full of logs. Flow generally brought the paper.

At the end, when all shore-based ratings were leaving on board the *St Ninian*, all the heads of the various departments at the base were on the quayside and the Marine band was playing. All the ratings had been trying to drown their sorrows and as the boat was leaving they all sang out together: 'Oh, my name is Macnamara I'm the leader of the band' and the old Admiral had a handkerchief out wiping his eyes, and so were a few more, such was the comradeship amongst all his staff at Scapa. Everyone thought a lot of old Mac – he ran the base like a Lord Mayor with a town council.[2]

*   *   *

¶ The war ended and the base gradually disintegrated. The huts emptied one by one, the Wrens departed, and many of the remaining officers and men became infected with a sort of Lyness *cafard*. I recall a young Lieutenant R.N.V.R. moodily drinking from a pint tankard of beer in the wardroom when

274

someone drew his attention to the clock on the far wall and reminded him that he should be reporting for duty. After a rude word about the clock, he flung his empty tankard at it clean across the wardroom, missed it by about two feet, and embedded his tankard firmly in the lath-and-plaster wall. Where it remained.[3]

The disintegration was slow and unhurried. There was much to undo. But the day had to come when the end of Scapa Flow as a base for the Home Fleet must be formally recognized. The death warrant had to be signed. It was 29 March 1957.

¶ I flew up from Lossiemouth where I was serving to attend the ceremony of hauling down the Flag. By now the base had been reduced to one retired Commander and a dozen ratings, and was finally to be closed.

Lyness was a ghost town. Many of the huts had been removed, leaving only the concrete standings. I went into the old wardroom. The floors creaked alarmingly. The pint pot was still embedded in the wall.[4]

Naval historians will search the national press in vain for a record of this historic moment – the end of the last chapter of a long and gallant story, a tale of hardship, heroism, patient endurance and loyal duty. *The Times* gave it an inch, the *Daily Telegraph* half an inch. There were no newsreel men, no official Admiralty photographer.

Fortunately for history, the local Orkney paper, the *Orcadian*, did the occasion justice. Perhaps it was because the editor had first come to Orkney as one of those down-hearted young soldiers from the south who had taken one look at the place and wondered how he was going to get through his nine-month tour of duty. Fifteen years (and four children) later, he was still there.

'We had almost come to take the base, and the advantages it brought to our island populations, for granted,' wrote the *Orcadian*, 'but the inexorable running-down went on and last Friday the end came.'

It was a typical Scapa day in springtime, grey and rather cold, with an impatient gusty wind which tugged at the Ensign and blew snell on the little group of islanders who waited for the last act.

An M.F.V. on the routine Houton to Lyness ferry run brought the official party across the grey, white-flecked waters of the Flow. As the little ship eased into Lyness only two tankers were to be seen alongside the wharf, and farther over at the jetty one solitary Naval vessel present in the base for the ceremony – the boom-defence ship, H.M.S. *Barleycorn*.

A detachment of Orkney Territorials, loyal to the last, were led by an officer wearing a sword from the old Volunteer days in Kirkwall. The Resident Naval Officer, Scapa, Commander C. C. S. MacKenzie, spoke of the history of the base during the war and the feelings of those who had served there:

The White Ensign which has flown every day through these years will be hauled down for the last time in a few minutes. Tomorrow morning we will hoist in its place the Union Flag of an Admiralty Civil Establishment. The formal dissolution of the Naval link with the Orkneys will not kill the affection in the hearts of two generations of the Royal Navy for Scapa – an affection which seems to grow warmer in retrospect than it did in those winter nights in the Flow.

Captain A. J. M. Milne-Horne, R.N., representing Flag Officer, Scotland, added his valediction and acknowledged the Navy's debt to the people of Orkney.

The name Scapa had a kind of mystical meaning for the Fleet: it conjured up all kinds of unusual feelings. Probably in the First World War this mystic word Scapa meant more to those serving there than it did in the last war. This had nothing to do with the place or personnel; it was more a subconscious appreciation that developments in waging war meant that Scapa no longer had the same value that it had had from 1914 to 1918. It is these developments indeed which have brought us to the end of an era . . .

Without the wonderful understanding and cooperation of the Orcadians, this place would have been impossible. The people of Orkney have helped to make this probably the finest naval base in the world.

The ceremony of Sunset takes place in every one of Her Majesty's ships and shore stations all over the world every day. Now it was to take place at Scapa Flow for the last time.

As the sad notes of the bugle died away, the White Ensign was lowered by a nineteen-year-old Ordinary Seaman, Ronald Henry, youngest member of H.M.S. *Barleycorn*.

Flying from the masthead throughout the ceremony was the 266-foot long white paying-off pennant (one foot for every month the establishment had been in commission, plus the length of the ship – in this case taken as one of the M.F.Vs).

Ensign and pennant fluttered down together. Two pipers played a lament. The order 'March off Parade' was given.

It was all over.

Scapa Flow has been out of the limelight for many years now. Thousands of people travel to Orkney every summer but Scapa has little or nothing to do with their coming. Now they journey north to fish in the lochs or the sea, to visit the remarkable archaeological remains of Skara Brae or Maeshowe, to taste the rare flavour of a world that is utterly remote from the noise and scurry of our big cities. They come to watch the sea dash itself against the rugged cliffs of Yesnaby, to wander through the narrow streets of Orkney's picturesque towns and enjoy the animation of its small but active harbours, to drive down to the Churchill Barriers and write their names in the visitors' book in the Italian chapel. Some of them arrive by British European Airways, which can fly them from London to Kirkwall between breakfast and lunchtime, but many sail by the more traditional Pentland Firth route to Stromness, little realizing that they travel in the wake of countless men and women for whom this crossing was a journey to a grim and demanding war. For the vast majority of these visitors Scapa Flow is merely one of the minor attractions of Orkney, a sombre and lonely expanse of water that perhaps brings Viking longboats to mind more easily than the battleships, cruisers and carriers of the twentieth century.

Yet – as this book shows – for a great company of British people Scapa Flow is and will remain an essential part of their lives. They are irrevocably tied to it by memories that will not be erased by time. Whether it is twenty-five or fifty years afterwards it makes no difference – Scapa is there in their minds ready to be evoked at the slightest twitch upon the thread.

¶ I remember vividly those dawns at Scapa, the mist on the hills on the surrounding islands. I can close my eyes to this day and be back – the waters of the Flow, placid in the early light, the awakening ships with their attendant noises signalling another day of war. Scapa was home to us then, a rough, tough, uncompromising home, but, after the rigours of the northern battles, still home.[5]

*   *   *

¶ I remember journeys up through those lovely, remote islands to the pub at Westray in a drifter; sundown in the Flow with the Last Post being sounded from each ship in turn on a calm evening; the Home Fleet going to sea through Hoxa Gate – two carriers, the destroyer screen, and the flagship – what an impression of power it gave. And what a sense of life and movement there was everywhere as a result of the Flow being the Fleet anchorage. Always launches coming and going, drifters on passage to and from various islands and the ships. And always ships to be visited: ferry to the flagship from Lyness Pier at 8.30, then a 'P.S.B.' from flagship to the ship you wanted to visit. A gin in the *Duke of York* while you waited. Launch alongside – then a jolly trip across the Flow to *Belfast, Mauritius, Sheffield, Renown* (so beautiful), *Nelson, Ajax*. Another gin on arrival – then down to business! There *were* people who made a profession of ship-visiting – Falstaff would have made a tremendous job of it![6]

*   *   *

¶ I recall how, one Sunday evening, I stood alone 800 feet above the Flow, on the top of Ward Hill, familiar to all who know Scapa, and gazed at the Fleet lying at anchor below. At ten o'clock, four bells rang out from one of the ships, followed by the 'Still'. Immediately, from the quarter-deck of every ship in the Fleet, came the sound of the Sunset bell, with perfect timing. The memory of the clarity of that call, as it came over the silent sea, stirs my heart even now. As I write about it after fifty years, and realize the likelihood that it may never be heard again, tears spring to my eyes, and many others must feel as I do, who knew Scapa in those days, when Britain's sea-power was spoken of with pride and was a reality accepted by the whole world.[7]

*   *   *

¶ I remember the Flow best when the light was failing – the huge black cliffs, the ships, the shining sea, and behind, the bare hills. Always the winds were high, invariably it was raining, but there were times when the thin sun shone across the shieling and gilded the round haystacks or a trembling rainbow would appear over the bare hills, and I was glad to have been there.[8]

*   *   *

¶ I spent a long time at Scapa and hated every minute of it, the weather, the loneliness, the weariness of the job, but because part of my life, and *young* life, was lived there, I find a sort of nostalgia, partly for the place itself, partly for the ships, but not least for the many good, fine men that I shared life and death with.[9]

*   *   *

¶ For generations of naval men Scapa holds a hallowed, if rueful, place in the memory. For two world wars it provided a stronghold, of sorts, for our men o' war, and there are very few matelots of any maturity who cannot establish an immediate link with an absent minded 'Old Ship' by claiming, 'Don't you remember? We were in Scapa together at the time . . . !'[10]

*   *   *

¶ Orkney made an impression on me which was never completely obliterated even by other, perhaps more important experiences later in the war, in Europe, and even now I still have a strong yearning to return. In fact, some mornings at certain times of the year and when the wind is in a particular direction, I remark to my wife that I can smell the breeze from Orkney![11]

* * *

¶ The long summer nights when you could read a book outside at midnight – views of Aurora Borealis – the utter silence outside – the tinny rattle as rats in the guardroom raced between the corrugated metal – the almost complete absence of trees and the absence of trains . . . These things were Orkney service. The hardships were relative – later service in Burma made me realize this – and taken all round they were outweighed by memories of the wind, wild seas, terns diving over the rocks and above all, the friendly Orcadians.'[12]

* * *

¶ To me this lonely outpost was sheer magic. I adored those bleak isolated moors and rolling treeless hills and sudden unexpected lochs. I met my husband there, too; he was in a destroyer which visited Scapa. My main memory is of the sheer beauty of the lonely islands, the lovely colours of the hills, the rare wild flowers, and seabirds and seals which followed me round my coastal walks, and above all of the kindly, friendly, local crofters.[13]

* * *

¶ The colours of Orkney are so soft and lovely and there seems to be a sort of pearly radiance over everything. I have heard Orkney called the Magnetic North and that's how it appeared to me. There was a kind of mystic light, a feeling I have never found anywhere else. And for all there were the normal noises of a busy Naval base and port, there seemed always to be an odd sort of quiet over the land, broken only by the soft lap of water.

Being interested in birds and flowers I went for long walks with my friend, an Edinburgh girl. We were fascinated by the fuchsias growing wild – such beauty they had – and the lupins. One day, we had wandered farther than usual and came upon a wonderful garden ablaze with golden daffodils. As we gazed in delight, a young girl came down the path and asked if we would like some. We said yes, of course, and she filled our arms. I can see those flowers still.[14]

* * *

¶ I remember the Merry Dancers – the Northern Lights that flickered across the sky on winter nights like the green patterns on a radar screen. And though those nights were very long, often starting about three o'clock in the afternoon, in summer there were the long, light, windy days, and Wideford Hill purple about midnight against a peaches and cream sunset, and that green glow of the sky between midnight and three A.M. that was all there was of a summer night.

There was the scent of salt and clover, the sulphurous smell of the ocean when you swam in it – is there underwater volcanic action up there? Winter or summer there was always a wind.

One evening in spring I passed a miniature glen beside the road to Grimsetter where a stream ran through unusually lush grass, and primroses were everywhere. And there I saw scores of rats gambolling in the twilight, fighting each other, washing themselves, sitting up like chipmunks to look around them and scuttling and sniffing this way and that on the scent of food.[15]

* * *

¶ Some day I hope to go back to the islands – see the Flow deserted by the Navy, visit Lyness and Flotta again and go back and see where we lived. I expect one can still see the outline of the sunken ships in the Flow when flying over and I wonder if parts of Hoy from the air look as I once thought they did: 'Like a waste land where no one comes, or hath come, since the making of the world.'[16]

* * *

¶ We left Orkney with many memories that may fade with the passing of the years, but which will never die entirely. The strange, even savage beauty of those lonely northern islands is still with me; I recall the stormy days with angry seas and driving rain; the days of sunshine with the sky resplendent in a medley of pastel tints; the nights of the aurora with eerie flickerings lighting up the darkness.

And the men who were with me in those days; I recall with gratitude the companionship of the men with whom the loneliness and sometimes the hardship were shared. Brave young men, some so soon to die, and now I scarcely remember their names.[17]

* * *

¶ I used to think to myself, one day when all this is over, if I survive, I'll bring my kids up here to Scapa Flow. But perhaps not now – how would they see it, this great area of water between the islands of Orkney? No doubt progress with its benefits has caught up with it, civilization with pylons, television aerials, etc. . . . Yet somehow echoing down the years are all the familiar sounds, bugle calls, pipes, shouted orders, the singing on the drifters returning from Flotta . . .

Scapa Flow – to this generation just a name in the history books but to others a home, a mistress, a legend.[18]

List of Contributors

Chapter 2 – The 'Jellicoes'
1. E. H. March
2. Albert Exell
3. Frank O'B. Adams
4. G. J. Plenty
5. J. C. Marsh
6. A. W. Lintern
7. Stanley Stiff
8. Tom Stoner
9. Bill Partington
10. H. Herring
11. Joseph Francis Gallagher
12. Edward G. Baker
13. H. Waring
14. H. A. C. Robey
15. Ron Whetton
16. Cyril Beech
17. Edward G. Baker

Chapter 3 – The Pentland Firth
1. James Lake
2. Reginald Brimicombe
3. Joseph Francis Gallagher
4. Leonard Clarke
5. Edwin F. King
6. Robert Barton
7. Rev. J. C. de la T. Davies, H.C.F.
8. Jimmy Morrison
9. Jack Lawrence
10. A. W. Lintern
11. William Stockley
12. John Rowe

13. James Lake
14. Frank Robert Jeffaray

Chapter 4 – 'A City of Ships'
1. Norman H. Hill
2. Richard H. Aldridge
3. William Kirk
4. K. R. Ridgway
5. Edward G. Baker
6. E. W. Clayton
7. John West Beardsley
8. Captain R. C. V. Ross R.N., D.S.O. (Ret.)
9. Patricia Begley
10. C. F. McMenemy
11. James Richard Lawrence

Chapter 5 – Setting Up the Base
1. John Wilson
2. C. E. Ede
3. W. L. Collins
4. D. Head
5. John Rowe

Chapter 6 – 'No World Outside the Ship'
1. J. C. Marsh
2. John West Beardsley
3. C. F. McMenemy
4. A. D. Murray
5. Frank O'B. Adams
6. T. Latham
7. Walter Burden

8. Captain R. F. Nichols R.N. (Ret.)
9. Frank Bowman
10. J. P. Harris
11. Andrew C. Barrie
12. C. F. McMenemy
13. S. T. Dent
14. Andrew C. Barrie
15. J. C. Marsh
16. J. P. Harris
17. S. T. Dent
18. T. W. Hudson
19. Sidney L. Hunt
20. John Rowe
21. A. W. Ford

Chapter 7 – 'Hands Coal Ship!'
1. D. Head
2. John West Beardsley
3. J. C. Marsh
4. F. W. Strike
5. Sidney Winsor
6. D. T. Surridge

Chapter 8 – Guarding the Fleet
1. John B. Milford
2. W. H. Taylor
3. Victor Steeple
4. Thomas Young
5. Squadron-Leader J. J. Teasdale, R.A.F. (Ret.)
6. A. P. Hickey, M.B.E.
7. H. L. Pugh
8. Andrew C. Barrie
9. F. R. Forster
10. Edwin F. King

Chapter 9 – Libertymen
1. C. F. McMenemy
2. Frank Bowman
3. W. L. Collins
4. Frank G. Briggs
5. Andrew C. Barrie
6. J. C. Marsh
7. Sydney S. Smith
8. C. H. Petty
9. J. P. Harris
10. Captain R. F. Nichols R. N. (Ret.)
11. J. P. Harris
12. Edwin F. King
13. C. E. Ede

Chapter 10 – Jutland
1. F. F. Clarke
2. Arthur W. Sneesby
3. Charles F. Gifford
4. J. C. Marsh
5. S. T. Dent
6. Sydney S. Smith
7. W. R. Nisbet
8. C. H. Petty
9. John West Beardsley

Chapter 11 – The Hampshire Disaster
1. S.T. Dent
2. John West Beardsley
3. Victor Steeple
4. H. Allsop
5. W. J. Penney
6. John West Beardsley

Chapter 12 – The Vanguard Disaster
1. Percy Ingleby
2. James Tuckett
3. C. E. Ede
4. Frank Bowman
5. Cyril V. Davey
6. Captain R. F. Nichols R. N. (Ret.)
7. J. P. Harris
8. E. Walker
9. Herbert Gallaher
10. C. E. Ede
11. Thomas Lee
12. Andrew C. Barrie
13. J. C. Marsh

Chapter 13 – 'Waiting for Them to Come Out'
1. Andrew C. Barrie
2. A. F. B. Bridges
3. J. P. Harris
4. Sidney L. Hunt
5. Frank O'B. Adams
6. T. H. Kinman
7. G. J. Plenty
8. S. T. Dent
9. John West Beardsley
10. Captain Geoffrey H. Freyberg R.N. (Ret.)
11. Sydney S. Smith
12. C. A. Pond
13. Andrew C. Barrie
14. Herbert Hoad

15. A. P. Hickey, M.B.
16. Herbert Gallaher

Chapter 14 – Strangers in the Flow
1. Geo. F. Sinclair
2. Sidney L. Hunt
3. Sidney Winsor
4. Thomas Young
5. R. C. Chadwick
6. Vice-Admiral Friedrich Ruge
7. C. F. McMenemy
8. G. H. Wild
9. Captain R. C. V. Ross, D.S.O, R.N. (Ret.)
10. Prebendary G. L. Bourdillon
11. H. T. Sneath

Chapter 15 – Loss of the Royal Oak
1. Charles B. Ford
2. Charles B. Ford
3. Wm. C. Powell
4. Commander C. H. A. Harper, O.B.E., R.N. (Ret.)
5. Captain R. F. Nichols, R.N. (Ret.)
6. Herbert Johnston
7. R. A. Rowley
8. Commander C. H. A. Harper, O.B.E., R.N. (Ret.)
9. James Lake
10. D. D. Williams

Chapter 16 – Bolting the Stable Door
1. Thomas McLachlan
2. W. E. Storey
3. Commander C. H. A. Harper, O.B.E., R.N. (Ret.)
4. John Atter, B.E.M.
5. James Lake
6. H. A. C. Robey
7. W. E. Storey
8. A. D. Southgate
9. Commander C. H. A. Harper, O.B.E., R.N. (Ret.)
10. Doreen West (*née* 'Pinkie' Vernon)

Chapter 17 – The Orkney Barrage
1. Stanley B. Emery
2. James Richard Lawrence
3. E. W. Jones
4. James B. Eustance
5. Frank Tait

6. Reginald Brimicombe
7. E. W. Jones
8. Paul A. Smith

Chapter 18 – 'In from Out'
1. Henry Lemmon
2. Robert C. Whittock
3. Bernard Campion
4. George W. Richardson
5. E. W. Clayton
6. E. L. Peck
7. E. W. Clayton
8. Lieutenant-Commander F. Williams R.N. (Ret.)
9. Robert C. Whittock
10. George W. Richardson
11. H. Waring
12. Richard G. Williams
13. Richard O. Hooker
14. Rev. P. G. Harrison
15. F. G. Hall
16. Douglas Grant
17. Donald Hewlett

Chapter 19 – *The Small Ships*
1. John Atter, B.E.M.
2. Colin V. Brindley
3. Colin V. Brindley
4. Rev. P. G. Harrison
5. W. L. Collins
6. Wilfred Hill Naylor
7. Charles A. Jones
8. Charles A. Jones

Chapter 20 – 'You Lucky People!'
1. Edward G. Baker
2. Les Prigg
3. James Richard Lawrence
4. Peter John Stainer
5. W. E. Storey
6. Peter J. Caine
7. Reginald Brimicombe
8. Marjorie Hunter (*née* Whitelaw)
9. Edwin Partridge
10. Stanley B. Emery
11. Peter J. Caine
12. Edward G. Baker
13. D. L. Roberts

Chapter 21 – 'Orkneyitis'
1. Ron Whetton

2. E. W. Jones
3. Wilfred Hill Naylor
4. D. D. Williams
5. Leonard Clarke

Chapter 22 – The Suicide Run
1. P. J. Spearing
2. P. J. Spearing
3. Richard H. Aldridge
4. E. L. Peck
5. E. L. Peck
6. Kenneth M. Stenner
7. P. J. Spearing
8. S. H. J. Hyan
9. W. L. Collins
10. Kenneth M. Stenner

Chapter 23 – 'Six hundred Men to One Girl'
1. Iris C. Goody
2. W. H. Blackmore
3. Christine Miles (*née* Macdonald)
4. Doreen West (*née* 'Pinkie' Vernon)
5. Jeanne Frith (*née* Grain)
6. Emily Hall (*née* Bulman)
7. Dorothy Elks (*née* Crossland)
8. Jeanne Frith (*née* Grain)
9. Marjorie Hunter (*née* Whitelaw)
10. Ann Moseley
11. Jean ('Nin') Macdonald-Smith
12, Jean ('Nin') Macdonald-Smith
13. Jack Taylor
14. Reginald Brimicombe
15. Thomas Blount
16. Lorna B. McMath

Chapter 24 – Making the Best of It
1. E. W. Clayton
2. John G. Openshaw
3. Richard H. Aldridge
4. W. J. Abraham
5. John H. Marsden
6. H. A. C. Robey
7. Marjorie Hunter (*née* Whitelaw)

8. Richard G. Williams
9. Tony Corlett
10. P. J. Spearing
11. William Kirk
12. Jeanne Frith (*née* Grain)
13. Wilfred Hill Naylor
14. A. W. Lintern
15. Robert Barton
16. Reginald Brimicombe
17. Douglas Grant
18. Kenneth M. Stenner
19. S. D. Relph
20. Donald Hewlett
21. Kenneth M. Stenner
2o. Robert Barton
23. H. Herring
24. Hector C. Wray
25. D. D. Williams
26. G. E. Flavell
27. Alfred Holmes

Chapter 25 – Paying Off
1. Richard G. Williams
2. J. N. Walton (Lieut.-Commdr R.N.V.R.)
3. Commander C. H. A. Harper, O.B.E., R.N. (Ret.)
4. Commander C.H.A. Harper, O.B.E., R.N. (Ret.)
5. Richard H. Aldridge
6. Peter Dowden
7. Percy Ingleby
8. Edward G. Baker
9. Charles A. Jones
10. Bernard Campion
11. J. G. Forster
12. Donald Weatherby
13. Ruth Dodd (*née* Fitzmaurice)
14. Isabel Laverack (*née* Air)
15. Jean Edmiston
16. Jean ('Nin') Macdonald-Smith
17. Alec W. Sherwood
18. Richard H. Aldridge

286

Index of Ships

(References in bold refer to illustrations)

287

The History Press The destination for history www.thehistorypress.co.uk